SolidWorks For Dummies®

Cheat Sheet

Top Ten SolidWorks 2006 Dialog Boxes

Button	Name	Purpose
	New	Creates a new document (part, assembly, or drawing).
	Open	Opens a new document.
	Save	Saves the active document.
	Print	Prints the active document.
	Make Drawing from Part/Assembly	Creates a drawing from the active part or assembly.
	Make Assembly from Part/Assembly	Creates an assembly from the current part or assembly.
	Tools	Provides access to SolidWorks tools, such as Measure, Spell Checker, Statistics, and so on.
	Options	Defines system and document setup options.
	Help	Reads the Help file.
	Note	Creates a note.

Y0-CBF-172

SolidWorks Keyboard Shortcuts

Rotate the model horizontally or vertically: **Arrow** keys

Rotate the model horizontally or vertically 90 degrees: **Shift+Arrow** keys

Rotate the model clockwise or counterclockwise: **Alt+** left or right **Arrow** keys

Pan the model: **Ctrl+Arrow** keys

Zoom in: **Shift+Z**

Zoom out: **z**

Zoom to fit: **f**

Previous view: **Ctrl+Shift+Z**

Filter edges: **e**

Filter vertices: **v**

Filter faces: **x**

Toggle Selection Filter toolbar: **F5**

Toggle selection filters (on/off): **F6**

New SolidWorks document: **Ctrl+N**

Open document: **Ctrl+O**

Make drawing from part: **Ctrl+D**

Make assembly from part: **Ctrl+A**

Save: **Ctrl+S**

Print: **Ctrl+P**

Repeat last command: **Enter**

Access online help when in a Property Manager or dialog box: **F1**

Rename an item in the Feature Manager design tree: Select item and then **F2**

Expand or collapse the flyout Feature Manager design tree: **c**

Rebuild the model: **Ctrl+B**

Force rebuild the model and rebuild all its features: **Ctrl+Q**

Redraw the screen: **Ctrl+R**

Cycle between open SolidWorks documents: **Ctrl+Tab**

Undo: **Ctrl+z**

Cut: **Ctrl+ x**

Copy: **Ctrl+ c**

Paste: **Ctrl+ v**

Next window: **Ctrl+F6**

Close window: **Ctrl+F4**

For Dummies: Bestselling Book Series for Beginners

SolidWorks For Dummies®

Top Ten SolidWorks 2006 Functions

Button	Name	Purpose
	Select	Selects objects.
	Zoom to Fit	Zooms to see the entire document.
	Zoom to Area	Zooms to an area defined by two corners of a rectangle.
	Rotate	Rotates the part or assembly.
	Pan	Moves the center position of a graphics window.
	Previous View	Jumps to the previously used view.
	Standard Views	Displays common view orientations.
	Smart Dimension	Creates dimensions based on what is selected and where the text is placed.
	Sketch	Creates a 2D sketch.
	Rebuild	Updates the document based on changes to dimensions or features.

Top SolidWorks 2006 CommandManager Groups

Button	Name	Purpose
	Features	Commonly used feature creation tools (Extruded Cut, Extrude Base/Boss, Swept Base/Boss, Swept Cut, Fillet, Chafer, and so on).
	Sketch	Commonly used sketch tools (line, arc, point, circles, and so on).
	Assemblies	Common assembly feature (Add Component, Mate, and so on).
	Drawings	Common drawing view features (Model View, Standard 3 Views, Projected View, and so on).
	Annotations	Common annotation tools (Smart Dimension, Auto Dimension, Note, Balloon, Centerlines, and so on).
	Mold	Common features used for creating models (Create Mold folder, Parting Lines, Shut off Surface, and so on).
	Sheetmetal	Common sheetmetal tools (Base-Flange tab, Edge Flange, Hem, and so on).

For Dummies: Bestselling Book Series for Beginners

SolidWorks®

FOR DUMMIES®

by Greg Jankowski

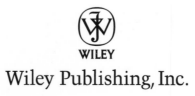

Wiley Publishing, Inc.

SolidWorks® For Dummies®

Published by
Wiley Publishing, Inc.
111 River Street
Hoboken, NJ 07030-5774

www.wiley.com

For general information on our other products and services, please contact our Customer Care Department within the U.S. at 800-762-2974, outside the U.S. at 317-572-3993, or fax 317-572-4002.

For technical support, please visit www.wiley.com/techsupport.

Wiley also publishes its books in a variety of electronic formats. Some content that appears in print may not be available in electronic books.

Library of Congress Control Number: 2005924605

ISBN-13: 978-0-7645-9555-4

ISBN-10: 0-7645-9555-5

Manufactured in the United States of America

10 9 8 7 6 5 4 3 2 1

1O/RS/QY/QV/IN

WILEY

About the Author

Greg Jankowski is the Customer Satisfaction Manager at SolidWorks Corporation. Greg is a veteran (translation — been doing this longer than he cares to admit) in the CAD industry with experience using SolidWorks, ProEngineer, and Computervision CAD systems in a variety of mechanical design and developmental positions. Greg was the Principal at CIMCo, a SolidWorks Solution Partner since SolidWorks 95.

Greg is the author of the book *SolidWorks for AutoCAD Users* and the e-book *Exploring SolidWorks*. In addition, he authored and developed the SolidWorks Workstation benchmark. Greg is also the author of the *Cadalyst* magazine column "Solid Thinking" and is a regular columnist in the *SolidWorks Express* newsletter.

Dedication

This book is dedicated to the three women in my life, my wife Sandy and daughters Alexis and Kaitlyn, who continue to put up with me and my crazy projects. I appreciate their patience, love, and understanding.

I also want to dedicate this book to all the hard-working folks at SolidWorks. It continues to be my pleasure to work with some of the best, hardest working, and brightest folks in the industry.

Author's Acknowledgments

Special thanks to Amy Castor, my technical editor, who helped turn much of my "engineer-ese" into something more Dummies-like. I appreciate your insight and comments (and you had more than a few).

To my project editor, Kelly Ewing, who kept us all on track and focused on task at hand, thanks. You really helped tie it all together. Kelly was other lucky recipient of my "engineer-ese."

To Terri Varveris, acquisitions editor, my thanks for helping to get this project off the ground and keeping the ball rolling.

Thanks also goes to my technical reviewers, Fred Koehler and Richard Doyle, who made sure what I did say was actually correct (to some extent).

Publisher's Acknowledgments

We're proud of this book; please send us your comments through our online registration form located at www.dummies.com/register/.

Some of the people who helped bring this book to market include the following:

Acquisitions, Editorial, and Media Development

Project Editor: Kelly Ewing

Acquisitions Editor: Terri Varveris

Technical Editors: Richard Doyle, Fred Koehler

Editorial Manager: Carol Sheehan

Media Development Manager: Laura VanWinkle

Media Development Supervisor: Richard Graves

Editorial Assistant: Amanda Foxworth

Cartoons: Rich Tennant (www.the5thwave.com)

Composition Services

Project Coordinator: Adrienne Martinez

Layout and Graphics: Carl Byers, Andrea Dahl, Lauren Goddard, Joyce Haughey, Ron Terry

Proofreaders: Leeann Harney, Jessica Kramer

Indexer: TECHBOOKS Production Services

Special Help

Amy Castor

Publishing and Editorial for Technology Dummies

Richard Swadley, Vice President and Executive Group Publisher

Andy Cummings, Vice President and Publisher

Mary Bednarek, Executive Acquisitions Director

Mary C. Corder, Editorial Director

Publishing for Consumer Dummies

Diane Graves Steele, Vice President and Publisher

Joyce Pepple, Acquisitions Director

Composition Services

Gerry Fahey, Vice President of Production Services

Debbie Stailey, Director of Composition Services

Contents at a Glance

Table of Contents

Introduction

. . . .

I started using SolidWorks when the very first version, SolidWorks 95, came out on the market. It's amazing to see how far solid modeling has come in ten years. Working within a 3D environment has transformed the way I create, iterate, and document a design.

One of the reasons I wrote this book was to help boil down much of the material that is out there and focus on not only what I believe to be important from my design experience, but also how I think the software should be used.

Now while many things are similar to what was done ten years ago, many things have changed. Even some of the saltier veterans out there will gain something from the ideas presented within this book.

SolidWorks is becoming a more mature application, and instead of getting harder to use, it makes modeling easier and, quite frankly, more fun.

One concept that recurs throughout this book is the ability of SolidWorks to reuse design information, saving you from having to do things manually. For example, SolidWorks can use the information in your part or assembly model to create manufacturing drawings automatically.

This way of creating products saves time and produces better end results. *SolidWorks For Dummies* shows you how.

Enjoy your journey with SolidWorks. You'll love the experience.

About This Book

This book isn't designed to be read from cover to cover, although it can be. *SolidWorks For Dummies* is designed as a reference book that you can use at any time.

This book isn't meant to be a complete reference for SolidWorks. If it was, you probably wouldn't want to drop it on your foot. Instead, I have focused on the key and commonly used elements of SolidWorks.

Conventions Used in This Book

I use the following conventions throughout this book:

- ✔ I use the term document to refer to SolidWorks drawing, part, or assembly files.
- ✔ The list of items across the top of the SolidWorks interface is the main menu. Each item in the main menu also has a hidden list, or pull-down menu. Whenever I want you to choose a series of commands from them, I use the phrasing, "Choose File➪Save."

What You're Not to Read

Sometimes this book can be a little technical. But I'm a nice guy, and I always warn you about the stuff you can skip with a handy Technical Stuff icon. Although the information next to this icon is interesting, you don't have to read it. The same holds true for sidebars, which are the little gray boxes that you see scattered throughout the book. While the information in the sidebars is interesting, it's really extra information that's nonessential to understanding the topic at hand.

Foolish Assumptions

When I wrote *SolidWorks For Dummies,* I assumed very little about you. Okay, maybe I did assume a few things, like that you're somewhat familiar with a computer and the Windows operating system. But I didn't assume that you have any prior SolidWorks experience.

If you're not comfortable working with your computer, then you may want to pick up a copy of *PCs For Dummies* by Dan Gookin and Sandra Hardin Gookin (Wiley), which walks you through the basics.

I also assume that you have a slight background with a CAD system. I've counted on a basic knowledge of geometry, lines, circles, points, and so on. I don't, however, assume that you can create these objects.

How This Book Is Organized

This book has five major parts. Each part contains several chapters, and each chapter contains several sections. You can read any section without reading the entire book or even earlier sections within that same chapter. Here's what you find in each part:

Part 1: Beginning the SolidWorks Journey

This part introduces SolidWorks and 3D design. You find out about the user interface, SolidWorks file types, and system setup. I also highlight the new features in SolidWorks 2006.

Part 11: Design Intent and the Virtual Prototype

This part contains the beef of the book. In this part, I talk about creating sound, robust, 2D sketches and examine design intent (do what I mean, not what I sketch). I also talk about the many ways to design and model a part and the virtual prototype.

Part 111: The Devil's in the "Drawing" Details

Drawings are a necessary part of the manufacturing process. In this section, I talk about how SolidWorks uses information captured in the model to create drawings automatically. I also cover several other SolidWorks drawing features that make your life easier.

Part 1V: Playing Nicely with Others (And Picking Up Your Toys)

If you can't find anything on your desk, this chapter may be a tough read. This part focuses on managing and sharing information with other team members so that your projects are more effective.

Part V: The Part of Tens

The Part of Tens provides examples, tips, and references for SolidWorks. You discover how you can become more proficient in SolidWorks, as well as how you can reuse design information and extend the capabilities of SolidWorks. Lastly, you find out about resources in the vast SolidWorks community.

About the CD-ROM

The CD included with *SolidWorks For Dummies* contains a product demo and add-on solutions. For more information on the CD, see the About the CD-ROM appendix at the back of this book.

Icons Used in This Book

Throughout this book, I use icons to flag information. Some icons mark topics that are useful down the line, while others warn you of geek topics ahead.

Here's what each icon means:

This icon flags useful tips and insight into the current topic. Read these tips carefully because they can save you time and effort.

Think of this icon as a message taped to your forehead. It serves as a gentle reminder to help reinforce a concept or idea.

This icon says, "Beware, potential problems lie ahead." Pay close attention to the text this icon flags to steer clear of trouble.

This one is for the techno-geeks out there. (I number myself as one.) If you get bored easily, skip this text.

Where to Go from Here

If you're ready to get started, turn the page and keep reading or, better yet, review the table of contents or index to find topics that interest you. No matter which approach you choose, you're well on your way to becoming a CAD operator. Creating products in 3D is a fun and efficient way to design. Enjoy!

Part I
Beginning the SolidWorks Journey

In this part . . .

Beginning the journey into 3D can seem daunting. It's not that bad, honest. In fact, it can actually be fun. This part introduces you to SolidWorks. You also find out about some of the new features in SolidWorks 2006, as well as how to set up SolidWorks before you start your first design project. You also delve into the topics of design layout and intent.

Chapter 1

Getting to Know (And Love) SolidWorks

. . . .

In This Chapter

▶ Becoming familiar with SolidWorks

▶ Discovering the advantages of the virtual prototype

▶ Figuring out where to start with SolidWorks

▶ Getting acquainted with new features in SolidWorks 2006

. . . .

SolidWorks is a tool that helps design engineers harness their imagination and add creativity to their designs. The true mark of a good tool is when it becomes part of your process without getting in your way. When you design, you need to do just that — design!

When SolidWorks was created, the power of 3D was not yet widespread. The company's original mission back in 1995 — and a goal that it still pursues today — is to bring the power of 3D to every engineer's desktop. Two early quotes of SolidWorks founders that still hold true today are

✔ "No matter how easy it is to use, it is never easy enough."

✔ "No matter how fast we make it, it is never fast enough."

In this chapter, I introduce you to SolidWorks, the wonderful world of 3D, and the virtual prototype. You discover the basic system requirements for SolidWorks and tips to keep the program running smooth. I also give you the lowdown on the newest features in SolidWorks 2006.

Exploring the Ins and Outs of 3D

As a design engineer, you need to be critical as to how you go about your craft and how you can do it better. As tools and technology continue to improve, you too need to evolve. And that means staying abreast of the latest design tool innovations.

Just as I wouldn't pound nails with a shovel, I also believe in using CAD tools for the purpose for which they were designed. Throughout this book, I emphasize how to use SolidWorks more effectively. It may be that designing in SolidWorks is different from how you've designed in the past. But keep an open mind to how you can sharpen your skills with 3D tools.

One of the biggest advantages to working in 3D is the ability to capture design intent early in the design process. Good designs are built on solid foundations. SolidWorks 3D modeling gives you a better understanding of your design, long before you create the first part. It also allows you to reuse design information downstream, for example, when it comes time to manufacture the design.

The SolidWorks advantage

When I reflect back on my early days as a designer, I realize that my greatest satisfaction came from creating a complex assembly on my computer, and then watching the darn thing actually come together on the shop floor just the way I designed it. Without the ability to create 3D solid models and assemblies, this goal isn't easily attainable.

SolidWorks lets you design 3D parts (see Figure 1-1) and assemblies and use them to generate manufacturing drawings. The drawings are based on the geometry defined in the original part or assembly.

Figure 1-1:
Here's an example of how a part is reused in the design process.

Embracing the virtual prototype

The virtual prototype is a concept that I refer to throughout this book. In the old days (I'm talking 20 years ago), designers drew their designs on paper. When a designer was done drawing, he built a physical prototype to test his design ideas in the real world. If things didn't work quite right, it was back to the drawing board. It took a lot of time building all those prototypes.

Nowadays, you do all that testing and simulating on a *virtual prototype*. When you design a product in SolidWorks, essentially you create a virtual prototype with all the characteristics of the real thing (dimensions, mass properties, screws and fittings, and so on). Your virtual prototype behaves in the computer realm as it would in the real world.

The power of the virtual prototype is that it allows you to test many, many, many design ideas quickly on your computer. And though the physical prototype has not vanished, you at least don't need so many.

Figure 1-1 shows a virtual prototype. Imagine if you had to draw this baby from scratch. In a drawing, changing the height from 100mm to 120mm requires major effort. In contrast, with a 3D design, you can modify and update key design attributes with ease.

If you think you can work faster in a 2D environment, you're probably right. But that's only because you can't include the detail required to fully manufacture the part. When I made designs on a drawing board with paper and pencil, I could easily radius any corner because I had my trusty ellipse template. In other words, I would fudge the corner and let the toolmaker properly fillet the corner. Sometimes this lack of detail is good, and sometimes it's bad.

People use SolidWorks because they can create a 3D part, place that part in an assembly the same way as if they were assembling physical parts, and then create a 2D drawing directly from that information.

Setting Up the System

SolidWorks comes to you on three CDs. When you are ready to install, put the first CD in your CD-ROM drive and follow the instructions. During installation or when you first run SolidWorks, the software asks for a registration code. This is different than the serial number, which is listed on the box. If a registration code does not automatically appear when you register the software, you can get one through your SolidWorks reseller (often called a Value Added Reseller, or VAR) or by visiting the registration page of the SolidWorks support site at www.solidworks.com/pages/services/Registration.html.

The minimum computer requirements boil down to the following:

- ✔ **CPU:** Get the fastest one you can afford. The performance of SolidWorks depends on your CPU speed. If you get a CPU that is too slow, you can add a second one later. But although a second CPU adds some performance increase, it doesn't come close to doubling performance, so it's best to start off big.

- ✔ **RAM:** SolidWorks lists minimum requirements, but I tell folks that a better way to gauge how much RAM you need is to open SolidWorks on your computer along with all the other applications you normally have open at one time, such as e-mail, word processing, a Web browser, and so on. Then open a good sampling of SolidWorks documents. (You can find some in the Tutorials folder in the SolidWorks program folder.) Open Windows Task Manager (Ctrl+Alt+Delete) and click the Performance tab. Check the available memory under Physical Memory. If available memory is not greater than 0, you need more RAM.

  The amount of RAM you have is important. If Windows runs out of physical memory, bad things happen. The system becomes sluggish and less stable. RAM is cheap, so make sure that you have plenty.

- ✔ **Graphics card:** Make sure that you have a certified graphics card and driver version. The SolidWorks support Web site lists certified graphics cards/driver combinations. For a listing of currently supported graphics cards/drivers, visit the hardware page of the SolidWorks support site at `www.solidworks.com/pages/services/VideoCardTesting.html`.

- ✔ **Hard drive:** Big and fast is where it's at. These days, folks who use SolidWorks typically have 60 to 80GB hard drives.

Keeping Your Computer Happy

A commonly overlooked means of making sure that your computer stays happy and healthy is regular system maintenance. The two most important items on this list are making sure you have sufficient disk space and routine disk defragmentation.

You should also check the backup settings in SolidWorks (Tools➪Options➪ Backups). Check the number of backup copies per document and the location of the backups. If you set the number of backup copies, keep this number low (1 or 2) because you will be creating copies of every document opened. It's best to store backups on a different computer or at a different site. Remember to check your backup directory regularly to make sure that you have enough disk space. If you run low on space, it's time to clean up your hard drive or buy a bigger one.

During your normal work on a computer, the disks become fragmented, which means that Windows can't store all of a file in one spot so it starts using a number of places on the hard drive to store documents. As you can imagine, fragmentation makes Windows run slower and causes stability issues with the system and the applications running on the computer. To alleviate this problem, use the Windows Disk Defragmenter (Start⇨All Programs⇨ Accessories⇨System Tools). I run a complete scan on a weekly basis. It does make a difference.

For more information on many of these administrative tasks, check out the *SolidWorks Express* archive. *SolidWorks Express* is a bimonthly electronic newsletter for the SolidWorks community. To view technical tips in the archive, visit www.solidworks.com/swexpress.

Things to Know Before You Start Designing

Before I start talking about SolidWorks, I want to explain a few basic items.

The first time you run SolidWorks, the Welcome to SolidWorks dialog box appears (see Figure 1-2) to ask you how you want to configure the Help and Workflow customization. You can set up SolidWorks based on your industry and skill level.

Figure 1-2:
Set up
SolidWorks
according to
how you
work and
what you
know and
don't know.

> **Welcome to SolidWorks**
>
> Welcome to SolidWorks. This is the first time you have run SolidWorks on this machine. We would like to give you an opportunity to customize your SolidWorks installation.
>
> Help customization
>
> ⦿ I am a new user. Show Quick Tips to help me get started.
> ◯ I am new to this version of SolidWorks. Show me Interactive What's New help.
> ◯ Do not show me any dynamic help.
>
> Work flow customization
>
> You can customize default visibility of toolbars and menus by your area of expertise. Select any, all, or none of the following categories.
>
> ☐ Consumer product design
> ☐ Machine design
> ☐ Mold design
>
> Note: You can change these options at any time in the SolidWorks application.
>
> [OK]   [Help]

The first section in the dialog box is Help Customization. If you're a new user, you can activate Quick Tips. *Quick Tips* are a set of pop-up messages that appear while you create SolidWorks documents. They display hints and options about what to do next. Figure 1-3 shows a Quick Tip that pops up when you create a new part document. The Quick Tip walks you through what is required to perform this task.

Figure 1-3:
Quick Tips
give you
an idea of
where to
go next.

What would you like to do?

Create a *solid part.*

Create a 2D *sketch.*

Create a sheet metal part.

How do I close this window?

You can turn Quick Tips on in each type of document (drawing, part, or assembly) by choosing Help⇨Quick Tips.

The second section is Work Flow Customization. If you make a selection here, SolidWorks displays toolbars and menus that relate to the type of work you do. The choices are Consumer Product Design, Machine Design, and Mold Design. You can select one, all, or none of these categories.

Based on the type of industry you select, SolidWorks displays a different set of tools in the CommandManager (see Figure 1-4). The *CommandManager* is a context-sensitive toolbar that dynamically updates based on the toolbar you want to access.

Figure 1-4:
The
Command-
Manager
automat-
ically
updates
to display
the toolbar
you need.
Here, the
Surface
toolbar
appears.

To change the icons shown within the CommandManager, right-click on the CommandManager and choose Customize CommandManager. A menu of available CommandManager icons appear. Select the ones that fit the type of work you most commonly perform.

Checking Out the Features

SolidWorks 2006 is the 14th version of SolidWorks to come out since the initial release of SolidWorks 95. Version updates, known as *service packs,* come out on about every six weeks, while major releases occur typically 10 to 12 months apart.

You can download service packs from the SolidWorks support Web site at www.solidworks.com/pages/services/downloads.html.

Getting started

A couple of resources can help get you started. The SolidWorks Resources tab (look for a house icon on the far right of the user interface) in the task pane, shown in Figure 1-5, displays links to the following:

- ✓ **Online Tutorial:** Online Tutorial offers a group of 30-minute step-by-step tutorials on a wide variety of topics. The first tutorial, Lesson 1, gives a quick overview of the basic features and functions with SolidWorks and is a good starting point if you haven't ever used the software.

- ✓ **What's New:** A document that describes the new features within the latest version of SolidWorks based on area (features, parts, assemblies, drawings, and so on). You can access the What's New document (PDF) in the Help menu.

- ✓ **Machine Design, Mold Design, or Consumer Product Design:** The title and contents of this tab relate to the industry type you chose in Workflow Customization. Figure 1-5 shows resources for machine design. If you chose mold design, other resources display. In this tab you find an overview of the industry and industry-specific tutorials.

- ✓ **Tip of the day:** This changes each time you open SolidWorks.

Figure 1-5:
Inside the
SolidWorks
Resources
tab in the
task pane
you find a
plethora of
learning
resources.

You can also find the following references under the Help menu:

✔ **SolidWorks Help Topics:** This takes you directly to the *SolidWorks Online User's Guide.* The guide is organized into chapters with an index you can browse through. A search tool guides you to information on just about any feature in SolidWorks.

✔ **Moving from AutoCAD:** An online guide designed to help those moving from AutoCAD to SolidWorks. AutoCAD is a popular 2D design program. Many SolidWorks user come from an AutoCAD background.

Finding out what's new to SolidWorks 2006

I based this book on SolidWorks 2006. Each version of SolidWorks has updates to accommodate new features and requirements. When you save a file in the new version, keep in mind that older versions can't read these newer files because the new features weren't available in the older version. However, you can open older versions in the new version.

Here's a taste of what's new inside SolidWorks 2006:

- ✔ **Spell Checker:** One of my favorites, as I am a typical engineer when it comes to spelling. This feature works similar to Microsoft application spell checkers. It checks a drawing for spelling errors and offers suggestions (see Chapter 7).

- ✔ **Multiple Viewports:** Gives you the ability to see your part or assembly in a two- or four-window configuration. Panning and zooming in one view cause the other views to update in scale and position. If you prefer to gaze over multiple views (isometric, top, front, and right side) at the same time, this feature may appeal to you (see Chapter 2).

  If you're used to working with another CAD system where multiple views (isometric, top, front, and right side) appear at the same time, this feature may be for you.

- ✔ **Text-in-a-Box:** Creates a bounding box to control the placement of notes in drawings. This feature makes it easier to place annotations in a drawing because you can define and change the size of the note based on the space available on the drawing (see Chapter 7).

- ✔ **3D Annotations Views (ASME 14.41-2003):** Makes it easier to control and organize the placement of 3D annotations in the model. This feature also automates the placement of 3D annotations in drawings (see Chapter 7).

  The dimensions are easier to read, and this standard helps define one of the other concepts that I stress in this book: When creating parts, make your sketches look how they should in the drawing. Then reuse these dimensions to create the drawing.

- ✔ **Display States:** Allow you to save your favorite visual settings (component color, component texture, Hide/Show state, and so on) in a Display States folder for reuse in different assembly components or drawing views (see Chapter 2).

- ✔ **Splines:** Graphical handles on splines (wiggly shaped lines) allow you to better edit and control the shape of the curves (see Chapter 4).

- ✔ **Sketch Blocks:** Similar to Windows block, lets you grab multiple entities in sketch mode and treat them as a single block. You can combine sketch blocks with other entities to create complex layouts. Sketch blocks are fully associative. If you change one instance, all instances update automatically (see Chapter 3).

- ✔ **Fastening Feature:** Adds common plastic part features (mounting bosses, snap hooks, snap grooves, and vents) to plastic parts automatically by selecting the new Fastening Feature command.

- ✔ **Smart Components:** Allow you to relate features and components to a part. For example, when you place a connector in an assembly, you can define smart components that automatically add mounting holes, nuts, and bolts to complete the assembly.

- ✔ **SolidWorks Design Checker:** Checks a drawing for a number of predefined criteria (dimension size, drafting standards, materials, custom proprieties, and so on) to ensure that the document meets your standards and practices. This option is included in the SolidWorks Office Professional and SolidWorks Office Premium software packages.

Chapter 2

Taking Control of SolidWorks

● ●

In This Chapter

▶ Getting around (the user interface, that is)

▶ Creating a new SolidWorks document

▶ Understanding the different SolidWorks file types

▶ Structuring and streamlining SolidWorks

▶ Creating templates for parts, assemblies, and drawings

▶ Saving and sharing SolidWorks files

● ●

*W*hen they first hit the market, 3D design programs were complex to learn and difficult to operate. Then SolidWorks came along and did everything that the other programs did, only it was less expensive and easier to use, enabling design engineers to get up and running fast. What gives SolidWorks a familiar look and feel is its Windows-like user interface and the use of other standard conventions, such as icon command buttons, menus, and toolbars.

This chapter is about the SolidWorks user interface: how to navigate it and how to personalize it to fit your needs. In this chapter, you discover how to open a new document and how to set up and maintain the SolidWorks program. Whether you work alone or in a group of 50 other engineers, the ability to define, save, and share document templates and common SolidWorks settings makes you more effective in using SolidWorks.

Working with SolidWorks Documents

SolidWorks is a *multidocument system,* which means that it uses different file types for different purposes. Part, drawing, and assembly files are some examples.

Many SolidWorks file types link to other files. A *drawing* references a part to create the detail views. An *assembly* references parts and other assemblies. The different types of documents are fully associative within SolidWorks, so a change to a part propagates to any drawing or assembly that uses the part.

Here's a list of SolidWorks document types that appear throughout this book:

- **Part:** The building blocks of every SolidWorks model. Each assembly and drawing you create is made from parts. Part files consist of a collection of part features (base, extrude, revolve, loft, and so on). SolidWorks attaches the extension .sldprt to part files.

- **Assembly:** A collection of related parts saved in one document file with an .sldasm extension. An assembly can contain anywhere from two to more than a thousand components, which can be parts or other assemblies called *subassemblies.*

- **Drawing:** 2D documents that convey a design to manufacturing. A drawing file consists of one or more sheets that contain different views of the model. SolidWorks gives drawings files the extension .slddrw.

- **Templates:** Documents that include user-defined parameters. When you open a new part, drawing, or assembly, you select a *template* to use for your new document. Templates have the extensions .drwdot, .prtdot, and .asmdot for drawing, part, and assembly documents.

- **Library Feature:** A frequently used part feature or combination of part features that you create once and save in a library for future use. You can use library features as building blocks to construct a single part to ensure consistency and save time. Library features have the extension .sldlfp.

- **Drawing Sheet Format:** You can save a border or a title block (which includes company name, material, sheet size, and other information) of a drawing in an .sldrt format to use in creating new drawings.

- **Block:** A group of 2D entities (such as standard notes, title blocks, label positions, and so on) that you can use in drawing files. *Blocks* can include text, any type of sketch entity, balloons, and imported entities. You can attach blocks to geometry or to drawing views and insert them into sheet formats. Blocks have the extension .sldblk.

- **Macro:** A set of keyboard commands that you can record and save in one file to automate redundant or menial tasks in SolidWorks. A macro is saved as a set of Microsoft Visual Basic for Applications (VBA) program code. SolidWorks *macros* have the file extension .swp.

You want to be sure to develop a consistent method for naming SolidWorks files that everyone on your design team can follow. SolidWorks follows the same filenaming conventions as Windows. As you develop your own naming style, here's what to keep in mind:

- Filenames aren't case sensitive. They can be upper- or lowercase.

- Filenames can include spaces.

✔ A filename can have up to 256 characters before the file extension.

✔ You can't include special characters (*, /, %, and so on) within the filename.

✔ Filenames that you store in the same data directory should be unique so that you don't accidentally choose the wrong file. For example, you don't name a connector part connector.sldprt because someone might use the same name for a part on another project. Filenames should include the part number, project name or number, and then a description.

Creating and Opening a Document

Before you explore the ins and outs of the SolidWorks user interface, you need to understand how to open a new document in SolidWorks. When you open a new part, assembly, or drawing document, you select a template to work with. A *template* is the foundation of the SolidWorks document. It stores the default document properties for each document. SolidWorks has default part, assembly, and drawing templates, but you can create your own templates, and the next section, "Working with Templates," tells you how.

To create a new SolidWorks document:

1. **Choose File⇨New.**

   The New SolidWorks Document dialog box appears.

   The New SolidWorks Document dialog box has two versions: Novice and Advanced. You can toggle between them by simply clicking the Novice or Advanced button at the bottom of the dialog box.

   Novice is the simplified version of the dialog box. It's also the default. In Novice mode, you have only three document templates (Part, Assembly, and Drawing) to choose from. In contrast, the Advanced mode shows the standard templates as well as any custom templates. The template icons appear in various tabs (see Figure 2-1). When you select a document template type in the Advanced mode, a preview of the template appears in the Preview box. You can find out how to create custom templates and add new tabs to the New SolidWorks Document dialog box in the next section, "Working with Templates."

2. **In the dialog box, select Part, Assembly, or Drawing.**

3. **Click OK.**

   A new document opens.

Figure 2-1:
The
Advanced
mode of
the New
SolidWorks
Document
dialog box
shows
document
templates
in tabs.

To open an existing SolidWorks document:

1. **Choose File⇨Open.**

   The Open dialog box appears.

2. **From the Files of Type drop-down list, select the type of document you want to open (.sldprt, .sldasm, or .slddrw for part, assembly, or drawing or a combination of SolidWorks files).**

3. **In the Look In drop-down list, find the folder that contains the document you want to open.**

   The files of that folder appear as a list in the middle of the dialog box.

4. **Click the file you want to open.**

   A preview of the document appears in the preview screen.

5. **Click Open.**

   The document opens in SolidWorks.

Working with Templates

A *template* is the foundation of a new SolidWorks document. Templates contain basic document information, such as document settings, custom properties, and so on. You can create a template out of any SolidWorks document by simply saving the document in a template format.

Templates are a good place to store company standards. For example, you can create templates that use inches and millimeters. You can create drawing templates that include a custom Title Block ready to go.

When you open a new document, the Advanced version of the New SolidWorks Document dialog box has tabs for templates. The default tab is Templates, but you can create your own tabs and add custom templates.

To create a new tab on the Advanced version of the New SolidWorks Document dialog box:

1. **In Windows Explorer, create a new folder.**

   For example, you can put a set of templates in a special folder called: *<SolidWorks install directory>*\data\templates\My Special Templates.

2. **Choose Tools⇨Options.**

   A dialog box appears, with tabs for Systems Options and Document Properties.

3. **Click the Systems Option tab.**

4. **Click File Locations.**

   The File Location options appear.

5. **In Show Folders For, click the arrow and, from the drop-down list, click Document Templates.**

   Document Templates appears under Show Folders.

6. **Next to the Folders box, click Add.**

   The Browse for Folder dialog box appears.

7. **Browse for the folder that you created in Step 1 and click to select it.**

8. **Click OK.**

   The Browse for Folder dialog box closes, and the new folder is added under Folders.

9. **Click OK again to close the Options dialog box.**

   After you save a template to the new folder, a new tab with the name of the folder you created appears in the advanced version of the New SolidWorks Document dialog box. Keep in mind, however, that empty folders do not appear.

To create a template:

1. **Choose File⇨New.**

   The New SolidWorks Document dialog box appears.

2. **In the dialog box, select Part, Assembly, or Drawing.**

3. **Click OK.**

   A new document opens.

4. **Choose Tools⇨Options.**

   A dialog box appears, with tabs for Systems Options and Document Property.

5. **Under the Document Property tab, select the options you want to customize in your new document template.**

   The most important are the following:

   - **Dimensions:** Set options for how you want dimensions handled in documents. Options include Snap to Grid, Arrow Style, and Text Alignment (horizontal or vertical).

   - **Notes:** Select how you want drawing notes to appear. Options include Text Alignment, Leader Anchor, Leader Style, and Border.

   - **Annotation Font:** Allows you to select the type and style of font to show in drawing and model annotations.

   - **Units:** Select the units for the document (IPS, MMGS, and so on), Length Units, Dual Units, Angular Units, and Density Units.

6. **Click OK.**

7. **Choose File⇨Save As.**

   The Save As dialog box appears.

8. **In the Save As Type drop-down list, select a template type (.prtdot, .asmdot, or .drwdot for part, assembly, or drawing).**

   Remember, you need to select the template type that matches the item you selected in Step 2.

9. **In the File Name box, type a name for your new template.**

   SolidWorks adds the extension automatically.

10. **In the Save In box, click the drop-down arrow to browse to the folder where you want to save your template.**

    Save the template in the new template folder if you want the template to appear under a different tab in the Advanced mode of the New SolidWorks Document dialog box.

11. **Click Save.**

    The new template appears in the New SolidWorks Document dialog box, and you can use it the next time you create a new document.

Understanding the User Interface

You won't feel like you're on alien landscape when you open SolidWorks. In fact, if you know Windows, then you're well on your way to learning SolidWorks. SolidWorks has many familiar Windows functions, such as dragging and resizing windows and so on. SolidWorks also uses Windows icons, such as print, open, save, cut, and paste.

Document windows

When you open a document in SolidWorks, two panels appear in the user interface. The right panel is the graphics window, where your model or drawing appears in all its glory. You can create and manipulate the document in the graphics window. The left panel contains the following SolidWorks document windows:

- **FeatureManager design tree:** Lists the structure of the part, assembly, or drawing. The FeatureManager design tree is similar to the Windows Explorer tree. You can expand or collapse the "tree" to see how a model or assembly is constructed or to examine sheets and views in a drawing.

- **PropertyManager:** Appears in the left panel when you select many SolidWorks commands, such as sketches, fillet features, assembly mates, and so on. The PropertyManager is a place for you to enter relevant command options, such as design data and parameters.

- **ConfigurationManager:** Appears in place of the FeatureManager design tree. Helps create, select, and view multiple configurations, or variations, of parts and assemblies in a document.

Menus, toolbars, and mice

You can access commands in SolidWorks using menus, toolbars, and your mouse. The SolidWorks interface is dynamic. Different menus and toolbars appear depending on the active document type. When you open a part, for example, the Feature toolbar appears with commands to build a part. Open an assembly (see Figure 2-2), and you see assembly commands.

Figure 2-2:
SolidWorks
displays
commands
relevant
to the
document
type.

The main elements of the SolidWorks user interface are as follows (see Figure 2-2 for the corresponding item numbers):

1 Title bar: Displays the name of the active document and the active document window, by default, with a colored title bar. Inactive document windows are shown, by default, with a gray, or faded, title bar. If you haven't saved changes in the document, you see an * after the document name.

2 Main menu: A set of items (File, Edit, View, and so on) across the top of the user interface. Each item also has a pull-down menu of functions and commands. The menu bar contents are task-dependent based on the active document type. You find these functions on SolidWorks toolbars. But while the toolbars contain commands you use more often, the menu bar contains the complete set.

3 Standard toolbar: Just beneath the main menu, you find a set of commonly used command buttons that make up the Standard toolbar. These buttons are for quick access to the commands you use most often, such as New (to open a new document), Open (open an existing document), and Print (print the active document).

4 View toolbar: The View toolbar features a series of commonly used command buttons that allow you to zoom, rotate, and view the part in different orientations.

5 Minimize window: Shrinks the document window. This command may come in handy when you want to view and work on two or more SolidWorks documents at the same time.

6 Maximize window: Enlarges the viewing window to full size.

7 Close window: Closes SolidWorks. If you've made any changes to your documents, SolidWorks prompts you to save the document.

8 CommandManager: Located beneath the Standard toolbar, the Command-Manager is a dynamic toolbar that lists command buttons for the type of document you are working on. (Read more in the upcoming "The CommandManager" section.)

9 FeatureManager design tree tab: Displays the FeatureManager design tree, similar to a Windows Explorer tree, where you can navigate the structure of your SolidWorks document.

10 PropertyManager tab: Displays the PropertyManager, where you enter the properties and other options for a SolidWorks command.

11 ConfigurationManager tab: Displays the ConfigurationManager design tree, available only for parts and assemblies. (You can find out more on how to manage configurations in Chapter 10.)

12 FeatureManager design tree: Displays the structure of your drawing, part, or assembly document.

13 Show Display pane: Expands or collapses the Display pane.

14 Graphics area: Displays the part, assembly, or drawing. Although SolidWorks allows you to open more than one document simultaneously, only one document is active at a time.

15 Pointer: Indicates the position of the mouse and lets you select items within the user interface. Note that the pointer changes based on where it's positioned in the interface.

16 ToolTip: Pops up to display an informational message about a feature or function and then disappears after a few seconds.

17 Status bar: Gives a more complete explanation of the selected function.

18 Status bar: Indicates the drawing, part, or assembly document that you're editing and helps you keep track of where you are. (See Chapter 6 for more information.)

19 Quick Tips Help: Indicates with a question mark button whether Quick Tips is on or off. Click the icon to toggle the state (on/off).

20 Resize window: Resizes the window if it isn't already maximized. Click and drag the window to its new size and then release the mouse.

21 SolidWorks Resources: Click to open the SolidWorks Resources tab, which contains links to resources, tutorials, tips of the day, and also command buttons to open or create SolidWorks documents.

22 Design Library: Click to open the Design Library. Inside you see the Design Library, Toolbox, and 3D Content Central, three resources that contain a plethora of standard design elements that you can drag and drop into your design. (Find out more about Design Library in Chapter 13.)

23 File Explorer: Duplicates Windows Explorer in your computer. Lists recently opened documents and currently open documents. You can drag documents from the File Explorer into the graphics area.

I prefer to maximize the document window so that I get a full view of what I'm working on. To ensure that SolidWorks uses this setting for all documents, choose Tools➪Options. In the dialog box that appears, click the Systems Options tab, select General, and select the check box for Maximize Document on Open.

The FeatureManager design tree

The FeatureManager design tree is to the left of the graphics window when you open a document in SolidWorks. You can think of the FeatureManager as command central for your SolidWorks design. The FeatureManager provides Windows Explorer-type selection and editing access to all the entities in your active document. In a part document, the FeatureManager displays part features, such as extrusions, fillets, boss, and so on. In an assembly, it gives you access to parts and subassembly components, and in a drawing, it provides access to drawing views, annotations, and constraints.

The FeatureManager offers several advantages:

✔ **Shows the order in which the elements of a document were created.** The newest element is on the top, while the oldest appears on the bottom.

✔ **Links to the graphic pane.** You can select an object by clicking on it either in the FeatureManager design tree or in the graphics area. Dynamic bidirectional highlighting occurs as you move the pointer over the members of the tree or the actual objects in the graphics pane.

✔ **Displays graphical feedback that describes feature or component characteristics.** For example, if an assembly component is hidden, its related icon in the FeatureManager tree looks empty. If the component is suppressed, it appears in gray.

✔ **Allows you to see the contents of folders in the tree.** You can click + or – to maximize or minimize a folder.

✔ **Gives you access to quick functions when you right-click.** The menu that appears changes based on each type of document and object (part features, drawing view, plane, and so on).

You can use arrow key navigation to walk through a design step-by-step if you enable this option: Choose Tools➪Options. In the dialog box that appears, click the Systems Options tab, select FeatureManager, and select the check box for Arrow Key Navigation.

If you want to understand how a design was built, select the rollback bar (a yellow-and-black line that turns blue when you select it) in the Feature-Manager design tree. Rollback temporarily reverts the model to an earlier state, suppressing recently added features. Drag the bar up or down the FeatureManager design tree to step forward or backward through the regeneration sequence.

If you're using arrow key navigation, the up and down arrows move the rollback bar.

The CommandManager

Located at the top-left corner of the user interface, just below the Standard toolbar, is the CommandManager, a smart toolbar that displays the menus you need for the task at hand. If you're editing an assembly, for example, the CommandManager shows the Assembly toolbar but hides the Feature toolbar because you can't edit a part feature until you open a part file.

The CommandManager is an efficient way to display SolidWorks numerous toolbars, which might otherwise clutter up the screen and block the graphics area. When you open a document, CommandManager appears with default tools for the file type you're working on.

The CommandManager is divided into two areas: the control area and an expanded toolbar. If you select a control area button, the corresponding toolbar displays in the toolbar area. For example, when you open a part document, the Features, Sketch, and Annotations buttons appear by default in the control area (see Figure 2-3). If you click Features, the Feature commands (Extruded Boss/Base, Extruded Cut, and so on) display in the toolbar area. If you click Sketch, the Sketch commands (Line, Rectangle, and so on) appear.

Figure 2-3:
Command-
Manager
displays the
tools you
want to see.

The CommandManager offers many advantages:

✓ **Reduces toolbar clutter.** Instead of having toolbars on the top, right, and left of the user interface, the CommandManager embeds them in a single toolbar and displays only the tools you need for a particular task.

✓ **Streamlines the work.** CommandManager keeps your workspace neat and tidy so that you can find what you need fast and work efficiently.

✓ **Minimizes mouse movements.** You can move more efficiently across the screen space as the CommandManager is at the top with the standard icons, the PropertyManager and FeatureManager design tree are on the left side, and the rest of the screen is available for the graphics window.

✓ **Minimizes the number of menu picks.** CommandManager puts the commands you need at your fingertips so that you don't have to navigate through menus and toolbars to find what you need.

If you find yourself squinting at the SolidWorks interface, try making the command buttons bigger. With a document open, choose View➪Toolbars➪ Customize. In the Customize dialog box, under the Toolbars tab, select Large icons. Click OK.

I also prefer to display the CommandManager without the descriptions below the command button, as shown in Figure 2-4. Using plain command buttons gives the CommandManager a cleaner look and allows room for more buttons. To turn off the descriptions, right-click anywhere on the CommandManager and deselect the check box for Show Description.

Figure 2-4:
You can
opt to
display the
Command-
Manager
without the
descriptions
below the
command
buttons.

Mouse buttons

One of your most used tools when working with SolidWorks is the mouse. SolidWorks uses three mouse buttons to access features, select objects, and perform tasks:

✔ **Left:** Selects menu items, entities in the graphics area, and objects in the FeatureManager design tree.

✔ **Right:** Displays context-sensitive options and shortcut menus so that you don't have to flounder around in a sea of menus looking for the right options.

✔ **Middle:** Rotates, pans, and zooms a part or an assembly. Scrolls in drawing documents.

If you use a wheel-type mouse, you can push down on the wheel to rotate a part. Scroll the wheel to zoom in on a model. Simply position the pointer on the object you want a close-up of and spin the mouse wheel toward you to zoom in on the object.

Here are a few notes on selecting objects:

✔ **To select a single entity:** Click the entity in the graphics window or in the FeatureManager design tree. Selected objects become highlighted in both the graphics area and FeatureManager tree.

✔ **To select a group of objects:** Hold down the left mouse button and drag a window around the objects.

✔ **To select more than one object:** Hold down the Ctrl key while clicking each object. If you want to deselect an object, click the object again.

✔ **To deselect all selected objects:** Click anywhere in the document window or user interface outside the part or assembly.

Getting a Better View of Things

One of the real beauties of SolidWorks is that once you build your model in three dimensions, you can move it around and play with it on-screen to ogle the design from a variety of angles. You can zoom in or out, you can turn the model upside down, or you can slice it in half to see what's inside. You can also vary the display state. You can view your model in its wireframe instead of solid form to get a better look at dimensions, for example. The ability to view a model in different ways gives you a better understanding of a design.

You control how a design appears on-screen using the View toolbar, which you find below the main menu, next to the Standard toolbar. The View toolbar is divided into three sections with commands for controlling orientation, display state, and display mode.

Orientation

The orientation section of the View toolbar offers several tools that allow you to move the model around on-screen, zoom in and out, pan, rotate, and so on. These manipulation tools include the following.

- ✔ **Previous View:** Switches back to the last view of the model. You can undo the last ten view changes.

- ✔ **Zoom to Fit:** Moves in or out so that your model or drawing fits entirely into the graphic display, and you can see the whole thing.

- ✔ **Zoom to Area:** Lets you zero in on the area you want to see. Click the area you want to view and drag the mouse to create a bounding box around the area. Let go of the mouse, and the area fills the screen.

- ✔ **Zoom In/Out:** Lets you move in close or far away. Drag the pointer up (toward the top of the screen) to zoom in or drag down to zoom out.

- ✔ **Zoom to Selection:** Zeroes in on a portion of a model or drawing that you select. Select an entity or hold down the Ctrl key to select multiple entities in the FeatureManager design tree and select Zoom to Selection.

- ✔ **Rotate View:** Allows you to rotate the model in space. Drag the pointer on the graphic display to rotate to the view you want.

- ✔ **Pan:** Scrolls the model or drawing in the document window. Drag the pointer in the direction you want to move the model across the screen.

Standard views

The Standards View toolbar is a flyout toolbar that is embedded in the View toolbar. (You can find out how to add flyouts to toolbars in the section "Adding flyout toolbars.") If you click the Standard View button in the View toolbar, you get a pull-down menu of several commands that represent standard engineering views. You can orient your model to one of these views manually by using the orientation tools in the View toolbar, or you can save time and click a Standard View command button.

Standard View commands include Side, Front, Top, Right, and Bottom. You can also choose the following perspectives: Isometric, Trimetric, and Dimetric. The difference between the perspectives is basically the angle of the model. The best way to understand each view is to just click on a button and see what happens to your model or drawing.

Display modes

The third section of the View toolbar offers the following display modes for model and drawing views in drawing documents. You can use the display modes to make your model look cool and to get a better understanding of it. These tools include the following:

- ✔ **Wireframe:** Displays all edges of the model.

- ✔ **Hidden Lines Visible:** Displays all edges of the model, but edges that are hidden from the current view display in a different color or font.

- ✔ **Hidden Lines Removed:** Displays only those edges of the model that you can see from the current view orientation.

- ✔ **Shaded View with Edges:** Displays a shaded view of the model with all of its edges.

- ✔ **Shaded:** Displays a shaded view of the model (no edges).

- ✔ **Shadows in Shaded Mode:** Displays a shaded view of the model with a shadow beneath the model.

- ✔ **Section View:** Displays a cutaway of a model using one or more cross-section planes (see Figure 2-5).

- ✔ **RealView Graphics:** Displays the model hardware accelerator shaders. Available with certain graphics cards, this mode uses realistic textures and highlights. In others words, chrome looks like chrome. (See the support section of the SolidWorks Web site for details on graphic cards.)

Figure 2-5:
The Section View displays a cut of the model.

You can set the default display mode of edges in all drawing documents. To do so, choose Tools⇨Options. In the Systems Options tab, under Drawings, select Display Style. In the options that appear, select the check box next to the display mode you want under Display Style for New Views. Click OK.

Exploring the SolidWorks Help Menu

If you get stuck in your quest to master SolidWorks, have no fear. The SolidWorks Help menu contains a plethora of information to get you back on track or point you in the right direction, at least.

Choose Help from the main menu. A pull-down menu, shown in Figure 2-6, appears with the following resources:

Figure 2-6: The SolidWorks Help menu offers a cornucopia of learning tools.

> SolidWorks Help Topics
> Quick Tips
> SolidWorks and Add-Ins API Help Topics
> Toolbox Help
>
> Moving from AutoCAD
>
> Online Tutorial
>
> What's New Manual
> ? Interactive What's New
> Service Packs...
>
> SolidWorks Release Notes
>
> About SolidWorks...
> About Toolbox...
>
> Customize Menu

- ✔ **SolidWorks Help Topics:** Takes you to the *SolidWorks Online User's Guide,* which addresses all the functions in the SolidWorks software. The guide includes context-sensitive topics, which you access from the PropertyManager, as well as additional topics and graphic examples. You can search the table of contents or the index. A glossary of SolidWorks terminology is also available.

- ✔ **Quick Tips:** Activates context-sensitive pop-up messages that appear while you're working on your document. These messages give tips on how to use the active command. Most of the messages have hyperlinks; click the hyperlink to see the associated item in the SolidWorks window.

- ✔ **Moving from AutoCAD:** Takes you to an online *Moving from AutoCAD* guide. Many new users switch from the 2D AutoCAD program to SolidWorks. This guide shows the differences between the two programs and helps to make the transition easier.

- ✔ **Online Tutorial:** Includes practical, step-by-step examples of more than 20 models you can build. These tutorials cover part creation, assembly operations, drawings, and several of the SolidWorks add-in programs, and are a good starting point for how to use the program.

✔ **What's New Manual:** Opens up a printable PDF manual. The manual explains new features and changes in the current version of SolidWorks.

✔ **Interactive What's New:** Provides links to topics in the What's New Manual on new menu items and new and changed PropertyManagers. The topics describe functionality added since the previous release of SolidWorks and often include examples with sample files.

✔ **SolidWorks Release Notes:** Contains information on new SolidWorks features that weren't available when the documentation was completed. For the most up-to-date information, refer to this document and to online help, which is updated with each SolidWorks Service Pack. You can find the release notes on the SolidWorks support site at www.solidworks.com/pages/services/subscription/index.html.

✔ **About SolidWorks:** Displays the version, service pack (minor version), and the serial number of your SolidWorks program. You can also access to Solidworks.com and the license agreement.

✔ **Toolbox Help:** Takes you to an online help resource for the Toolbox add-in, which addresses all the functions and features in Toolbox.

SolidWorks also offers context-sensitive help as you're working on documents. When you're working in a PropertyManager, for example, click the question mark in the top-right corner (see Figure 2-7) to link to information in the *SolidWorks Online User's Guide* about the active command.

Another way that SolidWorks walks you through the different program commands is with yellow message boxes, which appear now and again in the PropertyManager (refer to Figure 2-7). These boxes provide information on a particular feature and tell you what to do next.

Figure 2-7:
The yellow message box in the Property-Manager offers context-sensitive hints on using the program.

Customizing the User Interface

Every user has a preference on how the user interface should look. Fortunately, SolidWorks lets you customize keyboard shortcuts, toolbars, and icons to fit the way that you work. In fact, you may notice a couple of my own personal customizations (large icons and no description for the CommandManager) in screenshots throughout this book.

SolidWorks remembers the way that you configure the user interface and saves the settings in the document. (SolidWorks stores these settings in the Windows registry. I show you how to export and reload these settings in the upcoming section "Defining SolidWorks System Options.")

You can customize the CommandManager by adding or removing buttons to the control area of the CommandManager. But keep in mind that the changes you make stick for that document type only. You have to customize each document type separately.

To customize the SolidWorks CommandManager:

1. **Open a SolidWorks drawing, part, or assembly document.**

2. **Right-click anywhere on the CommandManager and select Customize CommandManager.**

   A menu of toolbar buttons appear with check boxes next to them. The toolbars with check marks next to them are the ones that already appear in the control area for this type of document. (In a part document, for example, Features, Sketch, and Surfaces are checked by default.)

3. **Select the check boxes next to the toolbar buttons you want to add to the CommandManager; deselect the ones you want to remove.**

   You want to select the toolbars you use most often. For example, if you make a lot of Molds, you want to select the Mold button.

4. **Click anywhere outside the menu to finish.**

You can also customize any of the other toolbars in SolidWorks by adding, deleting, or moving the command buttons. To customize other toolbar commands (but not CommandManager):

1. **With a document open, choose Tools⇨Customize.**

   The Customize dialog box appears.

2. **Select the Commands tab, as shown in Figure 2-8.**

Figure 2-8:
You can
drag a
command
button
from the
Customize
dialog box
and place a
copy of it in
another
toolbar
in the
SolidWorks
window.

Figure 2-8:
You can drag a command button from the Customize dialog box and place a copy of it in another toolbar in the SolidWorks window.

3. **Under Categories, select the toolbar that you want to change.**

   Under Buttons, you see all the buttons that appear in the toolbar that you selected. If you click a button, a description of what that button does appears under Description.

4. **Make your change to the toolbar.**

   What you do in this step depends on what you'd like to accomplish:

   • To place a copy of a command button in another toolbar, in the Customize dialog box, click and drag a command button to another toolbar in the SolidWorks window.

   • To remove a command button from a toolbar, in the SolidWorks window, click and drag the button from the toolbar to the graphics area.

   • To rearrange a command on a toolbar, in the SolidWorks window, click and drag the button from the toolbar to another area of the toolbar.

   • To move a command button from one toolbar to another, in the SolidWorks window, click and drag a button from one toolbar to a different toolbar.

5. **Click OK to close the Customize dialog box.**

Adding flyout toolbars

Another way to save space in the graphics area is with a flyout toolbar, which you can add to any toolbar including the CommandManager. A *flyout toolbar* makes functions accessible in one button, which takes up minimal space within the user interface and makes commands easy to access. When you click a Flyout button, the toolbar associated with that button appears, allowing you to conveniently scroll down and select the command you need. A good example of a flyout toolbar is the Standard Views flyout (see Figure 2-9) located on the View toolbar, which provides tools (Front, Back, Left, Right, and so on) to rotate the model, assembly, or sketch to a preset standard engineering view.

Figure 2-9: The Standard Views flyout is located in the View toolbar.

If you want to add a flyout toolbar button to another toolbar:

1. **With a document open, choose Tools⇨Customize.**

   The Customize dialog box appears.

2. **Select the Commands tab.**

3. **Select Flyout Toolbars under Categories.**

   You see several buttons appear on the right under buttons. These buttons are flyout toolbars that you can add to any other toolbar, including the CommandManager. Click a button to see a description of what the button does in the Description box.

4. **Under Buttons, drag a toolbar button to a toolbar in the SolidWorks window.**

5. **Click OK.**

Taking advantage of single-command mode

When you click a sketch or a dimension tool, the command stays active until you click it again, click another command, or press Escape on the keyboard. Known as *single-command mode,* this feature ensures that you're not stuck in a command. Once it's set, if you want to keep a command active for more than one use, double-click the icon when you select it.

To set single-command mode:

1. **Choose Tools⇨Options⇨Systems Options.**

   The Systems Options dialog box appears.

2. **Select General.**

   The General dialog box appears.

3. **Select the check box for Single Command Per Click.**

4. **Click OK.**

Defining SolidWorks System Options

Unlike Document Properties, SolidWorks system options relate to the system, not your document. Throughout this book, you find references on how to change various system options.

1. **Click Tools⇨Options.**

   A dialog box appears with two tabs, System Options and Document Properties. (The Document Properties tab only appears if you have a document open.)

2. **Under the System Options tab, select General.**

   Several options become available, as shown in Figure 2-10. The important ones to note are

   - **Open last used document(s) at startup.** Select Always or Never. Select Always if you want the documents that you used most recently to open automatically when you run SolidWorks again.

   - **Input dimension value.** Specifies that the Modify dialog box automatically displays when you create a new dimension. Otherwise, if you don't check this option, you must double-click the dimension to change its value.

- **Single command per pick.** Specifies that sketch and dimension tools clear after each use. (Double-clicking a tool causes it to remain selected for additional use.)

- **Show dimension names.** Displays the dimension's name as well as its value.

- **Show errors every rebuild.** Displays an error message each time you rebuild the model, if errors are present.

- **Maximize document on open.** Opens each document to its largest size within the SolidWorks window.

- **Use shaded face highlighting.** Displays selected faces in a solid color (green by default). To specify a different highlight color, click Tools, Options, System Options, <u>Colors</u>, and then select a different color for Selected Face, Shaded.

Figure 2-10:
Set the general system options in the System Options tab.

Chapter 3

Building Blocks for the Virtual Prototype

In This Chapter

▶ Planning the design and designing the plan

▶ Sketching it on paper

▶ Developing mistake-proof checklists

▶ Creating a design structure

*O*ne of the great strengths of SolidWorks is that it gives you the ability to create a complete virtual product on your computer screen. But don't let the word "virtual" fool you. No one is going to ask you to wear some high-tech headgear or relive an old sci-fi film (although I do like doing both).

By virtual, I mean that you can build a product in SolidWorks similar to how you would in the real world, from drawing an initial sketch to putting together parts and subassemblies to creating the final product. You don't get your hands dirty, and the final product you create looks as it would when rolling off the assembly line. Doing all this work in 3D has many advantages. You can see how components interact together and check that parts don't interfere with each other as they move. You can make sure that parts assemble properly on an assembly line and that they disassemble easily for maintenance. And you can show your customer how a final product will look even before it's built.

This chapter covers how to plan your design, the importance of drawing a hand sketch, and the basic building blocks for creating a virtual prototype.

As you read the sections on design layout sketches and skeletons, bear in mind that Chapter 4 (sketching) and Chapter 6 (assemblies) cover these topics in greater detail. Here, I introduce them only in the context of building a foundation for what's ahead.

Planning and Capturing Design Intent (Or, Think First and Then Do)

While throwing ideas onto a computer screen is certainly an easy way to start a project, starting with a plan is a better idea. The concept of think first and then design is key to building successful, re-usable designs. Applying some discipline to the design process is a good thing. A clearly defined, well-communicated *design intent* — what you want a design to do, how you want it to move, and how you want it to update when you make changes — results not only in a better design but one that, in my experience, gets out the door faster.

Some designers may argue that planning *is* extra work. They'd rather get on with hands-on work and complete the job as soon as possible. I'd argue that doing a job right the first time is worth the extra work up front. After all, everyone seems to make time to do the job right the second time! Just think how many times a design changes, not only during the initial development, but during the life of the product. The ability to easily understand and change the important elements of the design makes "getting on with it" easier.

So think first and then do. But thinking can be hard work. To make this part of the job a bit easier, I've come up with a handy list of tools that I use whenever I set out to build the foundation of a design I'm working on:

- Hand sketch of design intent
- Engineering journal
- Early brainstorm sessions
- Design reviews and checklists

These tools allow you to create a consistent and reusable design process, which helps you to define and document the key aspects of the initial design and to modify and create new versions of the product. They also can help you identify what you need to change and how the design will update as a result.

Starting the design with a hand sketch

When you start work on a design, you generally bump into more questions than answers, particularly when you're working on an all-new product as opposed to an improved version of one that's already out there, where you have access to existing information. So, assuming that you're not clairvoyant, how do you create and document a design so that you can easily modify it when new information becomes available? The answer: Simply grab a pencil and paper (or marker and whiteboard) and start sketching. When — and only when — you complete an initial hand sketch should you refer to Chapter 4 to find out how to turn that sketch into a SolidWorks model.

A simple hand sketch allows you to try different ideas and document what you know quickly. Believe it or not, you can capture even fairly complex systems in a design sketch. Sketching allows you to focus on the key design intent elements instead of hefty details that you have to address later. The key here is that the sketch should capture the essence of the design and not every minute detail.

Figure 3-1 shows a hand sketch of a machine design with motor and belts, key interface planes, and mounting hole locations. Similarly, your initial hand sketch should include the key functional areas of your design. You want to make sure to cover these key design issues:

✔ **Designed versus standard:** How many new versus existing or standard parts do you need for the design?

✔ **Major interfaces:** What are the interfaces between major design elements? This information comes in handy when you create the assembly structure.

✔ **Collaboration:** How many different people are going to work on the design? Are they in different locations? The logistics help determine who works on what parts.

✔ **Design reuse:** Are you going to base this design on an existing one? If so, update the old design to meet current standards so that you can re-use it.

✔ **Orientation:** What orientation depicts how you plan to manufacture or use the product in real life? It could be misleading, for instance, if you send your manufacturer a file that shows your assembly upside down. So be sure that front is front, back is back, and so on.

✔ **Specifications:** What information currently exists for the design? How big should it be? What is it made of? Are any important elements missing?

✔ **Manufacturing:** Include any additional design accommodations that need to be made for assembly fixtures, manufacturing, tooling, and so on.

✔ **Design notes and issues:** What additional notes, comments, or issues might the design group bring up? Be sure to capture and track these items.

✔ **Product life cycle:** How long do you plan to sell and maintain the product? If the design has a long life cycle, it may undergo a number of revisions in its lifetime, making design documents especially important.

Figure 3-1:
Your initial
hand sketch
should
cover the
major
design
elements.

Using an engineering journal and the SolidWorks Design Binder

As your design progresses, you need to answer a lot of questions and make many decisions. In the old days, before computers, engineers kept their thoughts and notes and other scribbles in a spiral notebook, or *engineering journal.* Nowadays, an engineering journal can be a Microsoft Word or Excel document. In SolidWorks, you have something even better, a virtual design folder called the *Design Binder,* where you can store links to documents that relate to the project. You'll never misplace your Design Binder because it's attached to your SolidWorks drawing, part, or assembly file. To link or attach a document to the Design Binder:

1. **Open the SolidWorks drawing, part, or assembly document.**

2. **In the FeatureManager design tree, right-click Design Binder and choose Add Attachment.**

   The Add Attachment dialog box appears.

3. **In the dialog box, type a path and filename or click the Browse button to navigate to the file you want to link or attach.**

4. **To link the file, check the Link option.**

   This option allows you to include a link to document. If you want to attach the physical document, leave this option blank.

5. **Click OK.**

   Your file or a link to your file shows up in the Design Binder. You can see what's inside the Design Binder by clicking the + sign to the left of the Design Binder in the FeatureManager design tree.

By default, the Design Binder also contains the Design Journal, a Microsoft Word document that helps to automate the journaling process. You can use the Design Journal to type notes and other thoughts on the design process. The document resembles an engineering journal with headings for File Name, Description, and Material. These fields link to the SolidWorks document properties and update whenever you open the journal. You can type text, paste images, and format text in the Design Journal just as you would in any Word document. When you open the Design Journal, SolidWorks captures a screen image of your design and attaches it to the Clipboard so that you can conveniently paste it into the document to help describe what's going on.

To make an entry into the Design Journal:

1. **Click the + sign to the left of the Design Binder icon (see Figure 3-2) within the FeatureManager design tree.**

   The folder maximizes to display its contents, which include the Design Journal and any other documents you add.

2. **Double-click the Design Journal to open the document in Microsoft Word.**

3. **Make your entries in the Design Journal.**

4. **Paste (Ctrl+V) an image of your design into the Design Journal.**

   SolidWorks takes a snapshot of the design and puts it in the Clipboard each time you open Design Journal, so you can paste it in the journal.

5. **Choose File⇨Exit.**

   Your document updates, Microsoft Word closes, and you return to SolidWorks.

Figure 3-2:
The Design Binder is a place to keep documents and files that relate to your project.

2D Layout
Annotations
Design Binder
Material <not specified>
Lights and Cameras
Front
Top
Right
Origin
Sketch1

The Design Binder is a tool that you can use consistently throughout the design process to capture ideas, issues, and decisions. You also may want to store engineering notes the old-fashioned way, in a good old spiral notebook. Find the option that fits your requirements and working style.

Capturing design intent: Brainstorming

Brainstorming is a fruitful approach to pulling collective ideas out of your design team. Have a meeting early in the design process and map out the design intent, including all the big elements of your product design on a large whiteboard. Write down ideas and functions the design should include. Document how the product should move. Make notes on potential issues and risks and include any other information that may be helpful.

These meetings are a great way to document some of that "tribal information" that lives quietly in everyone's head. Get everyone's ideas in writing. This review provides a consistent foundation for the design. The more you can identify before charging forward, the better.

Oh, and by the way, don't count on everyone to remember exactly what was said in the meeting. If you're using an electronic whiteboard, write a date over the top and print a copy. Otherwise, take a picture with your digital camera and pop the image into your Design Binder.

Making a list and checking it twice

Checklists are valuable tools in the design process. After all, if a checklist works for Santa Claus, why not for a design team? The purpose of the checklist is to provide a consistent basis or foundation for your design project and to reduce those (very avoidable) simple mistakes.

Your checklist should list common questions that the design team needs to address early in the design process, such as:

- Has anyone approved or sourced the material you want to use?
- Have you added engineering requirements to the RFQ (request for quotation)?
- Has your purchasing department submitted an RFQ?
- Have you completed and documented the design review?
- Have you checked design standards?
- Have you checked the assembly to ensure that the parts fit together properly and do not clash, or interfere, with one another when they move?
- Are you using standard hardware for all fasteners? (If not, you should be, unless you want to design them all yourself.)
- Have you completed the drawing title block and revision block? *Blocks* include standard information that you insert into drawings. A *title block* lists your company name and other basic information about the project. A *revision block* includes the revision number of the document. You

should include blocks in the drawing templates. (See Chapter 7 for more information on blocks.)

✔ Have you added custom properties to the document? *Custom properties* include information that identifies the project and the document. You can link custom property fields to the drawing title block so that information is consistent in both areas. (You can find more on custom properties in Chapter 10.)

✔ Is your testing and validation plan complete? This process should include a schedule of how and when you plan to optimize the design using analysis software or physical prototypes or a combination of both.

Quite often, you can use the same checklist from design to design. In fact, having a standard checklist ensures consistency throughout your design processes and makes documenting the design easier. Remember, a pilot has good reason to go over a checklist each and every time he flies a plane, so why not review a checklist each and every time you design?

The process for starting and documenting a design should be a well-worn and familiar path, not something you think up out of the blue each time you design a new product. Build reviews (like the design intent brainstorm listed in the preceding section) into your design process and subsequent design meetings. Planning for success is the best way to ensure that it happens.

Applying Layouts and Design Skeletons

After you've come up with a hand sketch (see the section "Starting the design with a hand sketch," earlier in this chapter), you're ready to translate it into a design layout sketch. The design layout sketch is related to — and often a subset of — the *design skeleton.*

Just to give you a couple of working definitions:

✔ **Assembly:** A collection of parts and other assemblies, known as sub-assemblies. A SolidWorks assembly file has a .sldasm extension.

✔ **Design skeleton:** A simple framework made up of design layout sketches and simple reference geometry (planes and axes) that document the important elements of the design.

✔ **Design layout sketch:** A 2D sketch that defines the key elements of the design. The design layout can be, and often is, a subset of the design skeleton.

This chapter describes how to create a framework for your SolidWorks *assembly* (your virtual prototype) using a design layout sketch or a skeleton. (For more information on layouts and skeletons, see Chapter 6.)

Your assembly can have anywhere from 2 to 1,000 or more components, which can be parts or other assemblies called *subassemblies.* Depending on how complex your assembly is, your skeleton may include one or more layout sketches.

The advantages of the skeleton include

✔ It gives you a better grasp of the design you're about to build. You can create and modify the assembly before you actually design any parts. Determining the most important aspects of the design early in the design process makes for a better design. The skeleton is the electronic version of the hand sketch discussed early in this chapter. (See the section "Starting the design with a hand sketch.")

✔ You can capture design intent in the design layout sketch so that you can collaborate better with team members. And the designer who works on this assembly can immediately see how parts fit together.

✔ As you create components for your assembly, you can design them so that they reference geometry in the layout sketch. If you change the layout sketch, those components that reference it update accordingly. A reference to geometry within the assembly is called an *in-context reference* and is a way of making sure that parts fit together correctly. You can design an assembly in two ways: top down or bottom up. In *top-down design,* you build parts in the assembly, using the geometry of one part to design the others. In other words, top-down design relies on in-context references. *Bottom-up design* is the opposite; you design each part individually and then assemble the components to make the assembly.

So which method is better, top-down or bottom-up design? In reality, a combination of both methods works best. By creating a skeleton first, you can design parts to reference the skeleton, instead of having them reference other parts, thereby giving you more control over the design. Other benefits include

✔ The assembly components reference the simple skeleton instead of complex parts or subassemblies.

✔ You can select a project leader to control important features. Too many cooks spoil the soup. I have worked on complex design where a skeleton controlled the interaction and location of the major subassemblies. It was too risky to allow just anyone to change the skeleton, which controlled the top-down design. Limiting the number of people responsible for the health of the skeleton worked very well.

✔ The entire assembly framework is collected into one skeleton, so even if you work on just the left widget assembly, you can see other important aspects of the design without having to look at the entire assembly.

WARNING! While in-context references are a very powerful feature, it's a stick with a sharp end. Too many external references affect performance due to the fact that SolidWorks needs to look at the original reference document to determine whether anything has changed. (For more information, see Chapter 6.)

Figure 3-3 shows a design layout sketch that controls the size, location, and design intent for two major sections (each section has its own separate components) within a larger assembly. The design layout sketch only captures essential design features. Too much detail can clutter up the design layout sketch and make it confusing. (And don't forget that all that clutter can make SolidWorks run slower, which can eat into your efficiency ratings.)

Figure 3-3:
A layout
sketch of
a belt
assembly
captures
major
design
elements.

REMEMBER You can find more information on the icons and toolbars that this section describes on the Cheat Sheet in the front of this book or in Chapter 2.

Here's how to create a design layout sketch of a 3D part in SolidWorks:

1. Choose File⇨New from the main menu.

The New SolidWorks Document dialog box appears (see Figure 3-4). You can choose to open a part, assembly, or drawing template.

TIP A *template* is what SolidWorks uses to begin a new document. You can modify templates or create new ones based on your needs. If you want to see what other templates are available, click Advanced in the New SolidWorks Document dialog box. The SolidWorks interface switches to Advance mode. To toggle back to a simpler version of the dialog box, click Novice.

2. Select Assembly and click OK.

A new SolidWorks assembly window appears, as shown in Figure 3-5.

Figure 3-4:
The New
SolidWorks
Document
dialog box
lets you
choose a
new
document
template.

CommandManager   2D Sketch

Figure 3-5:
The
SolidWorks
interface
appears
when
starting a
new part.

FeatureManager   Graphics Area

3. Choose Insert⇨Sketch.

The Edit Sketch PropertyManager appears. In the graphics area, the
FeatureManager design tree icon appears. If you click the + sign to the
right of it, you see Front Plane, Top Plane, and Right Plane. You can
sketch on these three planes. If you move the pointer over a plane in the
FeatureManager design tree, the border of the plane highlights in the
graphics window.

4. **Select the Front Plane in the FeatureManager design tree.**

   The Edit Sketch PropertyManager disappears. The display changes so that the front plane faces you and the Sketch commands appear in the CommandManager. Any entities you sketch attach to the front plane.

5. **Create your design layout sketch using the sketch tools.**

   Create the 3D sketch of your original hand sketch, making sure that you capture the important elements and design intent. (If you want to find out more about sketching, read Chapter 4.) The sketch tools follow. Choose a command and follow the instructions next to it.

   - **Line:** Sketch a horizontal or vertical line or an angle. Select orientation in the Insert Line PropertyManager. In the graphics area, click to begin the line. Double-click to end and click OK in the Line PropertyManager to accept the line.

   - **Rectangle:** Create rectangles whose sides are horizontal or vertical with respect to the sketch grid. Click and place the first corner of the rectangle. Drag and release when the rectangle is the correct size.

   - **Parallelogram:** Draw rectangles whose sides are at an orientation other than horizontal or vertical with respect to the grid. Click and place the first corner of the parallelogram. Drag and release when the rectangle is the correct size.

   - **Polygon:** Create equilateral polygons with 3 to 40 sides. Select the Polygon command. Set properties in the Polygon PropertyManager. In the graphics area, click to place the center and drag out the polygon. Click OK.

   - **Circle:** Sketch a center-based circle with this tool. Select the center or perimeter orientation in the Circle PropertyManager. Click the graphics area to place the center, move the point, and click to set the radius. Click OK in the Circle PropertyManager.

   - **Partial Ellipse:** Create a partial ellipse from a centerpoint, a start point, and an end point. Click in the graphics area to place the centerpoint. Drag and click to define one axis of the ellipse. Drag and click to define the second axis. Drag the pointer around the circumference to define the extent of the ellipse and then click to complete the ellipse.

   - **Parabola:** Create a parabolic curve. Click to place the focus of the parabola and drag to enlarge the parabola, which outlines the parabola. Click the parabola to define the extent of the curve.

   - **Spline:** Create a series of curves that run through points. Click to place the first point and drag out the first segment. Click to the endpoint and drag out the second segment. Keep going until the spline is complete. Click OK.

   - **Point:** Insert points into your sketch. Click in the graphics area to place the point.

- **Centerline:** Create symmetrical sketch elements. Click to start the centerline. Drag the pointer and click to set the end.

- **Sketch Fillet:** Trim away the corner at an intersection of two sketch entities to create a tangent arc. Click the Sketch Fillet tool and set the properties in the PropertyManager. Select two sketch entities or select a corner. Click OK to accept the fillet.

- **Sketch Chamfer:** Apply a chamfer to adjacent sketch entities in sketches. Click tool. Set Chamfer Parameters in the PropertyManager. Select two sketch entities to chamfer or select a vertex. Click OK to accept the chamfer.

6. **Choose Insert⇨Exit Sketch to exit the sketch.**

7. **Choose File⇨Save to save the assembly.**

   Don't forget to save your work. SolidWorks also asks whether you want to save any work in progress before you close down the program.

The preceding method creates the design layout sketch within the assembly, but that's not the only way to go. You can also create the design layout sketch in a part file and add the part to the assembly later. I cover this method in Chapter 6.

Assembly components can reference information (size or location) in the design layout or in the skeleton (next section). Both of these are examples of in-context references, meaning that when you change the design layout sketch or the skeleton, change the geometry that references those updates accordingly.

To reference parts to other parts, design layout sketches as in-context relations:

1. **Open the assembly file that contains the part to edit.**

2. **Click on the part to edit within the FeatureManager design tree or in the graphics area.**

3. **Click the Edit Component icon within the Assemblies toolbar.**

   The part you select appears normally; the other assembly components are transparent.

4. **Edit the part.**

   Make changes to the parts design. You can reference the assembly components to drive in-context relations.

5. **Click the Edit Component icon within the Assemblies toolbar to return to the original assembly.**

Thinking about Skeletons You Want in Your Closet

No, this section isn't about Uncle Bob at last year's Christmas party, but rather a SolidWorks feature that you can use to depict and document the major design elements of the assembly.

While a design layout sketch is great for laying out a single 3D part, you want to use a *skeleton* when creating something large and complex, such as a lawnmower. Similar to a sketch, a skeleton is saved as a SolidWorks part document (.slprt). However, a skeleton incorporates several design layout sketches and uses other elements (such as planes and axes) that allow you to simulate the location, important interfaces where parts fit together, and motion of the assembly components. Figure 3-6 shows an example of how you can extend 2D layout sketches into a 3D design skeleton.

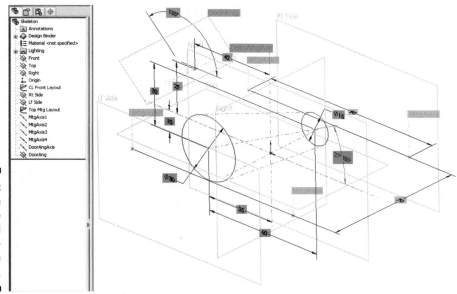

Figure 3-6:
You can reference parts and subassemblies to the skeleton.

You may opt to use a skeleton for several reasons:

- ✔ You can add more than one design layout sketch to the assembly. You may need a number of different orientations and functional design layout sketches to document the design intent for the assembly.

- ✔ You can add additional reference geometry (for example, 2D planes and axes) to the assembly to document other elements of the design that a layout design sketch cannot describe.

- ✔ Reference geometry can allow your virtual assembly to move or rotate as the real assembly would. If you've designed your assembly so that it moves or rotates, you can use the design skeleton to analyze how the assembly works in real life.

If working with a skeleton sounds intriguing, you may want to check out Chapter 6, which delves into the whole concept of design skeletons.

Part II
Design Intent and the Virtual Prototype

The 5th Wave   By Rich Tennant

With Dad's SolidWorks rendering of forest trolls, his campfire stories achieved new heights in realism.

In this part . . .

*E*asy-to-modify, or *robust,* designs provide a strong foundation for the design because you can create parts that are easy to understand and modify. You then use these parts to build functional assemblies. This design food chain is an effective means to build parts and assemblies.

It's the small things that count during the design process. This part builds on two main ideas: design intent (fit, form, and function) and the virtual prototype. SolidWorks creates the parts in 3D, which helps you get a better understanding of your design, long before you ever manufacture the first part.

Chapter 4

Do What I Mean, Not What I Sketch

*J*ust like building a house, your design needs to start with a sound and sturdy foundation. Sketches are the building blocks for your design. Before you start to build parts and assemblies, you need to know how to create a good sketch and to understand how a sketch impacts the rest of the design.

You may think it strange to talk about sketches before creating parts, but the ability to create sketches that capture design intent makes it easier to create the part. In other words, you need to walk before you run, so be sure that these concepts are clear before you go to other chapters in the book. Each step in the sketch process helps you think about how to create a better design and take the full advantage of the SolidWorks 3D modeling system.

In this chapter, I introduce what makes up a sketch: sketch entities (lines, arcs, and so on) and reference geometry (axes and planes). I also examine how part features use these objects.

Making and Editing a Sketch

A *sketch* is a collection of simple elements, such as lines, rectangles, and circles. Sketches can be 2D or 3D and serve a number of uses within SolidWorks, but most important, they are the basis for sketched features. *Features* (extruded bosses, cuts, and so on) are the geometrical shapes that you use to build parts. A model includes one or more sketches as well as one or more features (unless the part was created from imported geometry). This section focuses on how to create sketches to use as the bases of part features. Chapter 5 goes into detail on all the part features.

Here is the order to follow when you make a sketch:

1. Draw the sketch geometry.
2. Add relations.
3. Dimension the sketch.

Elements of a sketch

Before you find out how to draw the sketch, you should first become familiar with the sketch lingo that appears throughout this chapter. Refer to the following terms when you need to.

- ✔ **Origin:** Marks the center of the document. When a sketch is active, two red arrows appear in the middle of the graphic display and mark the (0,0,0) coordinate of the sketch. When you're working on a part, the arrows are blue. When a sketch is active, the origin appears red. Each part and assembly has its own origin. You can't delete the origin of a part or assembly.

- ✔ **Construction geometry:** Assists you in creating the sketch entities and geometry that you ultimately incorporate into a part. Points and centerlines are always construction geometry, but you can convert any other sketch entity into a construction geometry. Construction geometry appears as a dashed line. SolidWorks does not look at construction geometry when it creates part features.

- ✔ **Reference geometry:** Defines the shape or form of a surface or a solid in the model. SolidWorks uses reference geometry (planes, axes, coordinate systems, and points) as the basis for creating part features.

- ✔ **Plane:** Flat reference geometry. In a part or an assembly document, SolidWorks provides three default planes (front, top, and right). You can create your own reference planes as well. You must begin a sketch on either a plane or the flat, planar face of a part.

- **Axis:** An infinite straight dashed line that you use to create model geometry, features, or patterns. You can create an axis in a number of different ways, including by creating a line, a construction line, or by intersecting two planes.

- **Driving Dimension:** Known as *model dimensions,* driving dimensions define the size of a sketch, which drives the shape of the model. When you change a sketch dimension, the rest of the sketch updates accordingly. (Chapter 3 covers design intent in detail.)

- **Driven Dimension:** Sometimes called *reference dimensions,* these show the measurements of a model, but they don't drive the model, and you can't change them. You can add driven dimensions to sketches and drawings.

- **Sketch entities:** Simple objects, such as lines, points, and circles, that make up a sketch.

- **Relations:** Establish geometric relations for a single sketch entity and between sketch entities. For example, a parallel relation makes two lines parallel to each other; a tangent relation makes two lines tangent, and so on. Relations are an important method for capturing design intent.

Origins and orientation

How you kick off a sketch varies depending on how you want your design to look and the type and order of the design's features. Before you begin a sketch, you want to decide on the following:

- The reference plane or part face that you want to sketch on
- The origin of the sketch
- The relationships between the sketch entities
- The dimensions you need for the drawing

Every time you draw a sketch, you must first select a plane or a part face (such as the left side of a cube) to draw it on. The plane determines the orientation of your sketch. If you sketch on the front plane, you're sketching the front of a part. You don't want to end up with a part that is upside down or sideways, so choosing the right plane or surface is important.

The origin is where you start your sketch. In most cases, the origin of the sketch coincides with the origin of the document. The origin anchors your sketch. Centers of mounting holes, axes of rotation, and the mounting face are also good choices for an origin. Figure 4-1 shows examples of parts with origins defined with design intent in mind.

You can use the following list to determine the orientation or origin of your sketch:

- **Part origin:** Parts in an assembly can share a common origin. Parts are built with this common assembly location in mind.
- **Final assembly orientation:** You can position a part based on how it fits into the assembly.
- **Design layout:** You can position a part based on a design layout sketch or a skeleton.
- **Drawing views to create:** You can design a part based on how you want it projected in the drawing.

Origin

Figure 4-1:
Choose an origin that means something to the part.

Sketching with entities

After you've pondered over origins and orientation, you're ready to take your mouse in hand and draw. You begin a sketch in a part document by activating sketch mode. You can switch back into solid modeling mode by exiting sketch mode. Sketch entities are what you use to build the sketch. The sketch entities commands are located in the Sketch toolbar, which appears by default in the CommandManager when you begin a sketch.

Here's how to start a sketch:

1. **Open a new part document in SolidWorks.**

    The origin appears in blue in the graphic display area.

2. **Choose Insert⇨Sketch.**

    The Edit Sketch PropertyManager appears in the left pane. Three default planes (Front, Top, and Right) appear in the graphic display. If you place the pointer over a plane, the plane's edges highlight red.

3. **Click an edge of a plane or anywhere on a part face to sketch in the graphic area.**

    You can begin a sketch on a plane or a part face. You can select a default plane, or you can create your own. (See the section "Adding reference geometry," later in this chapter.) When you select a plane, the Edit Sketch PropertyManager disappears, and the plane turns to face you.

4. **Create your sketch using the sketch entities in Table 4-1.**

5. **Choose Insert⇨Exit Sketch.**

    You exit sketch mode and return to the part. The origin turns blue. Your sketch is saved with the part document.

When you finish creating a sketch entity, the sketch command is still active, and you just keep drawings circles and lines and so on. Double-clicking the button when you start a command keeps the command active after you place the first item. Right-click and choose Select or press Esc to place the entity and exit the command.

Table 4-1	Sketch Entities
Entity	**_Function_**
Line	A straight segment. Click Line on the Sketch toolbar and click the start and end points to define the line within the graphics area. Additional clicks creates a series of connected lines.
Rectangle	A box that consists of four lines. Click Rectangle on the Sketch toolbar and then, in the graphic area, click to place the first corner of the rectangle, drag to size the rectangle, and click again.
Circle	A full circle. Click Circle on the Sketch toolbar and click the origin and radius locations within the graphics area.

(continued)

Table 4-1 *(continued)*

Entity	Function
Centerpoint Arc	A partial circle defined by three points. Click Centerpoint Arc on the Sketch toolbar and click the origin, start, and end radius locations within the graphics area.
Tangent Arc	An arc tangent to a sketch entity. Click Tangent Arc on the Sketch toolbar and click the endpoint of an existing tangent entity (line, arc, ellipse, or spline) and the endpoint for the arc within the graphics area
Three Point Arc	A partial circle. Click Three Point Arc on the Sketch toolbar and click the three points on the arc within the graphics area.
Sketch Fillet	A tangent arc between two intersecting entities. Click Sketch Fillet on the Sketch toolbar and set properties in the PropertyManager. Hold Ctrl and select two sketch entities to fillet and select a corner.
Centerline	A straight line that is construction geometry. Click Centerline on the Sketch toolbar and click the start and end points to define the line within the graphics area.
Spline	A curvy line defined by a set of points. Click Spline on the Sketch toolbar and click the point locations within the graphics area to define the spline.
Point	An entity that defines a single location in space. Click Point on the Sketch toolbar and click the location for the sketch point within the graphics area.

Modifying sketch entities

Several additional commands on the Sketch toolbar allow you to make changes to your sketch if needed. For example, the Construction command turns any sketch entity into construction geometry.

You create your sketch in a part or an assembly document. When you open a document to edit a sketch, you need to switch back into sketch mode. To turn sketching on, choose Insert⇨Sketch. When you want to go back to solid modeling to create part features, choose Insert⇨Exit Sketch. If the sketch already exists, select the sketch in the FeatureManager design tree, right-click, and choose Edit Sketch.

The following sections cover the sketch modification commands (see Figure 4-2), which you find on the right side of the Sketch toolbar.

Figure 4-2:
The sketch
modification
commands
are on the
right side of
the Sketch
toolbar.

Mirror Entities

When you create Mirror Entities, SolidWorks mirrors the entities that you select about a centerline or line. If that sounds confusing, imagine that you're standing on the edge of a pond. You see a reflection of yourself in the water. The reflection is your mirror image, and the centerline, which you *mirror about,* is the edge of the pond. In SolidWorks, if you change a mirrored entity, its mirror image also changes.

To mirror one or more existing sketch entities in a sketch:

1. **Click Mirror Entities on the Sketch toolbar.**

   The Mirror PropertyManager appears, with the Entities To Mirror field active.

2. **In the graphic area, click the entities you want to mirror.**

   The entities display in the Entities To Mirror field. If you want to remove an entity, select it in the field and press Delete on the keyboard.

3. **Click inside the Mirror About field.**

   The field highlights, indicating that the next entity you select goes in this field.

4. **Click the check box for Copy to include both the mirrored copy and the original sketch entities. Clear the check box for Copy to add a mirror copy of the selected entities and remove the original sketch.**

   If you remove the original sketch, it's like removing the original object in a mirror and leaving only a reflection.

5. **Click the edge or line that you want to mirror about the centerline.**

   The edge or line appears in the Mirror About field.

6. **Click OK.**

   A mirror image of the entities you selected appears on the other side of the line or edge.

Convert Entities

You can create one or more curves in a sketch by projecting an edge, loop, face, curve, external sketch contour, set of edges, or set of sketch curves onto an existing sketch plane.

To convert sketch entities in an open sketch:

1. **Click a model edge, loop, face, curve, external sketch contour, set of edges, or set of curves.**

2. **Click Convert Entities on the Sketch toolbar.**

   The new sketch entities appear on the sketch plane.

3. **Click OK.**

Offset Entities

You can make a copy of a sketch entity so that the copy appears a specified distance on the sketch plane from the original object. To offset one or more sketch entities in an open sketch:

1. **Click Offset Entities on the Sketch toolbar.**

   The Offset Entities PropertyManager appears.

2. **In the Parameters section of the PropertyManager, type a value for the offset distance.**

3. **In the graphics area, click the entity or entities to offset.**

   To see a dynamic preview, hold down the mouse button and drag the pointer in the graphics area. As you drag the pointer, the size of the offset changes. When you release the mouse button, the Offset Entity is complete.

4. **Click OK.**

Trim Entities

You can trim entities to your liking with the Trim Entities command. The command allows you to create unusual shapes. For example, you can sketch a large circle with two small circles intersecting it at the top. You can then trim away the criss-crossing arcs of the three circles to end up with a shape that looks like Mickey Mouse. There are several options in the Trim Property Manager. The Power Trim option is a quick way to trim or delete any sketch entity. The Corner option lets you trim two entities to the nearest intersection. Both options allow you to "clean up" a sketch.

To trim sketch entities by using the Power Trim option:

1. **Right-click the sketch and choose Edit Sketch.**

   (For a new sketch, choose Insert⇨Sketch.)

2. **Click Trim Entities on the Sketch toolbar.**

   The Trim PropertyManager appears.

3. **In the Options section of the PropertyManager, click Power Trim.**

4. **Click and drag your cursor across the entities you want to trim.**

   The sketch entity trims the portion of the sketch you drag over. If there is no intersecting entity, the entity you select to trim is deleted.

5. **Click OK.**

To trim sketch entities using the Corner option:

1. **Right-click the sketch and choose Edit Sketch.**

   (For a new sketch, choose Insert⇨Sketch.)

2. **Click Trim Entities on the Sketch toolbar.**

   The Trim PropertyManager appears.

3. **In the Options section of the PropertyManager, select Corner.**

   This option trims two sketch entities to their intersection.

4. **Click two entities to trim in the graphics area.**

   Click the portion you want to keep.

5. **Click OK.**

   The two entities trim to the nearest corner.

Construction Geometry

You can change any sketch geometry to construction geometry by using the Construction Geometry command. Construction geometry serves as a guideline for creating the rest of the sketch. Construction geometry doesn't show in a part feature.

To change sketch geometry to construction geometry:

1. **Click the sketch entity that you want to change to construction geometry.**

   To select multiple entities, hold Ctrl and click. A sketch entity turns green when it's selected.

2. **Click Construction Geometry on the Sketch toolbar.**

   The selected entities appear with a dashed line to indicate that they are construction geometry. You can toggle back to sketch geometry by repeating the preceding steps.

Move Entities

You can move any sketch entity to a new location by using the Move or Copy Entities command.

To reposition sketch geometry:

1. **Click Move Entities on the Sketch toolbar.**

   The Move PropertyManager appears, with the Sketch items or annotations field active.

2. **Select the entities to move within the graphics area.**

   The entity names appear in the Sketch Items or Annotations field.

3. **Click the From/To or X/Y option from the Parameters field.**

   The base point (From/To) or delta x/ delta y (X/Y) fields, based on this selection, appear.

4. **Click inside the Base Point field (From/To) or enter the change in X and Y coordinates (X/Y).**

5. **Click the start point for the move in the graphics area for the From/To option.**

   The entity highlights green, and two green arrows indicating the base point X, Y coordinates appear near the pointer. As you move the pointer, the entities move with it.

6. **Drag the pointer and click to place the entity in its new location for the X/Y option.**

7. **Click OK.**

Adding reference geometry

When you sketch, axes and planes serve as reference geometry for the part you're about to build. *Planes* are flat surfaces that you draw your sketch on. *Axes* are straight lines that serve as the center of rotation for some shapes. You can create axes in many ways. For example, you can create an axis from a centerline or the intersection of two planes.

SolidWorks also creates temporary axes for cones and cylinders in the model. Sometimes confusion occurs about the difference between centerlines and axes. The difference is that a centerline is contained in a sketch, and an axis is in a part.

Here are a few other important aspects about reference geometry:

✔ To control the visibility for reference planes, axes, and temporary axes, in the main menu, choose View and select the reference type (Axes, Origin, and so on) that you want on or off. A checkmark next to a reference means that it's turned on.

✔ In the main menu, choose View and select Hide All Types to hide all types of reference geometry with a single selection. To turn on the display of all reference geometry, just deselect this option. A checkmark next to Hide All Types means that all types are hidden.

✔ When you create a plane or an axis, you should name it in the FeatureManager design tree to document how you intend to use it. To name a sketch entity, in the FeatureManager design tree, click the entity, press F2, and type a name. Naming items in the FeatureManager design tree is a key concept of capturing design intent.

Creating planes

In a part or assembly document, SolidWorks gives you three default planes to work with (front, top, and right). You can create additional planes to serve as the sketch planes or to create a section view of a model.

To create a reference plane:

1. **Open a part or an assembly document.**

2. **Choose Insert⇨Reference Geometry⇨Plane.**

   The Plane PropertyManager appears, with the Reference Entities field active.

3. **In the PropertyManager, select the type of plane you want to create.**

   You have several options, as shown in Figure 4-3:

   • **Through Lines/Points:** Creates a plane through a point and an edge, an axis, or a sketch line or through three points.

   • **Parallel Plane at Point:** Creates a plane through a point parallel to a plane or face.

   • **At Angle:** Creates a plane through an edge, an axis, or a sketch line at an angle that you specify to a face or plane. (If you choose this plane, enter the angle value into the spin box.)

   • **Offset Distance:** Creates a plane parallel to a plane or a face, offset by a distance you specify. This option is the default plane. (If you choose this plane, enter the offset value in the spin box.)

   • **Normal to Curve:** Creates a plane through a point and makes it perpendicular to an edge or a curve.

   • **On Surface:** Creates a plane on a nonplanar face or an angular surface.

4. **Click the items in the graphic that you want to create the plane with.**

   The items appear in the Reference Entities field. You must select valid entities. For example, if you choose Normal to Curve, you must select a point and an edge or a curve. If you want to remove a selection, select the item and press the Delete key.

   A preview of the new plane appears in the graphics area.

5. **Click OK.**

   The PropertyManager closes, and your new plane appears in the graphic display.

You can also copy planes offset at a distance. Select the plane in the graphics window by holding down the mouse button and the Ctrl key on the keyboard and then moving the pointer to a new location and releasing the mouse button.

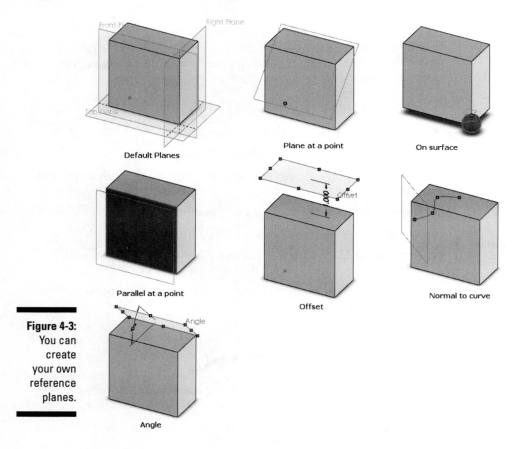

Figure 4-3:
You can create your own reference planes.

Default Planes

Plane at a point

On surface

Parallel at a point

Offset

Normal to curve

Angle

Working with axes

An *axis* is a type of reference geometry that you use to create a part feature. You can create an axis in a number of different ways by selecting different part geometry. Figure 4-4 shows the different axis types and the geometry required to create the axis.

On Edge

Two Planes

Plane and a point

Two points/vertices

Cylindrical/Conical face

Figure 4-4:
You can create axes from different part geometry.

Point and a face

Temporary Axes

To create a reference axis:

1. **Open a part or an assembly document.**

2. **Choose Insert⇨Reference Geometry⇨Axis.**

   The Axis PropertyManager appears with the Reference entities field active.

3. **Choose the type of Axis to create.**

   Your choices are as follows:

   - **One Line/Edge/Axis:** Creates an axis through a line, edge, or a temporary axis. Select a sketch line or an edge or choose View⇨ Temporary Axes and select the axis in the graphic area.

   - **Two Planes:** Creates an axis at the intersection of two planes. Select two planar faces or choose View⇨Planes and then select two planes in the graphics area.

   - **Two Points/Vertices:** Creates an axis through two points or part vertices. Select two vertices, points, or midpoints.

   - **Cylindrical/Conical Face:** Creates an axis based on an existing hole or cylindrical feature. Select a cylindrical or conical face.

   - **Point and Face/Plane:** Creates an axis that is normal (perpendicular) to a face through an existing point. Select two entities: a surface or a plane *and* a vertex point or a midpoint. The resultant axis is normal to the selected surface or plane through the selected vertex, point, or midpoint. If the surface is nonplanar, the point must be on the surface.

4. **In the graphics area, select the reference entities to create the axis.**

   The reference entities you select appear in the Reference Entity field. If you want to clear a selection, click it in the Reference Entity field and press Delete.

5. **Click OK.**

   The axis appears in the graphics display.

Defining the Sketch

A good sketch captures design intent. *Design intent* is all about how you want your model to behave when you make a change.

Say that you make a part with two holes. You want the holes to have the same diameter and to stay symmetric around the centerline of the part, even when you change the length of the part. You need to capture your intent in your sketches. The way to capture design intent is to *constrain* the design. (Another word for constraining a sketch is *defining* a sketch.)

SolidWorks offers two types of constraints: relations and dimensions. *Relations* establish geometric relationships (equal, tangent, and so on) between sketch entities. *Dimensions* constrain the length, width, or angle of a sketch entity so that it stays constant.

A sketch can by fully defined, underdefined, or overdefined.

 ✔ A *fully defined sketch entity* is fully constrained. Dimensions or relations (or both) describe the value and position of every line and curve in the sketch. In SolidWorks, fully constrained entities appear in black. A fully defined sketch ensures that your part updates more predictably.

 ✔ An *underdefined sketch entity* doesn't have enough geometric relations or dimension constraints to fully define its position and location. An underdefined sketch is okay if you plan to use it to create a feature, but you should fully define a sketch to complete a part. In SolidWorks, underdefined sketch entities are blue.

 ✔ An *overdefined sketch entity* has geometric relations and dimensional constraints that constrain it in more than one way, which creates a conflict. Overdefined entities appear in red.

Figure 4-5 shows an example of a sketch that is underdefined. Because this sketch isn't fully constrained and dimensioned, it doesn't modify predictably when you change a dimension value.

Figure 4-5: An underdefined sketch, such as this one, updates unpredictably.

In contrast, Figure 4-6 shows the same sketch fully constrained, which makes the design easy to modify. If you need to change the spacing or angle between the holes, you change a single dimension, and the sketch updates as intended.

The example shown in Figure 4-6 conveys the designer's intent as follows:

✔ The overall length and width is driven from other design elements, but is shown on the drawing with a tolerance of ±.03.

✔ All three smaller arcs are the same diameter.

✔ Tolerance between the two of the smaller arcs is ±.030. The tolerance between the other is +.000-.030.

✔ The two arcs on the bottom line up horizontally.

✔ The angle between the top two mounting holes is 75 degrees.

✔ The angle between the horizontal mounting hole and the right mounting hole is 30 degrees.

✔ The origin of the sketch is at the center of a bottom mounting hole.

✔ The designer added the three small and one large mounting holes as additional hole features after this sketch was complete, so they are easier to modify.

Figure 4-6:
A fully defined sketch updates predictably when you make a change.

Working with relations

Relations define how two sketch entities relate to each other. Relations are either inferred or added. SolidWorks infers relations as you sketch (see the upcoming section "Speeding sketch creating by using inferencing"), adding relations automatically, but you can also add your own relations.

Table 4-2 shows the major relation types.

Table 4-2	Relation Types
Relation Type	**Description**
Horizontal/Vertical	One or more lines or two or more points are horizontal or vertical.
Collinear	Two or more lines are linear.
Coradial	Two or more arcs share the same centerpoint and radius.
Perpendicular	The items are at 90 degrees to one another.
Parallel	The entities are parallel to one another.
Tangent	Two items remain tangent — for example, a line that intersects a circle or arc at a single point.
Concentric	Two or more arcs or a point and an arc share the same centerpoint.
Midpoint	The point or vertex (end of a line) remains at the midpoint of the line.
Coincident	A point lies on a line, arc, or ellipse.
Intersection	A point remains at the intersection of two lines.
Equal	Two entities remain of equal length or radius.
Merge Points	Two sketch points merge into one.

Adding a relation

To add a new relation to sketch entities in an open sketch:

1. **Click Add Relation on the Sketch toolbar.**

   The Add Relations PropertyManager appears, with the Selected Entities field active.

2. **In the graphic area, select the entity or entities you want to relate.**

   The entities appear in the Selected Entities field. The Existing Relations field shows any relations that already exist for those entities. The Add Relations section shows only the relation types that are valid for the entity or entities that you selected.

3. **To delete an existing relation, select the relation in the Existing Relations field and press Delete.**

   Use Display/Delete relations to see all relations.

4. **To add a new relation, select one of the relation types that appear in the Add Relations box.**

5. Click OK.

SolidWorks adds the relation to the entities.

SolidWorks places tiny icons on the graphics area to let you know what type of relation exists between sketch entities. For example, if two arcs have an equal radial value, SolidWorks puts an equal sign next to them. If a sketch entity has more than one set of equal constraints, SolidWorks places an instance number to the right side of the relation icon. The corresponding relation displays the same number on the right-hand side of the relation tag.

Using Relation Filters

It's useful to look at a sketch and tell at a glance what relations are where, especially when you need to edit a sketch that is overdefined. But things can get crowded, especially when working on a really big sketch, and that's when you want to use a relation filter. A *relation filter* shows only certain types of relations. The Display/Delete Relations command on the Sketch toolbar, shown in Figure 4-7, lets you choose the Relations types you want to see, and makes it easy to delete relations that you don't want.

To set a relations filter in a sketch:

1. Choose Tools⊅Relations⊅Display/Delete.

The Display/Delete Relations PropertyManager appears.

2. In Filter, select a relation to display in the drop-down list.

When you select a relation from the list, the appropriate sketch entities are highlighted in the graphics area. The options are as follows:

- **All in this sketch:** (Default) Displays all relations defined within the sketch. This list can be large based on the size and complexity of the sketch.

- **Selected Entities:** Displays relations only for the selected entities. This filter is the most commonly used.

- **Dangling:** Occurs when one of the references originally used to create the relation is missing (deleted entity).

- **Overdefined/Not Solved:** Indicates a redundant dimension or unnecessary relation.

- **External:** Displays relations created external to current sketch. It's often useful to reference existing part geometry.

- **Defined In Content:** Displays relations defined in the context of the assembly. This powerful feature has a number of performance considerations.

- **Locked:** Creates relations to locked external features or components. A locked external reference can no longer automatically update. Although not updating automatically can be a performance gain, you still need to ensure that changes are made correctly.

- **Broken:** Displays relations with broken external references.

3. **To delete a relation, highlight the entity in the graphic area and click Delete in the PropertyManager.**

   The relation changes to green in the graphic area.

4. **Click OK.**

   The PropertyManager closes.

Figure 4-7: The Display/Delete Relations command lets you display only the relations you want to see.

Scanning for equal size entities

You can save yourself time adding relations to a large sketch by using the Scan Equal command. Scan Equal looks for sketch entities with similar size lengths or radii and adds an equal relation to them automatically.

To locate sketch entities with equal radii or line lengths:

1. **In an open sketch, choose Tools⇨Relations⇨Scan Equal.**

   The Scan for Equal Line Lengths and Radius dialog box appears.

2. **Select the check box for the items you want to scan for.**

   Options are available only for those entities that exist in your sketch:

   - **Length:** Checks for two or more lines that are equal.
   - **Radii:** Checks for two or more arcs have equal radii.
   - **Both:** Checks for an arc that has a radii equal to a line length.

3. **Click Find Next.**

   The next set of equal entities becomes highlighted in the sketch. The length or radii of the entities displays in Value. The number of equal entities displays in Line Count and Arc Count.

4. **Click Set Equal to set the found entities as Equal.**

   An Equal relation is created between the highlighted entities.

5. **Repeat Steps 2 and 3 until you check all the entities in the sketch.**

6. **Click Close.**

Using Quick Snaps to create relations

When Quick Snaps are enabled, SolidWorks creates a relation (Nearest snap, Tangent snap, Perpendicular snap, Parallel snap, and so on) as you create the sketch geometry. SolidWorks creates relations automatically when sketching, but Quick Snaps give you more options and control.

For example, you may want a line to be as close as possible to another line. The nearest snap will complete the line based on the closest distance to the selected line. Quick Snaps help you better define the attributes, or behavior, of a sketch entity.

Available Quick Snaps are Point, Center (Arc/Circle), Quadrants (circle), Intersection, Nearest, Tangent, Perpendicular, Parallel, Horizontal or Vertical lock, Horizontal or Vertical point snap, Length snap, Grid snap, and Angle snap.

To create a sketch line using a Quick Snap:

1. **Open or create a sketch.**

2. **To display the Quick Snap toolbar, choose View⇨Toolbars⇨ Quick Snaps.**

   The Quick Snap toolbar appears.

3. **Click Line on the Sketch toolbar.**

   Quick Snap also works with other sketch geometry.

4. **Click the first point to define the starting point for the line.**

5. **Click Tangent on the Quick Snap toolbar.**

   Only tangent selections are shown as the cursor moves within the graphics area. Note that you can't select a Quick Snap until after you click to start sketching a new line, arc, circle, rectangle, spline, or point.

6. **Click the end point for the line.**

   The line appears, and the selected relation is added.

Speeding sketch creation by using inferencing

As you sketch, SolidWorks infers and creates certain types of relations between entities in a sketch automatically. For example, when you sketch a horizontal line, SolidWorks adds a relation to keep the line horizontal. With automatic inferencing, inferencing lines work together with pointers, Quick Snaps, and relations to graphically display how sketch entities affect each other and what type of relation SolidWorks is going to create.

Inferencing lines are dotted lines that appear when you sketch. When your pointer approaches highlighted cues, such as a midpoint, for example, green dotted lines appear to guide you relative to existing sketch entities. For some cases, SolidWorks automatically creates relations.

The pointer display indicates when the pointer is over a geometric relation, such as an intersection, what sketch tool is active, and dimensions. If the pointer displays a relation such as a horizontal relation, SolidWorks adds the relation automatically to the entity.

When creating a sketch, you may not want to use the automatically created inference relationships (see Figure 4-8). For example, you may not want SolidWorks to add a horizontal relationship to a line, or a coincident relationship to a line that goes over the top of a circle. To override the creation of these relationships, hold the Ctrl key down while creating the sketch entity.

Figure 4-8:
The pointer display changes to indicate the type of relation SolidWorks is about to add.

One reason why SolidWorks doesn't create all inferences automatically is that too many extra relations would exist, and the sketch would quickly become overdefined. A sketch entity is *overdefined,* either through dimensions or relations, when it's being told to define something twice. A warning appears when a sketch entity is overdefined.

Creating simple dimensions

You create sketches in three steps: You sketch, add relations, and then add dimensions to size and locate the sketch entities. You can create features without adding dimensions to sketches. However, dimensioning sketches is a good practice. You want to dimension in accordance with the model's design intent. For example, you may want to dimension holes a certain distance from an edge or a certain distance from each other.

You dimension sketch entities and other objects with the Smart Dimension tool. The type of dimension is determined by the items you click. For some types of dimensions (point-to-point, angular, and circular), where you place the dimension also affects the type of dimension that SolidWorks adds. You can also drag or delete a dimension while the Smart Dimension tool is active.

You can add other toolbars, such as the Dimension toolbar, to the Command-Manager. Right-click the CommandManager and choose Customize Command-Manager. In the menu that appears, select the check box next to the toolbar you want to add. Click anywhere in the graphic area to close the menu. The new toolbar button appears in the control area of the CommandManager. Click a button in the control area to activate that toolbar in the CommandManager.

To dimension an entity in a sketch:

1. **Click Smart Dimension on the Dimensions/Relations toolbar.**

   The pointer changes to a dimension icon.

2. **Depending on the entity to dimension, select the items as indicated.**

   - **Length of a line or edge:** Click the line.
   - **Angle between two lines:** Click two lines or a line and a model edge. How you place the dimension affects how the angle is measured. It's based on which quadrant of an imaginary circle you place the final dimension text on.
   - **Distance between two lines:** Click two parallel lines or a line and a parallel model edge.
   - **Perpendicular distance from a point to a line:** Click the point and the line or model edge.
   - **Distance between two points:** Click two points. One of the points can be a model vertex.

- **Radius of an arc:** Click the arc.

- **True length of an arc:** Click the arc and then the two end points.

- **Diameter of a circle:** Click the circumference. The dimension displays as linear or diameter, depending on where you place the pointer.

A preview of the dimension appears in the graphic area as a blue line with arrows on either end and the measurement value on top. As you move the pointer, the dimension moves with it.

3. **Move the pointer and click to place the dimension.**

   The Modify dialog box appears.

4. **Enter a value for the dimension in the Modify dialog box, as shown in Figure 4-9.**

   You do not have to enter a value; you can accept the existing value.

5. **Click Rebuild in the Modify dialog box to see the model updated with the new value.**

   If the value isn't correct or you want to change it, change the values and click Rebuild in the Modify dialog box again.

6. **Click OK.**

   The Modify dialog box closes and the dimension appears in the graphic display. The model updates accordingly.

Figure 4-9:
You can change a dimension by entering a new value in the Modify dialog box.

Marking a dimension for drawing reuse

When you create dimensions in part sketches, you can specify whether the dimension should be included in the drawing. In the Modify dialog box, after you enter the dimension value, the button Mark Dimension To Be Imported Into A Drawing is checked by default, as shown in Figure 4-10. Clicking this option flags the dimension for import into a drawing using the Insert Model Items feature (see Chapter 8).

Figure 4-10:
The Modify
dialog box
shows a
dimension
value
marked for
drawing
import.

Because the dimensions are reused within your drawing, spend some extra effort positioning the dimensions the way you want to see them in your drawing. You should also add any tolerances, notes, and symbols to the sketch dimensions in order to eliminate duplicate work on the drawing and include the information in the part where it belongs. You can read more on how to add annotations to models in Chapter 7.

Before you finish your sketch, give it some exercise. Click and drag entities to see if the sketch updates as you intend. If you resize an arc by dragging one of its end points, do the attached lines stay tangent? If the sketch does not capture design intent, you may want to add constraints.

Chapter 5

Making Better Parts

In This Chapter

▶ Creating better parts and features

▶ Making parts more robust with parents who understand their children

▶ Naming features and dimensions

▶ Making parts more robust using function feature order

▶ Documenting designs using comments and the design binder

*P*arts are the basis of drawings and assemblies. Just as assemblies are made from individual parts, parts are made from individual features. This chapter tells you how to create a part and introduces the different types of features you can use to construct a part. This chapter doesn't cover every feature type that SolidWorks offers. Instead, it focuses on the most common ones.

Introducing Part Features

Parts consist of features. *Features,* or shapes, are the building blocks of a model. You begin a part with a flat sketch. You dimension the sketch to make sure that it's the proper size, and then you create features.

The first feature in a part is the *base feature* because it forms the base of the part. Generally, but not always, the first feature is a *base extrusion.* An *extrude* adds material by pulling the shape out. If you extrude a rectangle, for example, you get a cube. After you have a lump of material to work with, subsequent features add or subtract material by scooping, rounding, and so on. Eventually, your part takes shape.

SolidWorks features are of two types: sketched and applied. A *sketched feature* is based on a 2D sketch. An *applied feature* is one that you apply directly to the model. The next sections cover each of these feature types:

✔ **Boss/Base:** Adds material to the model (extrude, revolve, sweep, loft). The first feature is a *base,* and subsequent features are each a *boss.* This feature is created from a 2D sketch.

✔ **Cut:** Removes material from the model (extrude, revolve, sweep, and loft). This feature is created from a 2D sketch.

✔ **Feature:** Performs a specific modeling task (fillet, chamfer, draft, shell, holes, and more). These features act upon existing geometry.

✔ **Pattern/mirror:** Copies features in a linear or circular pattern, or mirror (symmetry) features or the entire part. These features act upon existing geometry.

The examples in the figures throughout this chapter are meant to give you some ideas on starting a part and crafting the final part design. Figure 5-1 shows how part features produce a model. You can refine a design by adding, changing, or reordering features.

The general steps to create the example part shown in Figure 5-1 are as follows. (I include the feature name in parenthesis.)

Figure 5-1:
Individual
features
combine to
make a part.

1. **Create the sketch for the feature (Side Profile/Sketch1) and extrude the profile using an Extruded Boss/Base.**

2. **Shape the profile (Shape Face) by using the Shape feature.**

3. **Round the four corners (Corners) by using a Fillet.**

4. **Round the top edge (Outer Edge) by using a Fillet.**

5. **Hollow out the part (Inside Shell) by using a Shell.**

6. **Create the sketch for keypad cutout (Keypad/Sketch8) by using an extruded cut.**

As you create a feature, you see a preview of what the model will look like in the graphic display. The absence of a preview is an indication that SolidWorks can't create the feature. If you don't see a preview, change the parameters in the PropertyManager.

The Features toolbar

A handy tool to have around when working on parts is the Features toolbar. SolidWorks offers an extensive set of feature commands to shape your model, and not all of them show up on the default Features toolbar. But you can add or remove command buttons to customize this toolbar to suit your needs. (Chapter 2 explains how to customize toolbars.)

The Features toolbar, shown in Figure 5-2, shows the commonly used feature commands that appear in this chapter. This section assumes that you know how to create a sketch. (If you don't know how to create a sketch, see Chapter 4.)

Figure 5-2:
In a part document, by default, the Features toolbar appears in the Command-Manager.

The following is a list of what appears in the CommandManager, as shown in Figure 5-2, when you first open a part document in SolidWorks. Notice that the Features toolbar is active, so most of these are Feature toolbar commands.

- ✔ **Features toolbar button:** Changes the toolbar shown to the right of the CommandManager icons to feature related commands.

- ✔ **Sketch toolbar button:** Changes the toolbar shown to the right of the CommandManager icons to sketch (lines, arcs, rectangles, points, centerlines, and so on) related commands.

- ✔ **Annotations toolbar button:** Changes the toolbar shown to the right of the CommandManager icons to annotation (dimensions, notes, geometric tolerance, and so on) related commands.

- **Extruded Base/Boss:** Click to start an extruded feature.

- **Extruded Cut:** Click to start an extruded cut feature.

- **Revolved Base/Boss:** Click to start a revolved feature.

- **Revolved Cut:** Click to start a revolved cut feature.

- **Swept Base/Boss:** Click to start a swept feature.

- **Lofted Base/Boss:** Click to start a lofted feature.

- **Fillet:** Click to start a fillet feature.

- **Rib:** Click to start a rib feature (not covered in this chapter).

- **Shell:** Click to start a shell feature.

- **Draft:** Click to start a draft feature.

- **Hole Wizard:** Click to start the Hole Wizard feature.

- **Linear Pattern:** Click to start a pattern feature.

- **Circular Pattern:** Click to start a pattern feature.

- **Mirror:** Click to start a mirror feature.

- **Reference Geometry:** Click to display a menu of common reference geometry features (not covered in this chapter).

- **Curve:** Click to display a menu of common curve features (not covered in this chapter).

Sketched features

You must create a 2D sketch as the basis for a sketched feature (extrude, revolve, sweep, and loft) in SolidWorks. Sketched features can add or remove material from a part. A sketched feature that adds material is a *base* or a *boss*. A sketched feature that removes material is a *cut*.

When you design a part, imagine that you're a machine tool cutting away at a solid hunk of metal. In SolidWorks, a base feature gives you that solid hunk. Pick the most prominent section of the part as a base and choose a shape to best describe it. The most common base feature is a *base extrude,* but you can also create base features with a sweep, revolve, or a loft.

Your 2D outline for a sketched feature generally requires a profile. A *profile,* or sketch, is the flat shape that pulls out, revolves about, and so on.

If you click a sketched feature before you sketch the profile, SolidWorks takes you into sketch mode automatically. For example, if you click Extruded Base/ Boss before you sketch the extrude, SolidWorks takes you directly to sketch mode. When you complete the sketch, click the confirmation corner in the upper right corner of the graphic display. SolidWorks extrudes the part and displays the Extruded Cut PropertyManager.

Extruded features

An *extrusion* is like making a cookie from a cookie press. You place a shape (or profile) in the press, and the dough comes out in that shape. An Extruded Boss/Base adds material; an Extruded Cut removes material. The material added is extruded along a specified direction. SolidWorks bases the direction of the extrusion on a distance normal (perpendicular) to the plane of the 2D sketch or along a selected vector (direction).

The FeatureManager design tree displays the individual features of a part. You may find it easier to select the feature in the FeatureManager design tree rather than in the graphic display, especially if it's a tiny feature that you have to zoom in on to spot. When you select a feature, the feature is highlighted in both the graphic display and the FeatureManager design tree.

In the PropertyManager that appears for sketched features, a field turns pink to indicate that it is active and waiting for you to select one or more entities in the graphic area. If the field accepts only one entity, the next field activates automatically after you make a selection.

In some PropertyManagers and dialog boxes that appear when you choose a command, you enter values for a distance, angle, and so on in a spin box. You can click the up arrow or down arrow to increase or decrease the value incrementally. To change the default spin box increments, choose Tools⇨Options. Under the System Options tab, select Spin Box Increments and enter the new increment values.

To create an extruded-base/boss or cut feature:

1. **Sketch the profile that you want to extrude.**

   You can sketch on a plane or the face of a part.

2. **Choose Insert⇨Exit Sketch.**

   You exit sketch mode.

3. **In the FeatureManager design tree, select the sketch to extrude.**

   You can preselect a sketch.

4. **Click Extruded Boss/Base or Extruded Cut in the Features toolbar.**

   The Extrude PropertyManager appears (see Figure 5-3), and the shape extrudes by the amount that appears in the Depth field. SolidWorks prompts you for the parameters of the extrusion.

Figure 5-3:
A preview
of this base
extrude
feature
appears in
the graphic
area.

5. Set From to Sketch Plane.

The feature extrudes from the sketch plane. You can also set From so that the feature extrudes from a surface, face, or a vertex and offset. For a base extrude, you want to extrude from the sketch plane.

6. Set End Conditions to Blind.

This setting means that you want to specify the exact depth of the extrusion. Click the arrows to the right of Blind to change the direction that the part extrudes from. You can also set End Conditions so that the feature extrudes up to the vertex, up to the surface, and so on (see Figure 5-4).

7. Set the width in the Depth field.

Enter a parameter for how far you want the shape to extrude.

8. Click OK.

Figure 5-4:
You can
select end
condition
type for
extruded
features.

Revolved features

A revolve rotates a sketch profile around an axis to create a 3D shape. A door knob and a bedpost are shapes you can create with revolve. You can set the angle of revolve to 360 degrees for a full revolve or less than that — for example, when you want only a quarter of a door knob.

The sketch you create for a revolve feature must include _centerline_. The centerline serves as an axis of rotation. (The axis of rotation can be a centerline, line, edge or axis.) On one side of the centerline, you sketch the profile of the revolve. Don't let your sketch cross the centerline (see Figure 5-5). Otherwise, the profile may self-intersect, and SolidWorks isn't able to create the feature.

To create a revolved feature:

1. **Sketch a centerline and a profile.**

   A more complex shape can have one or more profiles and a centerline, line, or edge to use as the axis around which the feature revolves.

2. **Choose Insert➪Exit Sketch.**

   You exit sketch mode.

3. **On the Features toolbar, click Revolved Boss/Base or Revolved Cut.**

   The Revolve PropertyManager appears, and a preview of the revolve feature appears in the graphic display. The Axis of Revolution field is active.

4. **Select an Axis to serve as an axis of revolution.**

   This axis can be the centerline you created in your sketch, a line, or an edge. The name of the axis or sketch appears in the Axis of Revolution field.

5. **In the Revolve Type field, select One-Direction.**

   Your revolve is created in one direction from the sketch. You can also choose these other types of revolves:

   - **Mid-Plane:** Creates the revolve in the clockwise and counterclockwise directions, which is located at the middle of the total revolve angle.

   - **Two-Direction:** Creates the revolve in the clockwise and counterclockwise directions from the sketch plane. You need to set two angles that do not exceed 360 degrees.

6. **Enter a value for the angle in Angle.**

   This step defines the angle covered by the revolve, which can't exceed 360 degrees. If you selected Two-Direction in Step 5, you need to enter values for Direction 1 Angle and Direction 2 Angle.

7. **Click OK.**

Swept features

When you create a base extrusion, you extrude a shape straight out so that a circle becomes a cone, for example. In contrast, a sweep extrudes a shape along a *path*. Sweeps create curvy ergonomic shapes. You need to create a profile and a path to serve as the basis for a swept feature. (In Figure 5-6, a rectangle serves as a profile for the sweep feature.) Because the profile and path must be on different planes, you need to create two sketches. You can also add guide curves to the path to further define the shape of your sweep. Guide curves can be on the same plane as the path.

Your sweep sketch needs to adhere to these rules:

- ✔ If you're adding material (base/boss), the profile must be closed; the profile may be open or closed for a surface sweep feature.

- ✔ The path may be open or closed.

- ✔ The path may be a set of sketched curves contained in one sketch, a curve, or a set of model edges.

- ✔ The start point of the path must lie on the plane of the profile.

- ✔ Neither the section, the path, nor the resulting solid can be self-intersecting.

To create a swept feature:

1. **Sketch a profile for the sweep.**

   If the sweep is your base feature, sketch on a plane; otherwise choose a face of the existing part to sketch on. Your profile can be as simple as a square or circle or something more complex.

2. **In a second sketch on a different plane, sketch a path for the Sweep.**

   You can add guide curves for a more complex shape. If you add guide curves, you need to create coincident or pierce relations between the guide curves and the profile.

3. **Choose Insert⇨Exit Sketch.**

   You switch to part mode.

4. **Select Swept Boss/Base or Swept Cut from the Features toolbar.**

   The Sweep PropertyManager appears with the Profile field activated.

5. **Select the sketch to use for the profile.**

   The sketch appears in the Profile field. The Path field activates.

6. **Click a sketch to use for the Path.**

   The sketch name appears in the Path field. A preview of the sweep appears in the graphics area.

7. **If you're using a guide curve, under Guide Curves, click the Guide Curves field.**

   The field activates, turning pink. If you're not using a Guide Curve, skip to Step 9.

8. **In the FeatureManager design tree, select the sketch to use for the Guide Path Curve.**

   The sketch name appears in the Guide Path Curve field.

9. **Click the up or down arrows under Guide Path Curve to indicate the order that the guide curves are evaluated.**

10. **Click OK.**

Figure 5-6:
Sketch a
profile and
a path to
create a
sweep
extrude.

Lofted features

A *loft* feature is similar to a sweep, but instead of a single profile in the sketch, it has two or more profiles, and the loft transitions between them. A loft can add material or take it away. If you want to create a more complex shape, you can include guide curves and end conditions in your sketch.

When you create your sketch for a loft:

- ✔ Only the first, last, or first and last profiles can be points.

- ✔ If you create a solid loft, the first and last profiles must be model faces or faces created by split lines, planar profiles, or surfaces.

Consider the following when creating lofts with guide curves:

- ✔ You can use any of the following items as a guide curve: sketched curves, model edges, or curves of any kind.

- ✔ Guide curves must intersect all the profiles.

- ✔ There is no limit to the number of guide curves you may use.

- ✔ Guide curves can intersect at points.

Always select profiles on the same general area of the profile. In the example shown in Figure 5-7, the lower right-hand corner of the profile is selected. Otherwise, the profile twists in a way that you may not want. Always watch the preview in the graphics window and reselect profiles if necessary.

To create a loft feature:

1. Sketch two profiles and any guide curves for the feature.

Faces, curves, and edges can serve as profiles. You don't need to sketch two or more profiles if one is on the model.

2. Choose Insert⇨Exit Sketch.

You exit sketch mode and return to part mode.

3. Click Lofted Base/Boss or Lofted Cut in the Features toolbar.

The Loft PropertyManager appears with the Profile field active.

4. Select the two profiles in the graphic area.

The items appear in the Profile field. You can use the up/down arrows in the Profile section to switch the profile order.

5. Select the Guide Curve field to activate it.

The field is highlighted in pink.

6. **Select the guide curves in the graphic area.**

   The items appear in the Guide Curves field. A preview of the loft appears in the graphic area. You can use the up/down arrows in the Guide Curves section to change the order of the guide curves.

7. **Click OK.**

Figure 5-7:
A lofted feature is similar to a sweep but with two profiles.

Applied features

After you create a base feature, you have a solid hunk of material sitting in your graphic display. You can add some character to this hunk by using applied features (fillet, chamfer, rib, shell, and draft). Unlike sketched features, applied features don't require a sketch. You apply them directly to your part. Imagine that the following applied features are various machine tools drilling away at your part. One tool rounds off the edges, another scoops out the middle, leaving a hollow shell, and so on. Your part is taking shape.

Fillet/Round

The *Fillet/Round* command rounds off the sharp corners of your part or adds volume by rounding off an inner corner.

For all intents and purposes, *fillet* and *round* are the same thing, and you can use the terms interchangeably, although I use fillet in this chapter. You can create many different types of fillets. The most common is the multiple fillet, shown in Figure 5-8.

Fillets are not functional design elements. Typically, you add them for cosmetic reasons — to pretty up the part. You want to add cosmetic fillets at the end of the modeling process to minimize unwanted parent/child relations and to produce a more robust model. A *parent/child relationship* simply means that a fillet that references an edge is a child of that edge. If you remove the edge, the child becomes homeless and fails when you rebuild the part.

Figure 5-8:
Fillets
mainly add
cosmetic
appeal to
a part.

SolidWorks displays heads-up labels, shown in Figure 5-8. The heads-up label includes the radius value (Radius: 01.in) and is editable. Double-click the numeric text part of it to change the radius value.

To create a fillet feature in a part:

1. **Open a part document.**

2. **Click Fillet in the Features toolbar.**

3. **Select the edges or faces on the part that you want to fillet.**

   The Fillet PropertyManager appears, and you see a preview of the fillet in the graphic area, as shown in Figure 5-8.

The order in which you select multiple edges affects the way the fillet *blends* (how it looks when finished) and how far it goes (known as *tangent propagation*). For the example shown in Figure 5-8, the designer selected the larger 0.2 radii first. When the designer chose the smaller radii edges, those edges propagated all the way around the outside edge of the part because they didn't have to stop at the sharp corner.

4. **Select the Fillet type.**

   Your options include

   - **Constant radius:** Creates fillets that have a constant radius for their entire length. After you select Constant Radius, you can set parameters in the PropertyManager to create one of the following: Multiple radius fillets, Round corner fillets, or Setback fillets.

   - **Variable radius:** Creates a fillet with variable radii values. Control points allow you to define the fillet.

   - **Face fillet:** Blends nonadjacent, noncontinuous faces.

   - **Full round fillet:** Creates fillets that are tangent to three adjacent faces' sets (with one or more faces' tangents.)

5. **Set other options in the PropertyManager.**

   Your options include

   - **Radius:** Enter the default radius value.

   - **Edges:** Select the edges, faces, or loops to fillet.

   - **Multiple radius fillets:** Select to create multiple radius value, as shown in Figure 5-8.

   - **Tangent propagation:** Select to continue the fillet until it runs into a sharp corner.

   - **Preview:** Select Full Preview to see a preview of the fillet in the graphic area.

   You can take advantage of the preview option in the PropertyManager to get a clear idea of how the radius will look when you change the entities you select, the order of selection, and values. (However, this option can also really slow you down, especially if you're using Full Preview.)

6. **Click OK.**

Chamfer

Chamfer creates a beveled edge on selected edges of a part at a given distance and angle (or two distances). You often use a chamfer to break a sharp edge of a part or to provide a lead-in for mating assembly components. (You can read more about mating assembly parts in Chapter 6.)

To create a chamfer feature:

1. **Open a part document.**

2. **Click Chamfer in the Features toolbar.**

   The Chamfer PropertyManager appears with the Edges and Faces or Vertex field active.

3. **In the graphic area, select the edges and faces or vertex to chamfer.**

   The selections appear in Edges and Faces and Vertex, and the chamfer displays as a preview in the graphic area, as shown in Figure 5-9. In the preview, a tag pointing to the chamfer lists the distance and angle distance.

   In the graphic preview, you can click the arrow that points to the chamfer to flip the direction of the chamfer. You can do the same by selecting the check box for the Flip direction option in Chamfer Parameters in the Chamfer PropertyManager.

4. **Select other options in Chamfer Parameters.**

   Other options include

   - **Chamfer style:** Select a check box for an angle-distance or distance-distance type chamfer.

   - **Flip direction:** Select this check box to flip the direction of the chamfer.

   - **Distance:** Enter a distance value for the chamfer.

   - **Angle:** Enter an angle for the chamfer.

   - **Preview:** Select Full Preview to see how the part looks.

5. **Click OK.**

Figure 5-9:
A chamfer displays as a preview.

Draft

You can use the *draft* feature to add an angle to part faces. This feature is useful when making an injection mold for a plastic part. Imagine a cake pan: If the angle of the pan sloped inwards, your cake would stay forever stuck in the pan. You would have to cut it in pieces to get it out. It's the same with plastic molds. A proper draft angle, shown in Figure 5-10, ensures that a part slips out easily.

Figure 5-10:
A draft
angle
ensures
that a part
will slip out
of its mold.

To create a draft on a neutral plane:

1. **Open a part document.**

2. **Click Draft in the Features toolbar.**

   The Draft PropertyManager appears with the Neutral Plane field active.

3. **Click a face on the part that you want as a Neutral Plane.**

   The item appears in the Neutral Plane field. (Imagine this field as the top of the cake pan where the cake slides out.) The Faces to Draft field becomes active.

4. **Click the faces of the part you want to add a draft angle to.**

   The items appear in the Faces to Draft field. (Imagine these are the sides of the cake pan.)

5. **In Type of Draft, use the pull-down arrow to select Neutral Plane.**

6. **In Draft Angle, set a value for the number of degrees.**

   The draft angle is measured perpendicular to the neutral plane.

7. **In Face, select an item in Face Propagation if you want to propagate the draft across additional faces.**

   Your options include

   - **None:** Drafts only the selected faces.
   - **Along Tangent:** Extends the draft to all faces that are tangent to the selected face.
   - **All Faces:** Drafts all faces extruded from the neutral plane.
   - **Inner Faces:** Drafts all inner faces extruded from the neutral plane.
   - **Outer Faces:** Drafts all outer faces next to the neutral plane.

8. **Click OK.**

You can select the arrow in the graphics area on the neutral draft plane to flip the direction of the draft angle.

Shell

A *shell* feature hollows out a part, leaves out the faces you select, and creates thin-walled features on the remaining faces. If you don't select any face on the model, you can shell a solid part, creating a closed, hollow model. You can shell a model in one thickness, or you can define multiple shell thicknesses.

Before you shell a part, be sure to apply any fillets to the part first. The shell feature uses any existing features in the shell.

To create a shell feature with uniform thickness:

1. **Open a part document.**

2. **Click Shell on the Features toolbar.**

   The Shell PropertyManager, shown in Figure 5-11, appears.

3. **Set the following options under Parameters:**

   - **Thickness:** Enter a thickness for the faces you keep.
   - **Faces to remove:** Select one or more faces in the graphics area that you want to remove when the part is hollowed out.

- **Shell outward:** Select the check box for this option to increase the outside dimensions of the part.

- **Show preview:** Select the check box for this option to get a wireframe preview of the shell feature in the graphic area.

4. **Click OK.**

If you run into trouble creating a shell, run Error Diagnostics in the Shell PropertyManager to pinpoint problems.

Figure 5-11:
You can scoop out part innards using the shell feature.

Hole Wizard

The Hole Wizard lets you create holes in your part that you can use to insert fasteners. The Hole Wizard can create the following hole types: Counterbore, Countersink, Hole (simple holes), Tap, Pipetap, and Legacy.

You don't have to dig out the Machinery's Handbook to figure out how big you need to make the holes. The Hole Wizard creates the holes based on the type of fastener you plan to put there.

To add a hole to a part using the Hole Wizard:

1. **Open a part document.**

2. **Select a face on the part in which you want to insert holes.**

3. **Click Hole Wizard in the Features toolbar.**

   The Hole Definition PropertyManager appears.

You can preselect or postselect a face when using the Hole Wizard. When you preselect a face and then click Hole Wizard on the Features toolbar, the resulting sketch is a 2D sketch. If you click Hole Wizard and then select a face, the resulting sketch is 3D. Unlike a 2D sketch, you cannot constrain a 3D sketch to a line.

4. Select a tab for the hole type.

Your choices are Counterbore, Countersink, Hole, Tap, Pipe Tap, and Legacy. The Legacy tab allows you to make holes for files created in older versions of SolidWorks. In each tab, you see a table with three columns. The first column lists a property (Description, Standard, Screw Type, and so on), and the other columns are for property parameters.

Figure 5-12 shows a counterbore hole made for a #10 binding head machine screw.

5. Select the parameters for the type of fastener you want to add.

You can use the pull-down arrows next to the parameters box to select the exact parameters you want.

For each hole type (except Legacy), you can create and save hole types to include in your favorite property parameters. In the Hole Placement dialog box, after you select the parameters for a fastener, click Select Add under Favorites. Next time you want to add holes to a model, click the arrow under Favorites to select the hole type to add.

6. Click the Positions Tab.

The Hole Wizard closes, and the Hole Position dialog box appears and prompts you to enter the sketch points in the model where you want to place the holes. (Figure 5-13 shows three points dimensioned to define the three hole locations.) You're taken into sketch mode.

7. Use the Point tool to mark the spots in the model where you want holes.

You're automatically using the Point tool on the Sketch toolbar to add the holes. If you preselected a planar face, the holes must be on the same face.

8. Add dimension and relations to locate the hole centers.

See Chapter 4 for more detail.

9. Click OK.

The Hole Positions PropertyManager closes. The holes appear in the model and in the FeatureManager design tree.

SolidWorks uses two sketches to define Hole Wizard features. You can view the sketches in the FeatureManager design tree by clicking the plus sign to the left of the hole feature. The first sketch defines the centers of the hole. You can edit the first sketch to move holes. Simply right-click the sketch and choose Edit Sketch. You should not edit the second sketch. The second sketch is the profile for the hole defined by the Hole Wizard.

Figure 5-12:
Hole Wizard
creates hole
sizes to
match your
fastener.

Figure 5-13:
Points in
the sketch
determine
where to
insert holes.

Pattern and Mirror features

Pattern and Mirror features are applied features, in that you can apply them directly to the part geometry. But they're a unique type of applied feature, so I am putting them in their own section. Pattern and Mirror features allow you to create a pattern of features in a model, such as a pattern of teeth in a gear.

Linear patterns

A *linear pattern* creates features along a straight line, and a *circular pattern* creates features around a circle.

To create a linear pattern feature:

1. **Open a part document.**

2. **Click Linear Pattern in the Features toolbar.**

   The Linear Pattern PropertyManager, shown in Figure 5-14, appears with the Pattern Direction selection field active.

3. **Select an edge to define Direction 1.**

   The edge appears in Direction 1, and Direction box 2 is active.

4. **If needed, select an edge to define Direction 2.**

   The edge appears in Direction 2.

5. **Set the remaining options in the PropertyManager.**

   Here's what you need to do:

   • **Pattern Direction:** Select an edge that defines the direction for the pattern.

   • **Spacing:** Enter the distance between the pattern instances.

   • **Instances:** Type the total number of pattern features, including the original feature.

   • **Direction 2:** Creates a pattern in another direction. Follows the same process as the first direction.

   • **Pattern seed only:** Patterns only the original feature in the second direction.

   • **Faces or Feature to pattern:** Select either pattern in the Feature to Pattern field and select features to pattern or select specific faces to pattern using the Faces to Pattern field.

6. **Click OK.**

Figure 5-14:
Linear patterns repeat shapes along a straight line.

Circular patterns

Circular pattern (see Figure 5-15) is similar to linear pattern with the exception that you need to select an existing axis to serve as an axis of rotation, axis, temporary axis, angular dimension, or linear edge for the feature.

Figure 5-15:
The circular pattern feature repeats a shape in a circle.

To create a circular pattern feature:

1. **Open a part document.**

2. **Click Circular Pattern on the Features toolbar.**

   The Circular PropertyManager appears with the Pattern Axis field active.

3. **Select an axis, model edge, or an angular dimension in the graphic area.**

   The item appears in the Pattern Axis field. The Feature to Pattern field becomes active.

   Remember to display axes and temporary axes first. In the main menu, choose View and then select Axes and Temporary Axes from the list. A checkmark next to the item means that it's already visible.

4. **Select one or more features to pattern in the graphic area.**

   The features appear in the Feature to Pattern field. You can also repeat faces or bodies. If you choose to repeat one of these, you can highlight fields for Faces to Pattern and Bodies to Pattern and click the graphic to enter the items in those fields.

5. **In the Parameters section, enter values for the following:**

   - **Number of Instances:** Enter the number of times to repeat the pattern.

   - **Angle:** Indicate the angle of the features.

   Select the check box for Equal Spacing to save time when creating a pattern that goes all the way around the part. This option automatically sets the angle based on the number of instances you select.

6. **Click OK.**

You can use the Geometry pattern option in the Options section to create the pattern using only the geometry instead of the complete feature. The pattern feature contains only the geometric representation of the feature (faces and edges). This option speeds up the rebuilding of the pattern feature.

Mirror features

You can use the Mirror feature to create a copy of a feature (or a group of features) and mirror it around a plane or a part face. The advantage to mirroring an object is that you can create symmetrically similar features. You can manipulate the features by changing the original (or parent) feature.

You can mirror the body of a part, so you don't have to select individual features or faces to mirror. A *body* is the entire solid body. In other words, Bodies to Mirror is used to mirror the part. Expand the Bodies folder (+) within the FeatureManager design tree to see the body(s) within the part.

To create a mirror feature:

1. **Open a part document.**

2. **Click Mirror in the Features toolbar.**

   The Mirror PropertyManager, shown in Figure 5-15, appears with the Mirror Face/Plane feature active.

3. **Select the face or plane in the graphic area to mirror on.**

   The item appears in the Mirror Face/Plane feature. The Features to Mirror field becomes active.

4. **Select a feature in the graphic area that you want to mirror.**

   The feature appears in the Features to Mirror field.

   Try to create a mirror pattern with the Geometry Pattern option in the PropertyManager selected first. With this option selected, SolidWorks mirrors only the faces and edges of the features, rather than the whole feature, speeding up the creation of the pattern. If SolidWorks can't solve the geometry pattern version, uncheck this option. For some cases, geometry pattern may be required to solve the cases that nongeometry pattern features cannot solve. Either way, if the feature can't be built with the options selected, SolidWorks explains the problem in the What's Wrong dialog box.

5. **Click OK.**

Figure 5-16:
Example
mirror
feature and
Property-
Manager.

Building a Part

You construct a part in SolidWorks much like you do in the real world. Here are the steps to follow when making a part.

1. **Select a plane and orientation for your part.**

   You don't want your part to appear upside down or sideways. Typically, you begin your part with one of the default planes (front, top, or right).

2. **Draw a sketch on the plane.**

   This sketch is the basis of the first feature in your part, so be sure to give it an appropriate shape. You want to fully dimension your sketch so that all the lines appear in black.

3. **Create a base feature.**

Use one of the sketched boss features (extrude, revolve, sweep, or loft) to create the first feature in your part based on your sketch. Your base feature is the solid hunk of material that all the other features go on top of.

4. **Add additional sketched and applied features.**

5. **Add round/fillets and other cosmetic features last.**

Always try to break a design into definable segments. I recall many times in my design youth when I had no idea about how I was going to solve a complex design problem. But here's the secret: Start with what is important and what you know about the design. "Keep it simple, stupid" (KISS) is an adage that applies well. Even the most complex part is manageable when you break the job down into simple steps.

To get a visual grasp on how to build a part, peruse the following example parts. Each part uses a different sketched feature as its base. You can follow the feature creation order of each part by studying the FeatureManager design tree. The base feature is on the top, and the most recently created feature is on the bottom.

Example part #1

For the example part shown in Figure 5-17, the base feature is a revolve because the original profile is circular.

Figure 5-17: A Revolved Base/Boss is the heart of this part.

Example part #2

The part in Figure 5-18 found its beginnings with an extrusion feature because the original profile was a planar extruded profile.

Figure 5-18:
An extrusion
marked the
birth of this
model.

Example part #3

This little darling, shown in Figure 5-19, began life as a sweep. The sweep feature sweeps the original sketch profile (Sketch2) along a Profile Helix (3DSketch2), which formed the basis for path.

Figure 5-19:
A sweep
marked the
early life of
this part.

Example part #4

This art piece, shown in Figure 5-20, began as a loft feature because the part shape was created from several 2D sections. This example shows only a portion of the design. Lofts created the handle portion of the drill body.

Building a Better Part

Although you can build your model in numerous ways, no matter how you put it all together, you can do certain consistent things to make your model more readable and easier to modify. This section includes tips on ways that you can make your part model even better.

Figure 5-20:
Two sketch profiles served as the basis of this loft.

Naming features (Or, you call it tomato, I call it tomato)

After you make your part, you may want to rename some of its features in the FeatureManager design tree. SolidWorks gives features default names, such as Extrude1 and Extrude2, but these don't offer much clue to what a feature does — not to mention that this naming scheme can get messy if your part has 100 features. To find the meaning behind Cut-Extrude20, you'd have to review the sketch and features, as well as the part geometry. On the other hand, a feature with a name like "Upper Boss Relief" may give some idea of its purpose.

Relevant names make a feature easier to find in the FeatureManager design tree. But you need to be sure that the name relates to what the feature does. (Names such as Gandalf and the Big Pookie are not helpful.) A good naming system makes design intent clearer and parts easier to modify.

Be especially sure to name a feature that is an important design element that you're likely to change later. You should only name fillets and chamfers only when you use them for noncosmetic purposes.

To name the feature when you create it, choose Tools⇨Options. In the Systems Options tab, select FeatureManager. In the options that appear on the right, select the check box for Name Feature on Creation. This method is my preference because I'd rather name the feature right as I create it than to have to go back and rename it later.

To rename the feature within the FeatureManager design tree, double-click the feature in the FeatureManager design tree and type a new name. You can also right-click the feature in the tree and choose Feature Properties from the menu that appears. This command gets you to the Properties dialog box, where the name is highlighted, and you can change the name of the feature.

The best time to name a feature is right after you create it. If you don't name a feature, most likely nobody is going to do it for you when the project is complete. Make it a habit to name features and reinforce the habit by checking names in the FeatureManager design tree at design checks.

Naming features is a way to organize a design. The example in Figure 5-21 shows two versions of a FeatureManager design tree from the same part. One part (the left side) uses the default feature names, and the other (the right side) uses the named features. Which design would you rather work on when your boss comes in and tells you to modify a design immediately?

Along with features, you also want to name some dimensions. If you use a dimension in a design table or if an equation references that dimension, then give the dimension a meaningful name. To change the name of a sketch dimension, first make the dimension visible. In the FeatureManager design tree, right-click the feature and choose Edit Sketch. Then right-click the dimension you want to rename and choose Properties. In the Name field of the Properties dialog box, type a name for the dimension. The full dimension name appears as <dimension name@feature name>. Instead of a dimension D2@Cut-Extrude1, you can rename the dimension "outside" and the feature "MtgBoss" so that the new dimension name is outsideDia@MtgBoss.

Figure 5-21:
It's easier to locate and modify named features.

Thinking about feature order

Another method of documenting a design is feature order. The FeatureManager design tree shows features in the order in which they were made. The feature on the bottom is the newest. The order of features in the FeatureManager design tree should communicate your design intent.

When you change a sketch, you need to rebuild to see how the change affects the model. You can press Ctrl+Q to completely rebuild all the features in the model. Click Rebuild on the Standard toolbar or press Ctrl+B to rebuild only new or changed features and their children.

You can change the order in which features are rebuilt by dragging them in the FeatureManager design tree. Place the pointer on a feature name, press the left mouse button, and drag the feature to a new position in the list. (As you drag up or down the tree, each item that you drag over is highlighted. The feature name that you're moving drops immediately below the currently highlighted item when you release the mouse button.)

Moving a feature or folder can cause the model to change. If you don't like the results, click the Undo button to return the feature to its original location.

Organizing features with folders

Just as you use folders and file cabinets to organize paperwork, you can use folders in the FeatureManager design tree to organize your SolidWorks part and assembly data. The part features in Figure 5-22 are broken into four main functional areas based on their function: Profile, Mounting, Molding, and Cosmetic. When working on a specific area of the design, you can expand or collapse a folder by clicking the plus symbol to the left of the folder name.

Figure 5-22: Folders make a Feature-Manager design tree more manageable.

You can drag part features or assembly components in the FeatureManager design tree to group them into functional folders. To add a new folder in the FeatureManager design tree, right-click a feature and choose Add to New Folder. A new folder appears in the FeatureManager design tree. The feature you right-clicked is now in the new folder. You can rename the folder and drag additional features into the folder.

Name your folders according to their function or role in the model. You do not have to put every part feature or assembly component in a folder. If you group features or components into a folder, you can act upon them as a group. SolidWorks lets you suppress part feature or assembly components in a folder as a group. In the example shown in Figure 5-22, you can turn off the mounting features by selecting the folder, right-clicking, and choosing Suppress. You can use the Suppress command for multiple versions of the same design or just for visualization purposes.

When you select a folder in the FeatureManager design tree, the features in the folder are highlighted in the graphics area. Similarly, when you select a feature in the graphics area that is in a folder you created, the folder is expanded to show the highlighted feature in the FeatureManager design tree.

Grouping features has several advantages:

- ✔ **It makes the design easier to read.** You can look at the FeatureManager design tree and find features by how they relate to function (mounting location, profiles, and so on) because they're in the same area. Using folders also makes the length of the features listed within the FeatureManager design tree shorter.

- ✔ **It enhances performance.** When you work on larger parts, feature order can be a performance enhancer. For example, if you're working on a particular functional area, you can move that folder higher up in the FeatureManager design tree so those features rebuild first, and you can see the changes in the model sooner.

Using the Rollback feature

The Rollback bar, a yellow-and-black line in the FeatureManager design tree, turns blue when you select it. You can drag the bar up the FeatureManager design tree to suppress features one by one and revert the model to various earlier states.

The example shown in Figure 5-23 shows the part rolled back to show all features up to the Inner hinge. You see the model as it looked at the time the designer added the Inner hinge. The features created after the Inner Hinge do not appear in the model. In this case, the designer used the Rollback bar to go back and insert a new feature after the Inner hinge.

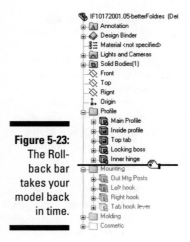

Figure 5-23:
The Roll-
back bar
takes your
model back
in time.

Using comments

You can add comments to the FeatureManager design tree to document design intent. (See Figure 5-24.) These comments appear when you place the cursor over the feature name in the FeatureManager design tree.

Figure 5-24:
Comments
are another
way to
document
design
intent.

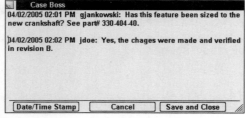

To create and edit a feature comment

1. **Open a part.**

2. **In the FeatureManager design tree, right-click a feature and select Comment⇨Add Comment, Edit Comment, or Delete Comment.**

   If a comment doesn't already exist, you see Add Comment in the menu. If a comment does exist, you see Edit Comment and Delete Comment. Select Delete Comment to delete the existing comment.

A comment box, which resembles a yellow sticky note, appears. The name of the item is at the top of the note. If you selected Edit Comment, you see the existing comment, and you can change or respond to it.

3. **Click Date/Time Stamp at the bottom of the comment box.**

   The date, time, and your name are added to the comment.

4. **Type your comment.**

5. **Click Save and Close.**

   When you roll the pointer over the item in the FeatureManager design tree, the note appears.

Consider adding a comment to a folder so that you know the purpose of the folder. Otherwise, you may have little indication of why the folder exists and what it contains.

Knowing How Much to Model

One question that folks often ask is, "How much detail should I include in my model?" For example, if you're making a ruler, do you need to include the metal edge insert and the all the detailed text and ruler markings?

My answer is this: "Just because you can doesn't mean you should." Yes, you can make parts look just like they would in real life, but you'll pay the piper at some point in terms of assembly performance and the time it takes to maintain that level of detail.

If you need all kinds of tiny details to document or to manufacture the part, then by all means, add them to the model, particularly if it helps someone else to make the part. However, you don't need as much detail if you plan to make the part yourself.

Use Feature Statistics to determine which features take the most time to open and rebuild. Choose Tools⇨Feature Statistics.

Here's a simple example. Figure 5-25 shows two screws. The screw on the right is loaded with features, including chamfers and fillets on all edges to make it look real. The screw on the left is plane and simple. This screw is a standard part, and the only item that counts is the threaded cut for the screw threads. Even if this part were made in-house, you don't need the detailed geometry to create the screw.

Here is the difference in file size between the simple versus detailed version of the screws. Also listed is the effect on a medium assembly (50 fasteners) and a large assembly (250 fasteners):

- ✔ 1 fastener = 115KB versus 470KB (408 percent larger than the simple version)
- ✔ 50 fasteners = 5.7MB versus 23.5 MB (17.8MB difference)
- ✔ 250 fasteners = 28.7MB versus 117.5 MB (88.8MB difference)

Figure 5-25:
While a detailed screw may look pretty, it's a waste of time.

Now some may argue that the detailed screw does not have enough detail. My response is, unless it's an art project, include only the detail that some-one really needs. I would rather start simpler and add any detail later if needed.

Designing standard parts is a waste of time. SolidWorks Toolbox includes a library of standard fasteners. You can find other standard part models at www.3dcontentcentral.com.

Chapter 6

Putting It All Together

*O*ne of the advantages of 3D design is that it gives you a complete virtual product that you can assemble and analyze. SolidWorks lets you create a functional assembly so that you can see how your design looks and works before you build a single part. This way, you can quickly identify mistakes before spending time and resources to create the actual parts.

The SolidWorks virtual assembly mimics the location and movement of the components to determine their fit and function and lets you see how the assembly looks in its assembled and exploded states.

Creating and Modifying the Assembly

An *assembly* is a collection of components that consist of parts and other assemblies, called subassemblies. You create an assembly in SolidWorks the same as you build a product in the real world. *Mates* position a component in an assembly precisely with respect to each other. Mates defines how the components move and rotate together. Assembly reference geometry, such as sketches, planes, and axes, controls the shape and position of components.

Figure 6-1 shows a complete virtual assembly of a Sea Scooter in its final stage before going to the manufacturer.

Figure 6-1:
A designer
can see
assembly
parts in this
Sea Scooter
fit together.

The following is a list of items that you use to create an assembly:

- ✔ **Components:** Refer to both parts and subassemblies. You insert components into an assembly to show their orientation and the order in which manufacturing needs to assemble the final product. You can evaluate the form, fit, and function of a component in relation to other components in the assembly.

- ✔ **Mates:** Create geometric relationships between assembly components. As you add mates, you define the allowable directions of linear or rotational motion of the components. You can move a component within its degrees of freedom, visualizing the assembly's behavior.

- ✔ **Planes:** Define the location of an assembly component or provide a construction plane for an assembly object.

- ✔ **Axes:** Define the location of an assembly component or a construction reference for an assembly object.

- ✔ **Layout sketches:** Control the size and/or location of assembly components and reference geometry.

- ✔ **Skeleton:** Consists of 2D layout sketches, axes, and planes. The assembly references these simple sketches, as well as reference geometry, to define location, size, and position of assembly components.

When an assembly or part file is open in SolidWorks, the triad (colored X-Y-Z arrows) in the lower left-hand corner of the graphics panel indicates the positive direction of each axis with arrows.

Throughout this chapter, you use the Assembly toolbar, shown in Figure 6-2. When you're working on an assembly document, the Assembly toolbar appears in the CommandManager. (You can read more about the CommandManager in Chapter 2.)

When active in the CommandManager, the Assembly toolbar includes the following functions:

1 Insert Components: Inserts new component into the current assembly.

2 Hide/Show Components: Turns the display of a component on or off temporarily. Even when you can't see a component, it's still in memory and other assembly components can reference it.

3 Change Suppression State: Allows you to set a component as Suppress, Resolve, or Lightweight. When a component is suppressed, it doesn't load into memory, and other components can't reference it. When a component is lightweight, only a subset of its model data is loaded into memory and the rest is loaded on an as-need basis. A resolved model loads completely. (Read more on suppression states in Chapter 10.)

4 Edit Component: Allows you to edit a part or a subassembly while the rest of the assembly is visible in an opaque display in the graphics area.

5 No External References: Lets you create a model in an assembly window without creating external references. This chapter covers external references later in the section, "In-context assembly modeling."

6 Mate: Adds geometric references in between assembly components to position and constrain them.

7 Move Component: Allow you to drag an assembly component to a new location.

8 Rotate Component: Rotates an assembly component.

9 Smart Fastener: Automatically adds fasteners (such as bolts, nuts, and washers) to assembly holes.

10 **Exploded View:** Creates a view of the assembly showing the components pulled apart so you can see how components fit together. You can use this view in assembly drawings and manuals.

11 **Explode Line Sketch:** Adds lines to components in an Exploded View to show the direction and final location of the exploded component.

12 **Interference Detection:** Checks the assembly to ensure that parts don't clash into one another when they move.

13 **Features:** Creates assembly level features, such as Extruded Cut and Hole Wizard. Features a flyout toolbar in the Assembly toolbar that contains only the features that you can use in an assembly.

14 **Physical Simulation:** Performs a motion study by applying Linear Motor, Rotary Motor, Linear Spring, and Gravity to an assembly and animates the results. Physical Simulation is a flyout toolbar in the Assembly toolbar.

Planning your assembly

A number of factors influence how you go about creating an assembly in SolidWorks. Resist the urge to start modeling immediately. Instead, step back and take time to plan your assembly. Planning pays off later in the design process.

The following are items that help define the starting point of an assembly. This chapter covers each of these items in more detail.

✔ **Define what is known.** Every project has certain requirements, such as the product's purpose, size, weight, cost, and so on. Capture these requirements before you start. Where you keep these requirements (for example, in Microsoft Word or Microsoft Excel) doesn't particularly matter, as long as you capture them consistently and store them in a shared location if you're working with other designers.

Well-defined requirements ensure that you go in the right direction. They also save time and let you know in advance whether you have all the information you need to complete the project.

✔ **Create the structure.** Define the principle components of the assembly and create configurations that show each major subassembly component and suppress everything else. Because a suppressed component doesn't load into memory, these configurations allow other designers to examine the major areas of an assembly without having to resolve the entire kit-and-kaboodle.

✔ **Collaborate.** Think about how to break up the assembly in order to distribute the workload if you plan to work with several designers on a project.

✔ **Review and capture the design intent.** Use a skeleton to capture and control the functions of your design if you plan on creating a complex assembly. Test the skeleton before you begin adding components.

✔ **Review existing information.** Check to see what designs and standard components exist so that you can use them in your assembly design.

You can set document properties (dimensions, standards, text size, unit of measurement, and so on) and custom properties in an assembly template that you can reuse. Defining custom properties in advance helps when it comes time to create the drawings. (To find out more about templates, see Chapter 2.)

Designing an assembly

You can use two basic methods to design an assembly: top-down or bottom-up. With either method, your objective is to position and mate the components. Mates position the components and define how they move. (Read more on mates in the "Understanding Your Mates" section, later in this chapter.)

In *top-down design,* you start work on the assembly, and you build parts to fit into the assembly. The geometry of one part defines the geometry of others. You start a top-down design with a skeleton that defines fixed part locations, planes, and so on, and then design the parts referencing these positions.

Bottom-up design is a good plan if all parts come from suppliers. You don't need to create references that control the size and shapes of parts, because the parts already exist. You simply insert them into the assembly and mate them together. Because components are designed independently, their relationship to each other is simpler than in top-down design.

In most cases, you work with a mix of custom and standard parts, so the best design method is a cross between top-down and bottom-up. Read the sections "Using skeletons and layouts" and "In-Context Assembly Modeling" for specific techniques on how to design top-down.

The following sections give you three ways to begin work on an assembly. Depending on what documents you have open, one method may be more straightforward than another. In other words, they all work, but the one that works best for you depends on the project you're working on at the time.

Creating an assembly

You can create an assembly by starting with an assembly document and then adding parts one by one. Start with a component that doesn't move with respect to the other components. That way, you can anchor the component to the assembly origin. Anchoring the first component ensures that the planes in both documents are aligned.

To create a new assembly in SolidWorks:

1. **Choose File⇨New.**

   The New SolidWorks Document dialog box appears.

2. **Click Assembly.**

   You select the standard Assembly template. (If you want to select a custom template, click Advanced in the dialog box to display other templates that are available.)

3. **Click OK.**

   A new assembly document opens. The Insert Component PropertyManager appears in the left panel (see Figure 6-3). Any part or assembly files that are already open appear under Open Documents.

   Select the check box for Graphics Preview in the Insert Component PropertyManager to see a preview of the part that you're inserting.

Figure 6-3: The Insert Component Property-Manager lets you insert a part or assembly file into your assembly.

4. **Under Part/Assembly to Insert, click Browse.**

   The Open dialog box appears.

5. **Navigate to the part or assembly file that you want to insert.**

   A preview of the model appears in the Preview section of the dialog box. Any configurations appear in the Configurations box.

6. **Select the file and configuration (if one exists) and click Open.**

   The Open dialog box closes, and the model appears in your assembly. The origin of the new component aligns with the assembly origin.

7. **Click View and select the check box next to Origins to display the assembly origin.**

   The assembly origin appears in blue.

8. **To anchor the part to the assembly origin, click OK.**

   The component anchors to the assembly origin. When you place a component this way, the component origin is located coincident with the assembly origin, and the planes of the part and assembly are aligned, which helps establish an initial orientation for the assembly. An (f) appears next to the component in the FeatureManager design tree to indicate the component is fixed into place.

Creating an assembly from a part

You don't need to begin an assembly from an assembly document. In many cases, you may want to start building an assembly from an existing part. To create an assembly from a part or assembly:

1. **Open the model to use as the first assembly component.**

2. **On the Standard toolbar, click Make Assembly from Part/Assembly.**

   A new assembly document opens, and the Insert New Component PropertyManager appears.

3. **In the main menu, choose View and select the check box next to Origins to display the origin in the graphic area.**

   The blue origin appears.

4. **In the PropertyManager, under Options, select Graphics preview.**

   A preview of the model appears in the graphic area.

5. **Move the pointer over the origin in the graphic area.**

   The model moves with your pointer, and the pointer changes to indicate an inference to the assembly origin.

6. **Click to place the component.**

   The component anchors to the assembly origin.

Adding components to an assembly

Once you begin building your assembly, you want to load additional components and position them. You can position components anywhere in the graphics area and then use the Move Components tool to drag each component closer to the first anchored component. You should leave some space between the components to view the relevant component areas. In many instances, you can use the Rotate, View, and Pan tools in the View toolbar to change the orientation of the components to facilitate selecting the edge, face, or other entity needed to apply mates.

To insert a part or subassembly into an existing assembly:

1. **Click Insert Components on the Assemblies toolbar.**

    The Insert Component PropertyManager appears.

2. **Under Part/Assembly to Insert, click Browse.**

    The Open dialog box appears.

3. **Navigate to the part or assembly file that you want to insert.**

    A preview of the model appears in the Preview section of the Open Dialog box. Any configurations appear in the Configurations box.

4. **Select the file and configuration (if one exists) and click Open.**

    The Open dialog box closes, and the model appears in your assembly. The origin of the new component aligns with the assembly origin.

5. **To place the part in the center of the assembly, click OK.**

    The new component aligns with the origins of the assembly. (If you can't see the blue origins, click View and select the check box next to Origins.)

6. **To place the part in a different location, move the pointer and click.**

    SolidWorks anchors the component into place. The new file appears in the FeatureManager design tree.

After you insert a new component, you want to mate it to another component. Read the section "Understanding Your Mates," later in this chapter, to find out how to mate two components together.

Another way to add components to the assembly is to drag them in from File Explorer in the SolidWorks Task Pane and place them into the assembly. This method allows you to add several components quickly. You can use the Move command to position them later.

Organizing your assembly

When you're creating a large assembly, you want to group components into manageable subassemblies. The advantages to breaking up the assembly this way are multifold:

✔ **It distributes the work.** Design team members can collaborate on the same design by working on the subassemblies separately. It would be a huge train wreck to have a number of designers in the same subassembly.

✔ **It organizes the assembly based on manufacturing considerations.** You may want the components to appear in the bill of materials list in the same order in which you want to build them. (Find out more about inserting a bill or materials table into a drawing in Chapter 8.)

✔ **It minimizes visual clutter.** You can use the Change Suppression State command to display only the subassemblies you're working on in order to minimize the visual clutter and the amount of information loaded into computer memory. Select a part or subassembly in the FeatureManager design tree and on the Assembly toolbar click Change Suppression State and select Suppress, Lightweight, or Resolve. A suppressed part doesn't load into memory. Only graphical information loads for a lightweight part, and a resolved part is fully loaded.

✔ **It replaces a subassembly easier.** A subassembly behaves as a single component. You can replace an entire subassembly with another one and fully constrain it with only three mates, making it easier to deal with than lots of individual parts.

✔ **It limits the number of top-level mates within the assembly.** The more subassemblies in a design, the fewer top-level mates. When SolidWorks opens an assembly, it solves mates at the top level first, so the more top-level mates, the longer it takes to open a file. By default, SolidWorks doesn't solve mates inside the subassemblies.

It takes three mates to fully constrain a part, so if you do the math, you need only 15 mates to constrain an assembly of 150 parts, if you break the assembly into five subassemblies. In contrast, you need 150 mates to fully constrain that same assembly if it were flat (no subassemblies). You may need to wait a long time for the second one to load.

The RC car assembly in Figure 6-4 has two example FeatureManager design trees (see Figures 6-5 and 6-6).

Figure 6-4:
Breaking a large assembly, such as this RC car assembly, into sub-assemblies makes the assembly easier to work with.

The following two FeatureManager design trees show different versions of the assembly. The first one shows parts and assemblies at the top level, and the second one shows functionally grouped subassemblies. The second assembly is easier to work on — for example, to work on the front suspension, you only need to open a subassembly instead of the entire assembly.

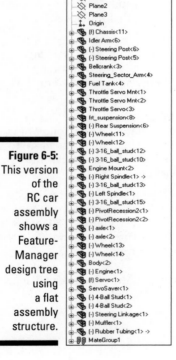

Figure 6-5:
This version of the RC car assembly shows a Feature-Manager design tree using a flat assembly structure.

Figure 6-6:
This version of the RC car shows a Feature-Manager design tree broken into functional sub-assemblies.

You can use the following commands to change the level and grouping of assembly components at any time. You can access all these commands by right-clicking a component in the FeatureManager design tree:

- ✔ **Insert New Sub-assembly:** Create a new assembly at the level you select. Select the top icon in the FeatureManager design tree, right-click the icon, and choose Insert New Sub-assembly.

- ✔ **Dissolve Sub-assembly:** Dissolves the subassembly you select. Select the sub-assembly in the FeatureManager design tree, right-click, and choose Dissolve Sub-assembly.

- ✔ **Add to New Folder:** Creates a new folder within FeatureManager design tree. To move the assembly component into the new folder, right-click the icon and choose Add to New Folder.

- ✔ **Drag and drop:** Selects parts and subassemblies. Hold down the mouse button and drag the component to the new top-level assembly or assembly location.

Understanding Your Mates

A *mate* is a feature in SolidWorks that controls how parts move with respect to each other. Without any connecting mates, a pair of components can move with six unrestricted degrees of freedom relative to one another. (Each mate reduces the degrees of freedom by two. You need only three mates to fully constrain a part so that it can't move at all.)

Mates also create geometric relations (such as coincident, perpendicular, tangent, angle) between two parts or subassemblies. Mates let components act and react like the ones in a real-world assembly.

For example, if you want a door to open from 0 to 90 degrees within a product (see Figure 6-7), you can add an angular mate that allows a component to open and close within an assembly.

Figure 6-7: Mates define the movement of the tops of these inkjet cartridges.

Mates allow you to not only review and document fit and form, but also to simulate how parts function within the assembly. When you design assemblies that move, you can perform fit and interference checks in the open or closed state of a part and at any point in between.

The following concepts make your assemblies more effective and easier to modify:

- **Make the mate mimic reality.** Mates that mimic the way the part will be assembled in the actual product ensure realistic motion studies and easier editing later on.

- **Know what you're mating and why.** When creating a mate, don't just pick a reference without understanding what you're creating. Otherwise, you may create a mate reference that doesn't reference what you actually wanted.

- **Mate as high as possible in the assembly structure.** Again, try to keep the references between components simple. Choose references for mates that you plan to keep around. If you mate haphazardly, your mates may end up referencing components that don't exist in other configurations of the assembly or that you may remove or change later.

- **Name important mates.** Names make mates easier to identify and to change.

- **Understand warnings and errors.** The FeatureManager design tree gives you feedback on problems with mates. Figure 6-8 shows examples of a couple of mate issues. To understand a problem, in the FeatureManager design tree, right-click the mate and choose What's Wrong. The What's Wrong dialog box gives a more complete description of the issue and potential sources of the problem.

Figure 6-8:
The Feature-Manager design tree lists errors next to the mates.

- **Mate Diagnostics.** When problems do occur with mates, as shown in Figure 6-8, use Mate Diagnostics to review the mate errors and warning. To diagnose mate issues, right-click the Mates icon and choose Mate Diagnostics. Click Diagnose and review the mate issues.

✔ **Constrain only the degrees of freedom required.** For example, if you insert a screw, you only need to mate the screw axis and the bottom of the screw head to the assembly component. You can leave the screw free to turn in the hole. The screw will appear as underconstrained in the FeatureManager design tree, but that is okay.

Getting familiar with mate types

Each mate is valid for a specific combination of geometry, such as cones, cylinders, planes, extrusions, and so on. For example, you can only use coincident, concentric, and distance to mate a cone to another cone.

The Mategroup folder in the FeatureManager design tree looks like a pair of paper clips. If you expand the folder, you see a list of all the mates in your assembly. Figure 6-9 shows a mate, pointer indication, and the Mategroup in the FeatureManager design tree.

Mates are broken down into the following three basic categories:

✔ **Geometry-based mates:** When you drag a component into an assembly, you can use the SmartMates command to create mates automatically. SmartMates adds mates according to the type of geometry and references that you select.

For example, in Figure 6-9, when I select the inside edge of the washer in the graphic area and drag it into the assembly, as the washer passes over the hole on the boss, my pointer changes to indicate the type of mates that will be created. When I drop the washer (by releasing the mouse button), two mates, both concentric to the holes and edges, appear automatically.

⊟ 𝄃𝄃 Mates
    ◣ ✎ Coincident16 (89-NOAO-4200-0052<1>,89-NOAO-4200-1058<1>)

Figure 6-9:
Your pointer changes when it is ready to attach a mate.

✔ **Feature-based mates:** A feature-based mate is created between a boss and a hole. The example shown in Figure 6-9 is a feature-based mate (you know this because the pointer is over a cylindrical face). The pointer gives feedback based on the type of geometry and the reference that you select. The pointer type shown in Figure 6-9 shows that a feature will be used for the mate.

✔ **Pattern-based mates:** You can also create SmartMates by referencing a circular pattern of holes on a planar face. (These apply only to true pattern features, not those you create manually.) Align the component to the match circular edge. Use the Tab key to align its patterns and release the mouse button to drop the component into place.

For a pattern-based mate, you can create three mates: a Concentric mate between the circular edges, a Coincident mate between the planar faces, and a Concentric mate between the selected part and pattern within the assembly.

You can use feature-based and pattern-based mates to create SmartMates (see the "Working with SmartMates" section, later in this chapter). You use the geometry-based mates to create basic mates. The types of basic mates are as follows:

✔ **Coincident:** Places two items (faces, edges, or planes in combination with each other or combined with a single vertex) so that they touch.

✔ **Parallel:** Places two items so that they remain a specified distance from one another.

✔ **Perpendicular:** Places two items so that they're 90 degrees from one another.

✔ **Tangent:** Places a curve and another item so that they meet at a single point. One of the selected items must be a cylindrical, conical, or spherical face.

✔ **Concentric:** Places two items so that they share the same center axis.

✔ **Distance:** Places two items at a specified distance from one another.

✔ **Angle:** Places two items at a specified angle to one another.

Adding a mate

To add a mate:

1. **Open a SolidWorks assembly document.**

2. **Click Mate in the Assembly toolbar.**

   The Mate PropertyManager, shown in Figure 6-10, appears, with the Entries Selections field active.

Figure 6-10:
The Mate
Property-
Manager
shows valid
mate types
for the
entities you
select.

3. **In Options, select the check boxes for Show Preview and Show Pop-up Dialog.**

4. **In the graphic area, click the two faces, edges, vertices (corners/points), or planes that you want to mate together.**

   In the graphic area, the Mate pop-up toolbar, shown in Figure 6-11, appears with default mates for the entities you selected.

Figure 6-11:
Default
mate types
appear in
the Mate
pop-up
toolbar.

5. **In the toolbar, click the type of mate you want to add.**

   The two components move into place to give you a preview of the mate type.

   Under Mate Alignments, in the Advanced Mates section of the Mate PropertyManager, you can select Align or Anti-Aligned to switch parts so that the faces of the two parts point together or in opposite directions.

6. **Click OK (the green checkmark) in the pop-up toolbar.**

   The Mate pop-up toolbar closes. The Mate PropertyManager stays active so that you can continue adding mates.

7. **Click OK to close the Mate PropertyManager.**

You can test a mate by clicking Move Component on the Assembly toolbar and then click a component and drag it to see how it moves. If a component doesn't move, it's fixed or fully constrained. If a component is fixed, it has a (f) before its name in the FeatureManager design tree. A floating, or underdefined, component has a (-). A fully defined component doesn't have a prefix. To fix or float a component, right-click the component in the FeatureManager design tree and choose Fix or Float.

Editing a mate

You can edit an existing mate at any time. To edit an existing mate:

1. **Open an assembly file.**

2. **In the FeatureManager design tree, expand the Mategroup.**

   You can also select the mate under the Mates folder for the component.

3. **Select the mate to edit.**

   The items (faces, edges, and so on) that the mate references are highlighted within the graphics area.

4. **Right-click the mate.**

   The right mouse button menu appears.

5. **Choose Edit Feature.**

   The Mate PropertyManager appears. The name of the PropertyManager is based on the type of mate.

6. **Edit the mate properties and selections.**

7. **Click OK.**

You can use the middle mouse button to rotate your model to see what you're selecting or working on. If you have a wheel mouse, use the wheel to zoom in and out as you rotate the model. You can use these mouse buttons while in the command without going to another area of the interface.

Working with SmartMates

If you prefer to spend as little time as possible mating components, SmartMates may be your thing. *SmartMates* apply mates automatically when you drag and drop components into an assembly. SmartMates chooses a mate based on the geometry of the part.

SmartMates works with part edges and faces. Depending on what you select, an edge or face, SolidWorks determines a valid mate type as you drag your pointer over the component or select other geometry.

The example in Figure 6-12 shows a washer and a bolt. I selected the washer edge and bolt diameter for SmartMates. In this case, SmartMates creates a concentric mate, which constrains the bolt to the washer.

SmartMates did not fully constrain the bolt in Figure 6-12. To fully constrain an assembly component, all size degrees of freedom (front/back, right/left, up/down) must be constrained. You can constrain them by using three mates. In Figure 6-12, the base of the bolt and the top of washer do touch, and the hole and bolt diameter do align, but there is still a degree or two of movement left. The bolt head can still spin around its axis. In this case, I wouldn't add another mate to completely fix the component. Why create the last mate if it doesn't make a difference?

You can activate SmartMates when you drop an assembly component into the assembly, in order to eliminate the extra steps of first adding the assembly component and then manually adding more mates.

Figure 6-12:
SmartMates
creates a
concentric
mate for
this washer
and bolt.

To activate SmartMates when you pull a component into the assembly, hold down the Alt key and drag a component over potential mate partners. The component becomes transparent and the pointer changes when it is over a valid mate partner. Drop the component to apply the mate.

To add a SmartMate to an existing assembly component in a SolidWorks assembly:

1. **Click Move Component on the Assembly toolbar.**

   The Move PropertyManager appears.

2. **In the PropertyManager, under Move, click SmartMates.**

3. **Double-click a component and then click a valid mate partner.**

   The pointer turns into a paper clip, indicating that SmartMates is active. The Mate pop-up toolbar appears, with the default mate types to fit the geometry you selected.

4. **In the Mate pop-up toolbar, click a mate type.**

5. **Click OK in the Mate toolbar.**

   The components move into place, and the SmartMates PropertyManager stays active for you to add other mates.

6. **To add other mates, repeat Steps 3 to 5.**

7. **Click OK in the PropertyManager.**

   The SmartMates PropertyManager closes.

To add a SmartMate to a new component by dragging and dropping it into an existing assembly:

1. **Open a SolidWorks assembly document.**

2. **Open another SolidWorks part or assembly document.**

3. **Choose Windows⇨Tile Vertical.**

   Both windows appear side by side so that you can see both open files at the same time. You can zoom into either model to get a close look at the areas you want to mate.

4. **Hold down the Alt key, click the model, and drag it into the main assembly document to where you want to mate it.**

   The pointer changes to a mate type when the parts are ready to mate.

5. **Release the mouse button.**

   The Mate pop-up toolbar appears with the default mate types for the two parts.

6. **Click a mate type in the toolbar.**

7. **Click OK.**

    The parts mate and the toolbar closes.

After SmartMates mates your two components, you can flip a part if it doesn't point in the right direction by clicking the part and pressing the Tab key. If the orientation isn't what you want, press the Tab key again to flip the components back around without exiting the mate function. If you're mating a pattern feature, clicking the Tab rotates the part about the center of the pattern rather than flipping the mate alignment (aligned or anti-aligned).

Working with mate references

Mate references specify one or more entities of a component to use for automatic mating. When you drag a component with a mate reference into an assembly, SolidWorks looks for other combinations of the same mate reference name and mate type. If the name is the same, but the type doesn't match, SolidWorks doesn't add the mate.

Here are a few things to keep in mind about mate references:

- ✔ **Components:** You can add mate references to parts and subassemblies. In subassemblies, you can select assembly geometry (such as a plane in the assembly) or component geometry (such as the face of a component).

- ✔ **Multiple mate references:** A component can contain more than one mate reference. The MateReferences folder in the FeatureManager design tree holds all mate references. For example, you can have a component in an assembly with two mate references, bolt and washer. When you drag a fastener with a mate reference named bolt into the assembly, SolidWorks adds mates between the entities with the same mate reference name.

- ✔ **Multiple mated entities:** Each mate reference can contain up to three mated entities: a primary, secondary, and tertiary reference entity. Each of these entities can have an assigned mate type and alignment. The primary reference entity on one component must mate to the primary reference entity on another. For example, a shaft can have its cylindrical face assigned to a concentric mate and its planar end face assigned to a coincident mate. When you drag that component into an appropriate location in an assembly, SolidWorks adds both mates.

- ✔ **SmartMates:** When the SmartMates PropertyManager is open, SolidWorks adds mates via mate references before it adds geometric SmartMates.

You need to set up the mate reference ahead of time in the original document (part or assembly) and the target assembly. You want to use mate references mainly in situations where there is a common component that you plan to use and change to another component often.

In Figure 6-13, the selected face is the primary reference. The axes named Axis1 and Axis2 are the secondary and tertiary references. You can add these three references to the engine to allow you to drag new exhaust systems into the assembly and automatically mate them.

Figure 6-13: The muffler assembly shows the three references (primary, secondary, and tertiary) used to mate to the engine assembly.

To define a mate reference:

1. **Open a SolidWorks part or assembly document.**

2. **Choose Insert⇨Reference Geometry⇨Mate Reference.**

   The Mate Reference PropertyManager appears with the Primary Reference Entity field active.

3. **Under Reference Name, type a name for the mate reference.**

   Always give the mate reference a meaningful name.

4. **Select a face, edge, vertex, or a plane for the Primary reference entity.**

   The entity appears in the Primary Reference Entity field. Select the most important mate for the primary reference. SolidWorks uses the entity for potential mates when you drag a new component into the assembly.

5. **In Mate Reference type, use the pull-down menu to select a default mate type for the Primary reference.**

6. **In Mate Reference Alignment, use the pull-down menu to select the default reference alignment for the Primary entity.**

   This selection determines which way the part flips or aligns when a mate is applied. The Mate Reference Alignment uses a vector that's perpendicular and pointing away from the face to help to determine how to flip the component when its mated. Options include:

   • **Any:** Positions the components either aligned or anti-aligned based on their current position.

- **Aligned:** Positions the components so that the normal vectors of the selected faces point in the same direction.

- **Anti-Aligned:** Positions the components so that the normal vectors of the selected faces point toward each other.

- **Closest:** Positions the components depending on the condition that can be met, aligned or anti-aligned, with the least movement.

7. **If needed, repeat Steps 3 to 6 to add secondary and tertiary entities.**

   The mate referenced appears in the FeatureManager design tree in the MateReferences folder. Each mate can have up to three reference entities. All three references are required to fully constrain the component within the assembly.

8. **Click OK.**

After you define the mate references, just drag a part or an assembly into the new assembly. If the name and type of the new component match the reference, SolidWorks mates it automatically.

Understanding the FeatureManager design tree Mategroup

The FeatureManager design tree displays a range of information about the assembly components and their status. Figure 6-14 shows an assembly with the Mategroup and a component expanded to show the mate features.

Figure 6-14: The Feature-Manager design tree shows the Mates component folder and mategroup.

Clutch (Default<Display State-1>)
- Annotations
- Design Binder
- Lights and Cameras
- Front
- Top
- Right
- (-) Outer Basket<1> (Default<Display State-1>)
- (-) Inner Clutch Pack<1> (Default<Display State-1>)
- (-) AP(KAM)<1> (Default [last saved])
- (-) AP Bearing<1> (Default<Display State-1>)
  - Mates in Clutch
    - Coincident6 (Outer Basket<1>,AP Bearing<1>)
    - Concentric9 (Outer Basket<1>,AP Bearing<1>)
  - Plane1
  - Plane2
  - Plane3
  - (-) Bearing Half<1> (Default<Display State-1>)
  - (-) Bearing Half<2> (Default<Display State-1>)
- MateGroup1
  - Concentric7 (Outer Basket<1>,AP(KAM)<1>)
  - Concentric8 (Outer Basket<1>,Inner Clutch Pack<1>)
  - Parallel1 (Outer Basket<1>,Inner Clutch Pack<1>)
  - Distance2 (Outer Basket<1>,Inner Clutch Pack<1>)
  - Distance3 (Inner Clutch Pack<1>,AP(KAM)<1>)
  - Coincident6 (Outer Basket<1>,AP Bearing<1>)
  - Concentric9 (Outer Basket<1>,AP Bearing<1>)

You can infer the following from the display of the FeatureManager design tree objects within the assembly in Figure 6-14:

✔ All top-level components (Outer Basket, Inner Clutch Pack, and so on) are underconstrained as indicated by the (-) next to the component name, indicating there are still some degrees of movement. You can add more mates to fully define the location of the assembly component.

✔ You find only one instance of each component in the top level of the assembly, noted by the *<1>* after the component name. A subassembly, AP Bearing, has two subassembly instances — <1> and <2> — of the Bearing Half assembly.

✔ The mates for each component appear in the Mategroup in the Mate in <Assembly name> folder. The AP Bearing has two coincident mates (Coincident6 and Coincident9).

✔ The mate name defaults to the type (Distance, Concentric, and so on) followed by [reference 1 (parent), reference 2 (child)]. For example, AP Bearing has two mates (Coincident6 and Coincident9). The names of these mates define the location of the AP Bearing (child, reference 2) using The Outer Basket (parent, reference 1).

✔ A total of seven mates appear in the assembly, as shown under Mategroup1.

Assemblies created in older versions of SolidWorks name Mategroups Mates.

You can click the plus and minus signs on the left side of the object icon in the FeatureManager design tree to expand or collapse a folder.

Working with Your Virtual Prototype

Designing an assembly is a complex task that can involve the work of several designers. SolidWorks offers tools that allow you to plan your design and implement your plan. Layout sketches and skeletons indicate the location of components. Other tools allow you to build parts inside the assembly window to reference them to other part geometry. And tools that load only the assemblies you need to see make it easier to share the workload.

Using skeletons and layouts

You can use skeletons and layouts to control the location and orientation of assembly components, and define important mates. Layouts contain one or more 2D sketches and skeletons consist of several 2D sketches along with planes and axes. Both are important components in top-down design.

Layout sketches

You can use 2D layout sketches to define parts or the major components of subassemblies. You can construct a sketch to show where each component belongs. Then you can modify the sketch before you add any parts.

The major advantage of designing an assembly using a layout sketch is that if you change the layout sketch, the assembly and its parts update automatically.

Another advantage is that layout sketches reduces the amount of parent/ child relationships. Components are related by one sketch in the assembly, so parts are more robust and easier to change and redefine.

To use an assembly layout sketch, do the following:

- ✔ Create a sketch in the assembly in which various sketch entities represent parts in the assembly.
- ✔ Indicate a tentative location for each component, capturing the overall design intent.
- ✔ Reference the geometry in the layout sketch when you create each component.
- ✔ Use the layout sketch to define the component size, shape, and location within the assembly and make sure that each part references the layout sketch.

While a layout sketch is good for some designs, it may not be great for all designs. Figure 6-15 shows an assembly that uses linkages. You can use the layout sketch to design and test out the linkage. You can use a sketch like the one shown in Figure 6-16 to drive the position of the assembly components.

Figure 6-15:
The major mounting joints in this backhoe are good candidates for inclusion in a layout sketch or skeleton.

Figure 6-16:
You can
reference
parts to
the layout
sketch.

Assembly skeleton

An *assembly skeleton* is a simple structure that uses layout sketches, planes, and axes to relate assembly components and define their movement. An assembly skeleton is saved as a part file.

The benefit of a skeleton is that it captures design intent. You use a skeleton in top-down design when most of the assembly components are custom made. A skeleton ties components together so that if one changes, all the related components change.

A skeleton should define mates, functionally important surface, axes, or edges for the assembly. You build your components on these features.

Here are the advantages of an assembly skeleton:

- ✔ A skeleton is easier to understand and modify because it's built on 2D sketches and planes and axes.

- ✔ You can analyze assembly fit, form, and function in a skeleton long before you add a single part. (You can't test movement and function in a layout sketch.)

- ✔ A skeleton makes it easy to break a very large assembly into subassemblies that multiple designers can work on.

- ✔ You can capture your assembly structure in a skeleton and save configurations that resolve major subassemblies and suppress others so that the configurations load into memory faster.

- ✔ You can name major geometry in the skeleton so that you know which parts reference certain areas of the skeleton when you want to make a change.

Creating the skeleton and layout

You create the skeleton as a separate part document and use it as the first component in an assembly, anchoring it to the origin. (See "Creating an assembly," earlier in this chapter.) Instead of inserting the skeleton as a regular part, you insert it as an envelope by choosing Insert⇨Envelope so that the skeleton component doesn't appear on the bill of materials table as a part that someone needs to order from a supplier. An *envelope* is a special type of assembly reference component. It's ignored in global assembly operations, such as the bill of materials and mass properties.

If desired, make the skeleton part read-only for everyone except an administrator or project lead. This way, you limit access to add or change this important design element.

Using blocks in your layouts

A new feature in SolidWorks 2006 lets you create blocks from sketch entities and use them in your layout sketches and in your assembly skeleton. *Blocks* let you group sketch geometry. The group updates and behaves as a single entity. The sketch must be active in order to create or edit blocks. You save blocks with the .sldblk extension so that you can easily import them into part, assembly, or other blocks files later.

To display the Block toolbar, choose View⇨Toolbars⇨Blocks. The Block toolbar, shown in Figure 6-17, includes the following functions:

Figure 6-17:
The sketch
Block
toolbar lets
you group
blocks of
sketch
entities.

   ✔ **Make Block:** Create a block from selected sketch geometry.

   ✔ **Edit Block:** Change dimensions and relations in a block.

   ✔ **Insert Block:** Insert a saved block into the current sketch.

✔ **Save Block:** Save a block to disk for re-use.

✔ **Explode Block:** Ungroup a block and convert to regular sketch entities.

You can use blocks to create an assembly by clicking Layout⇨Create Assembly from Layout. This function takes the sketch block names and creates components for the assembly.

To create an assembly from a layout sketch:

1. **Open a new part or assembly.**

   You want to use this as a starting point in your assembly layout sketch.

2. **Create or click the existing sketch within the FeatureManager design tree containing sketch blocks to define the assembly.**

   See Chapter 4 for more information on creating sketches.

3. **Choose File⇨Create Assembly from Layout Sketch.**

   The Create Assembly from Layout Sketch dialog box appears. The Create Assembly from Layout Sketch command is only selectable when a sketch has been selected in the FeatureManager design tree.

4. **Click the source block to include on the new assembly and whether to create a new top-level assembly within the Create Assembly from Layout Sketch dialog box.**

   See Figure 6-18 for an example. The block names appear under Sketch1 and are used for the default component names.

   Use the Browse button to optionally change the path for the new assembly. The Target Component name is based on the block name, and you can change it by clicking inside the Target Component field.

Figure 6-18:
The Create Assembly from Layout Sketch lets you create an assembly from a layout sketch.

5. **Click OK.**

   The new assembly is creating in the location specified using the sketch blocks

Using advanced selection

You can use two tools in SolidWorks to control how components appear in an assembly: Advanced Component Selection and Advanced Show/Hide.

You can use these tools together to create assembly configurations that hide or show components based on the component's mass properties (weight, volume, and so on) and custom properties. The ability to control what you can and can't see in an assembly is another example of why custom properties are so important to SolidWorks document types.

Advanced Component Selection allows you to define criteria and select assembly components based on those criteria. Advanced Show/Hide Components also allow for the components to be shown or hidden within the same command.

The example in Figure 6-19 shows how you can use Advanced Component Selection to select all of the fasteners (nuts, pins, washers, and so on) in an assembly based on the custom property IsFastener.

Figure 6-19: Advanced Component Selection lets you choose all the fasteners in an assembly based on their custom property values.

SolidWorks defines special properties to use within the select criteria:

- **Part Mass:** SW Special (numeric)
- **Part Volume:** SW Special (numeric)
- **Part is interior detail:** SW Special (is yes or is no)
- **Configuration name:** SW Special (string)
- **Document name:** SW Special (string)

Advanced Show/Hide is similar to the Advanced Component Selection, but you use it to specifically hide or show components in an assembly configuration. For example, you may want to create a configuration that doesn't show any of the standard hardware. You can use Advanced Component Selection to select the hardware based on a custom property.

The example shown in Figure 6-20 hides all the interior components in an assembly. Hiding the interior detail is useful for simplification and performance reasons.

Figure 6-20:
Advanced
Show/Hide
dialog box
with the
"part is
interior
detail"
criteria.

The advantage of using this feature is that it directly modifies the state of the selected assembly components. The options under the criteria definition section is where the difference between the functions lies. You can also use the criteria in the previous section in this function.

To show or hide components based on advanced selection criteria:

1. **Click the ConfigurationManager tab at the top of the FeatureManager design tree.**

   The FeatureManager design tree disappears, and the ConfigurationManager appears in its place. The ConfigurationManager lists the different configurations in the assembly.

2. **Right-click a configuration and choose Advanced Show/Hide.**

   The Advanced Show/Hide PropertyManager appears.

3. **Define the Property and Condition values.**

   You can apply more than one condition using the Boolean values And and Or.

4. **Click the Add button.**

   The Properties and Conditions are added to the configuration.

5. **Click Apply to run the query.**

   You can save or load criteria using the Save Criteria and Load Criteria buttons.

6. **Click Close to quit.**

Creating assembly features

SolidWorks allows you to create certain features (Extruded Cut, Revolved Cut, Hole Wizard, and Linear and Circular Patterns) in the assembly.

You can use these features when you're modeling a cut or a hole at the assembly level. For example, in a welded assembly, you may want to add cuts and holes to the assembly after all the assembly components are in place.

Assembly features are added at the assembly level, not to the individual components. You add these features the same way you do part features. (You can read about part features in Chapter 5.) You can access the commands in the Features toolbar.

When adding an assembly feature, you can set the feature scope to specify which components should be taken into consideration when creating the assembly feature. So if you want to cut only certain parts with an assembly cut, you can define the scope to only include those components.

To set the scope for an assembly feature:

1. **Select an assembly feature to set the scope for that feature.**

   If you don't select a feature, you specify the feature scope for the next assembly feature that you create.

2. **Choose Edit⇨Feature Scope.**

   The Edit Assembly Feature Scope dialog box appears. The Feature Scope field is active.

3. **In the FeatureManager design tree or in the graphics area, click the components that you want the assembly feature to affect.**

   The selected component names appear in the Edit Assembly Feature Scope dialog box.

4. **Click OK.**

   The feature is applied to the selected components. The default feature scope is updated. The next assembly feature that you add inherits this feature scope.

In-context assembly modeling

In addition to creating or editing components in their own part windows, you create or edit components in the assembly window. The advantage to this method is that it allows you to build a part that references the geometry of another. If you update one part, the other updates as well, ensuring that the components fit together correctly. This method of design is called *in-context* design because you're working in the context of the assembly.

When you create a part in an assembly window, the part appears in the FeatureManager design tree as if you created it in its own window. SolidWorks also adds an item to the FeatureManager design tree that lists information about the part, such as what was used to create it and the referenced assembly component.

Parts created within the context of the assembly contain external references. SolidWorks creates an *external reference* when one document is dependent on another for its solution. The referenced document is known as the *parent,* and the document that references it is known as its *child.* If the parent document changes, its children update to reflect that change.

The ability to design in the context of the assembly is a powerful one. But if too many parts are tied to one another, managing the automatic update of changes to the original parts can be harder. I always like having more control over what changes and when.

You can use the following commands to work on parts in the context of an assembly. You can access all these commands when you right-click a component name in the FeatureManager design tree.

- ✔ **Edit Part:** Allows you to edit a part in the assembly window while the assembly geometry displays in the background.

- ✔ **Edit In-Context:** Recalls the assembly when only the part is active so that you can change, add, or remove references.

- ✔ **List External References:** Lists the references of a part and their current state (in or out of context).

- ✔ **Display/Delete Relations:** Allows you to list, review, delete, or replace an external reference.

The FeatureManager design tree indicates that a feature has an external reference by appending the -> symbol to the right of the feature name. If the external reference is locked, the symbol changes to ->*.

If you're editing in context of the assembly and you don't want to create external references, click No External References on the Assembly toolbar (see Figure 6-21).

Figure 6-21:
You can edit
a part in
the context
of the
assembly.

Creating a part in an assembly

To create a part while in the assembly:

1. **Choose Insert➪Component➪New Part.**

   The Save As dialog box appears.

2. **Type a name for the new part and click Save.**

   The new part is saved in its own document, and you can edit it separately. The dialog box closes, and the component pointer appears.

3. **Select a plane in the FeatureManager design tree or select a planar face on which to position the part.**

   The name of the new part appears in the FeatureManager design tree, and a sketch automatically opens in the new part. An Inplace (coincident) mate is added between the Front plane of the new part and the selected plane or face.

   The new part is fully positioned by the Inplace mate. No additional mates are required to position it. If you want to reposition the component, you need to delete the Inplace mate first.

4. **Construct the part features using the same techniques you use to build a part on its own and reference geometry of other components on the assembly as needed.**

   See Chapter 5 to brush up on part making skills.

5. **Choose File➪Save.**

   The changes save to the part file.

6. **Select the Resolve Ambiguity dialog box or select the assembly name to save the entire assembly and its components.**

7. **To return to editing the assembly, right-click anywhere in the graphic area and then choose Edit Assembly:<assembly_name> or click Edit Component.**

Editing a part in an assembly

Editing a part while in an assembly allows you to modify a component without leaving the assembly. You can create sketches for the new features that reference an edge or that you dimension to an edge in another part.

When you edit a part in the context of an assembly, the part turns blue, and the rest of the assembly turns gray.

To edit a part while in an assembly:

1. **Right-click the part and choose Edit Part.**

   The rest of the assembly becomes transparent in the background.

   You have several options for displaying component transparency when you edit a component in the context of an assembly. These settings affect only the component not being edited. Choose Tools➪Options. On the Systems Option tab, select Display/Selection. Under Assembly transparency for in-context edit, select an option for the type of transparency.

   The title bar shows the name of the part in the assembly that is open for editing as <part_name> in <assembly_name>.sldasm. Note that the message in the status bar indicates that you're now editing the part document even though the entire assembly is visible.

   When you edit a part in the context of an assembly, the referenced configuration in the assembly becomes the active configuration in all open windows (for example, if the part is open in its own window).

2. **Make the necessary changes to the part.**

   You can read more about how to make a part in Chapter 5.

3. **To return to editing the assembly, right-click the assembly name in the FeatureManager design tree, or right-click anywhere in the graphics area and choose Edit Assembly:<assembly_name> or click Edit Component.**

Getting information about your assembly

You can squeeze plenty of information out of your solid model. Similar to any real world product, you can measure your model, weigh your model, and examine how parts fit together and come apart — all this without getting your hands dirty. Isn't the virtual world grand?

Making sure that everything fits

Once you create an assembly, you want to make sure that components inter-act properly. *Interference checking* in SolidWorks lets you check to see whether any parts clash into one another. Interference checking is an under-used feature in SolidWorks, but don't underuse it in your work. Check for interference even after simple design changes. It's much easier to fix a virtual model than a real one, and you'll have less explaining to do.

Figure 6-22 shows an assembly where the shaft is too large for the gears and bearing. Thank goodness the designer caught it. Keep in mind, though, that interference is not always a bad thing. For example, a press fit is a designed interference.

Figure 6-22: Interference detection spots that the shaft is too large for the gears.

You can see two interferences in Figure 6-22 (Interference1 and Interference2). If you select the interference in the Results field of the Interference Detection PropertyManager, the interference volume highlights as shown. The names of the interfering components also appear under the interference.

To check the assembly for interferences:

1. Open an assembly document.

2. **Choose Interference Detection on the Assembly toolbar.**

   The Interference Detection dialog box appears with the Selected Components field active. The entire assembly appears in the field by default. You can clear the field and enter any subassemblies individually.

3. **Select (or don't select) the check boxes for these options:**

   - **Treat coincidence as interference:** Reports coincident entities as interferences.

   - **Show ignored interference:** Shows ignored interferences in the Results list, with a gray icon. When this option is cleared, ignored interferences aren't listed.

   - **Treat subassemblies as components:** Treats subassemblies as single components so that interferences between a subassembly's components aren't reported.

   - **Include multibody part interferences:** Reports interferences between bodies within multibody parts. (A *multibody* is a part file with two separate solid bodies that don't touch.)

   - **Make interfering parts transparent:** Displays the components of the selected interference in transparent mode.

   - **Create fasteners folder:** Segregates interferences between fasteners (such as a nut and bolt) into a separate folder under Results.

4. **Select Component View under Results.**

   Any interferences highlight in the model.

5. **Click Calculate.**

   The interference between components is calculated and the results appear in the Results field.

6. **Click OK.**

Measure your design

Just as with parts, you can measure the assembly by using the Measure tool.

To measure within an assembly:

1. **Open an assembly document.**

2. **Choose Tools⇨Measure.**

   The Measure dialog box, shown in Figure 6-23, appears. The dialog box is a toolbar that you can expand to display the measurement values.

3. **Select the items to measure.**

   The pointer turns to a ruler to indicate Measure is active. The items you select are highlighted, and values display in the graphics area. You can expand the measure box to display values in the box. New measurements update dynamically when you change selections.

TIP

While the Measure dialog box is in place, you can switch between different SolidWorks documents without closing the dialog box. The name of the currently active document displays in the title bar of the Measure dialog box. If you activate a document that has items already selected, the measurement information updates automatically.

 4. **Click X to quit.**

Figure 6-23:
You can
measure
your
assembly
with the
Measure
tool.

Just the facts, ma'am (Assembly Statistics)

When working with an assembly, especially one that someone else made, you may want to get some of the vitals of the assembly. You can quickly determine the number of parts, unique parts (only used once), subassemblies, mates, and so on using the Assembly Statistics feature.

For an assembly, the key thing to know is how big is the assembly? In other words, how many components does it have? You also want to know how many top-level mates exist. Too many top-level mates creates performance issues.

To determine the assembly statistics:

 1. **Open an assembly document.**

 2. **Choose Tools⇨Assembly Statistics.**

    The Assembly Statistics dialog box, shown in Figure 6-24, appears. Inside the dialog box, you can see how many components are in the assembly, what type of components, the number of top-level mates, top-level components, and so on.

 3. **Review the information.**

 4. **Click OK to close the dialog box.**

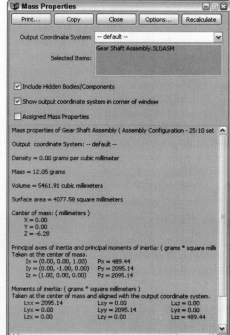

Figure 6-24:
The
Assembly
Statistics
dialog box
gives the
low-down
on this Sea
Scooter.

How big is that breadbasket (Mass Properties)?

Of course, you can use other ways to pry information from an assembly —
the Mass Properties tool, for example (see Figure 6-25). You can use Mass
Properties to find out your assembly's weight and volume and more.
SolidWorks calculates all of this information directly on the assembly based
on the materials that you assign to individual parts.

Figure 6-25:
Mass
properties
tells how
much this
Gear Shaft
weighs.

To calculate the mass properties for an assembly:

1. **Open an assembly document.**

2. **Choose Tools⇨Mass Properties.**

   The Mass Properties dialog box appears. The name of the assembly appears in the Selected Items field.

3. **Select the check box for Include Hidden bodies/components.**

   Hidden components are included in mass property calculations.

4. **Select any components, subassemblies in the FeatureManager design tree to get individual or combined mass properties.**

   By default, the active assembly is shown within the Selected Components field.

5. **Click Close.**

   The Mass Properties dialog box closes.

Part III
The Devil's in the "Drawing" Details

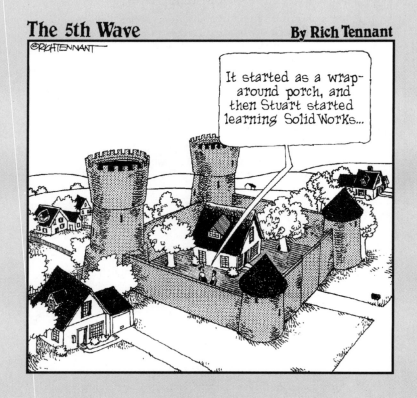

The 5th Wave   By Rich Tennant

It started as a wrap-around porch, and then Stuart started learning SolidWorks...

In this part . . .

After you create the parts and assemblies, you're ready to draw. *Drawings* are the means used to document the design intent and requirements for manufacturing.

You can reuse the information that defines the part or assembly to help produce the drawing. When a change does occur (and it will), you can modify the dimension within the part/assembly or drawings, and both documents update. The ability to easily change the design and have the changes update in the related document illustrates the power of 3D.

Chapter 7

Creating Drawings

● ●

● ●

Drawings formally communicate your design to manufacturing. While technology has come along promising to eliminate the need for them, drawings continue to serve an important purpose in design. Manufacturers need drawings to produce quotes, to determine the proper manufacturing processes, and to inspect the parts to ensure that they meet the requirements set forth in the drawings.

SolidWorks offers a number of different tools to automate the drawing process based on information that you capture in your 3D design. This chapter focuses on the basics of drawing creation. The next chapter expands on these topics and offers some insight on how to automate drawing functions.

Becoming Familiar with Drawing Elements

In essence, *drawings* are large sheets of paper that contain images of your model in various views and orientations along with dimensions, manufacturing symbols, notes, and other annotations.

Back in the good old days before CAD software, engineers created drawings on a drawing board with paper and pencil. First, you pulled out a preprinted drawing sheet that fit the drawing size you wanted (A, B, C, and so on). Then you created the drawing views that showed the part as it appeared from different angles (top, front, right, isometric, and so on). Finally, you inserted dimensions, filled in the title and revision blocks, and added notes and other annotations.

SolidWorks follows this same process, only virtually, so that you don't have to actually get up and sharpen your pencil or fumble around with large drawing sheets. The software does the heavy lifting for you.

And the best part of SolidWorks is that the drawing file is fully associative with the model. That means that if you change the part geometry after the fact, the drawing views update automatically so that you don't have to go in and redo them manually. Adding views is simple, and it's all tied together.

The following elements, shown in Figure 7-1, make up a drawing:

Figure 7-1:
Drawings display your model in all its glory.

1 Drawing format: You can edit the drawing format, which is the predefined background for a drawing, directly. The predefined background for a drawing may also contain title block text and other standard notes. Read the section "Editing the Drawing Sheet Format," later in this chapter, to find out how to change the drawing format.

2 Drawing sheet: A drawing in SolidWorks contains one or more sheets, like a set of drawings, allowing you to keep multisheet drawings in a single file. SolidWorks uses a simple tab organization method for multisheet drawings. You can add sheets at any time, using any format. Select a tab to activate a sheet. To add a new a new sheet, right-click a tab and choose Add Sheet.

3 **Scroll bars:** You can use the scrollbars on the sides of the drawings to scroll up or down and right to left.

4 **Title block:** This area is where the information concerning title, revision, material, drawing size, part number, drawn by, and so on appears. The title block is contained within the drawing format.

5 **Drawing format text (static):** Some text notes within the drawing format are static and don't change. The words, such as SIZE and REV, don't change from drawing to drawing.

6 **Drawing format text (dynamic):** This text changes with every drawing. These values are linked to custom properties.

7 **Drawing view border:** When you place a drawing view, a frame appears around the view.

8 **Pointer:** Other programs call the pointer a cursor. A tag next to the pointer tells you what drawing sheet is active. You can change drawing sheets by clicking a sheet tab at the bottom of the drawing.

9 **Drawing view (isometric):** Drawing views on drawings sheets show the model in different orientations and include dimensions and annotations. This drawing view shows a standard isometric view of the model. This view and the next two are the three standard views you can place on a sheet automatically using the Standard 3 Views command on the Drawings toolbar.

10 **Drawing view (right):** This view shows the model from the right.

11 **Drawing view (front):** This view shows the front of the model.

12 **Datum annotation:** This annotation was created within the part and inserted into the drawing automatically using the Insert Model Items command. (You can read the details of this command in Chapter 8.)

13 **Revision annotation:** Revision mark. This annotation is tied to the revision table.

14 **Dimension (driven):** Dimensions that appear in grey are driven dimensions that serve only as reference geometry. You can add driven dimensions to a drawing, but they don't change the model.

15 **Dimension (driving):** Black lines indicate driving dimensions in Solid-Works. You can insert driving dimensions from the model into the drawing automatically. If you change their values, the changes update in the model.

16 **Note:** You can create this type of annotation directly in the drawing. Notes contain text and symbols.

17 **Surface finish symbol:** This type of annotation indicates the type of surface finish. You can import these annotations directly from the model.

18 **Revision table:** A special table type is the revision block. This table also has special functions to add revision marks and new revisions.

SolidWorks supports a number of drawing standards, including ISO, ANSI, DIN, JIS, BSI, GOST, and GB. The standard you choose affects the appearance of drawing views. For example, if you choose ANSI, drawing view projections are third-angle, and the symbols meet the ANSI drafting standard. Likewise, if you choose DIN, the drawing view projections are first-angle, and the symbols comply with the DIN drafting standard. The drawing in Figure 7-1 is set to ANSI standard.

Default values and drawing standards are in the drawing template. You can change the standard template or make your own. Read Chapter 2 for more on how to define, save, and share drawing templates.

Opening a New Drawing Document

Drawings consist of one or more views generated from a part or an assembly. Views show the model in different orientations. SolidWorks lets you create a drawing from a drawing template or from within a part or assembly document. This chapter shows you how to make a drawing from a model.

Drawing files have the .slddrw extension. A new drawing takes the name of the first model you insert into it. The name appears in the title bar. When you save the drawing, the name of the model appears in the Save As dialog box as the default file name, with the default extension .slddrw. You can edit the name before saving the drawing.

You can create a drawing in many ways. The following method is my preference as it is the most straightforward:

To create a new drawing:

1. **Open the part or assembly document you want to use for the drawing.**

2. **Choose File⇨Make Drawing from Part or Make Drawing from Assembly.**

   A new SolidWorks drawing document appears. The Sheet/Format Size dialog box appears.

3. **If you don't want to use any sheet format, click Cancel and continue to Step 5.**

   The Sheet/Format Size dialog box closes, and the Drawing View PropertyManager, shown in Figure 7-2, appears in the left pane.

4. **If you do want to use a sheet, select the check box for Standard sheet size (or choose custom sheet size if you want to make your own).**

   If you selected Standard sheet size, the standard sheet sizes become visible. If you select Custom sheet size, the Width and Height fields become active.

Figure 7-2:
You can
select a
single view
orientation
in the
Drawing
View
Property-
Manager.

5. **Select a standard sheet size or type a width and height for the custom sheet size.**

6. **Select the check box for Display sheet format to display a border, title block, and so on.**

7. **Click OK.**

A new drawing appears in the graphics area, and the Model View PropertyManager appears. In the PropertyManager, you see your open part or assembly document listed in Open Documents.

If you're in a hurry, you may want to place three standard views instead of a single model view. If so, when the Model PropertyManager appears, ignore it and click Standard 3 Views in the Drawings toolbar. The Standard 3 Views PropertyManager appears, and the list of open documents is available. Click an open document and three standard views (front, right, and isometric) of the model appear on the drawing sheet. You don't need to select any other options.

8. **In the PropertyManager, double-click a part or assembly listed under Open documents.**

If you're creating a drawing from an open part or assembly, your file should appear in this field. If you want to use a different model, browse to select another file. Once you select a model, the Model View PropertyManager expands to show other options.

9. **In the PropertyManager, select a named view under Orientation (Front, Back, and so on).**

   The name is highlighted. If you select the check box next to Preview, you see a preview of the view next to your pointer.

10. **Click a Display Style.**

    You can choose from an assortment of display styles, such as hidden lines removed, hidden lines visible, and so on.

11. **Select a scale.**

    You have three options:

    • **Use parent view:** This option is only available after the first view. When you add views, you can use the parent view, which applies the same scale used for the parent view. If you change the scale of the parent view, the child view updates.

    • **Use sheet scale:** Your model appears scaled to fit the sheet that you're using. SolidWorks selects a scale based on the default sheet template and reduces the scaled based on the model size.

    • **Use custom scale:** Select a ratio from the drop-down list or enter in your own values.

12. **In Dimension Type, select a check box for Projected or True.**

    Projected shows 2D dimensions, and True displays those that are accurate model value.

13. **Click in the graphic area to place the view on the sheet.**

    As soon as you place the view, the Drawing View PropertyManager replaces the Model View PropertyManager. If you place an orthogonal view orientation, the Projected View PropertyManager appears, and you can place any number of projected views for any orthogonal view. But before you start placing more views, you many want to read the "Placing Drawing Views" section, later in this chapter.

14. **Click OK in the Model View PropertyManager or in the Drawing View PropertyManager.**

    The PropertyManager closes and the new drawing appears in the graphics area.

Editing the Drawing Sheet Format

You can think of the drawing sheet format (see Figure 7-3) as letterhead for your drawings. It contains your company name, the size of the sheet, title of the drawing, and other information that you think is important. You can customize the sheet format to match your company's standard format. The sheet format underlies the drawing sheet and is separate from the drawing sheet. You edit the sheet format directly before you place all the model views.

The drawing format has a scale of 1:1. If you use letter-sized paper, then that's the actual paper size, which makes setting up a drawing format simpler because the views aren't scaled. Figure 7-3 shows an A-size drawing format.

Standard sheets include links to system properties and custom properties. SolidWorks extracts custom properties from the model to use in the drawing.

Figure 7-3:
An example of an A-Size drawing format.

SolidWorks sheet formats have the file extension .slddrt. You can save sheet formats separately and use them to create future drawings. You can create drawing sheets in new drawing documents and in drawing templates.

Drawing templates have the extension .drwdot. A template forms the basis of a new document. You can create custom templates to include predefined views, multiple drawing sheets, and so on.

When you open a drawing with an existing drawing format, you can't change the information directly. When you edit the sheet format, the drawing views and other non-drawing format items are no longer visible because you're editing the sheet format (drawing background), not the other drawing information (views, notes, dimensions, and so on).

To edit a drawing sheet format:

1. **Open a drawing file or a drawing template file.**

2. **In the FeatureManager design tree, expand a sheet folder.**

   The sheet format and drawing views become visible.

3. **Right-click the sheet format you want to edit and choose Edit Sheet Format.**

   You're now in edit mode.

4. **To edit the title blocks, in the graphic area, right-click the text and choose Properties.**

   The Properties dialog box opens.

5. **Change any items in the Properties dialog box and then click OK.**

6. **Move, delete, or add lines of text.**

   To delete, click the line or text and press the Delete key. To move, click the line or text and drag to a new location. To add lines, click the Line button within the Sketch toolbar.

7. **To add text, click Note on the Annotation toolbar.**

8. **Specify the text properties and then click to place the text in the desired location.**

9. **When you're done editing, in the FeatureManager design tree, right-click the sheet and select Edit Sheet.**

   You return to your drawing default edit sheet.

Placing the Drawing Views

After you edit your sheet format, it is time to place the model views on the drawing sheets, as shown in Figure 7-4. A drawing view shows a model in a particular orientation, scale, and display state. These views are important because they convey information about how to build or assemble your model.

Your can create views of one or more parts and assemblies and include them in the same drawing. A perusal of the commands on the Drawings toolbar gives you an idea of the multitude of views you can include on a sheet.

Introducing the Drawings toolbar

When you open a drawing document in SolidWorks, by default, the Drawings toolbar, shown in Figure 7-5, appears in the CommandManager. (You can read more about the CommandManager in Chapter 2.) The Drawings toolbar contains commands that let you add various model views to your drawings.

Figure 7-4:
You can place several model views in a drawing.

Your first view must be a standard view, and from there, you create other views that are based on the standard views (section, detail, and so on.) The Model View command allows you to place any one standard view while Standard 3 Views places three standard views automatically.

Figure 7-5:
You can use the Drawings toolbar to place all of your views.

The following sections are the Drawings toolbar view commands with explanations of how to place each view. Remember that you need to have a drawing document open to use these commands.

When you place a view, you need to drag it into position. You can see a preview of a model view as you're dragging it by setting this option: Choose Tools⇨Options. In the Systems Options tab, select Drawings and select the check box for Show contents while dragging drawing view. (This option is generally set as a default.)

Model View

You can use the Model View command to place any standard view of your model. Standard views are just that: standard engineering views, such as front, top, isometric, and so on. Figure 7-4 item #1 shows an example of this view type.

To insert a model view into your drawing:

1. **Click Model View on the Drawings toolbar, shown in Figure 7-5 item #1.**

   The Model PropertyManager appears, as shown in Figure 7-6. Any model that is active in SolidWorks appears in Open documents.

2. **Double-click the model listed in Open documents to place a new view or click Browse to locate a different part or assembly file.**

3. **Select a view under Orientation (Front, Back, and so on).**

   Select the check box for preview to see a preview of the model before you place it.

4. **Set the options for display style and scales in the PropertyManager.**

5. **Click in the graphic area to place the view on the sheet.**

   As soon as you place the view, the Drawing View PropertyManager replaces the Model View PropertyManager. If you place an orthogonal view orientation, the Projected View PropertyManager appears, and you can place any number of projected views for any orthogonal view. But before you start placing more views, you many want to read the "Placing the Drawing Views" section, later in this chapter.

6. **Click OK in the Model View PropertyManager or in the Drawing View PropertyManager.**

   The PropertyManager closes, and the new drawing appears in the graphics area.

Standard 3 Views

The Standard 3 Views function creates three views (top, front, and right) and places them on your drawing automatically. This command is a good one to use if you're in a hurry. Standard views are generally the first that you place in a drawing. (Read the section "Opening a New Drawing Document," earlier in this chapter.)

Figure 7-6:
You first place one or more standard views in a drawing using Model View or Standard 3 Views.

To create three standard drawing views:

1. **Click Standard 3 Views on the Drawings toolbar, shown in Figure 7-5 item #7.**

   The Standard 3 Views PropertyManager appears. In the PropertyManager, any open documents appear listed under Open Documents.

2. **In the PropertyManager, double-click the model under Open Documents or choose Browse to locate a different one.**

   The three views appear in the drawing. The alignment of the top and side views is fixed in relation to the front view. You can move the top view vertically and the side view horizontally.

3. **Click OK.**

Projected View

This view allows you to create a new orthographically projected view from an existing, or parent, view. Figure 7-4 item #2 shows an example of this view type.

To create a projected view:

1. **Click Projected View on the Drawings toolbar, shown in Figure 7-5 item #2.**

   The Projected View PropertyManager appears.

2. **Select an existing view from which to project.**

   The new view is going to be projected normal (90 degrees) to the selected drawing view.

3. **Click in the graphic area to place the view.**

   The Projected View PropertyManager expands to include several options. You can project the new view in any direction (up/down, right/left, and isometric) from the selected view.

4. **Set options in the PropertyManager.**

   You can set the display style, scale, and dimension type. These options are the same ones covered in the earlier section "Opening a New Drawing Document."

5. **Click OK.**

Auxiliary View

This view is defined by folding the new view perpendicular to an existing view's part or assembly edge. Figure 7-4 item #6 shows an example of this view type.

To create an auxiliary view:

1. **Click Auxiliary View on the Drawings toolbar, shown in Figure 7-5 item #3.**

   The Auxiliary View PropertyManager appears.

2. **Select a reference edge.**

   Don't select a horizontal or vertical edge, which creates a standard Projection View.

   You can use an edge of a part, a silhouette edge, an axis, or a sketched line as a reference. If you sketch a line, activate the drawing view first.

3. **Move the pointer until the view is where you want and then click to place the view.**

   The PropertyManager for the drawing view appears.

4. **Set options in the PropertyManager.**

   You can set the display style, scale, and dimension type. These options are the same ones covered in the earlier section "Opening a New Drawing Document."

5. Click OK.

To override the default alignment of any view type, hold down the Ctrl key while placing the view. Section View

A section view shows the internal details of a part or assembly. Section views make details easier to read than when you use hidden line views. You create a section view by drawing a line through the parent part. Figure 7-4 item #9 shows an example of this view type.

To create a section view:

1. Click Section View on the Drawings toolbar, shown in Figure 7-5 item #4.

The Section View PropertyManager appears. The Line tool is active, and when you pass the pointer over an existing view, a box appears around the view.

2. Sketch a section line through an existing view.

Draw the section line completely through the box of the model in the view. If the section line doesn't completely cut through the box, you're asked whether you want it to be a partial section cut. If you click Yes, the section view is created as a partial section view. If you click No, a full section view is created for you. Once the line is complete, the section view appears as a preview.

3. Move the pointer until the view is where you want and click to place the view.

The section view is aligned to the source, so you can only place the new view above or below the section line in the graphic area. Once you place the view, the PropertyManager for that view appears.

4. Set options in the PropertyManager.

You can set the display style, scale, and dimension type. These options are the same ones covered in the earlier section "Opening a New Drawing Document."

5. Click OK.

Aligned Section View

You create an aligned section view similar to a section view, but instead of a single line, you sketch a section line that consists of two lines connected at an angle. The section view rotates the geometry on the angled segment so that the section can be projected. Figure 7-4 item #8 shows an example of this view type.

To create an aligned section view:

1. **Select Aligned Section View on the Drawings toolbar, shown in Figure 7-5 item #5.**

   The Aligned Section View PropertyManager appears. The Line tool is active, and when you pass the pointer over an existing view, a box appears around the view.

2. **Sketch two lines to define the section cut in a drawing view.**

   The two lines must connect at an angle. Once you draw the line, a preview of the section appears in the graphic area near the pointer.

3. **Move the pointer until the view is where you want and click to place the view.**

   The view is aligned to the sketch segment that you selected when you created the section line; the cut faces from the other segments are projected into the same plane.

4. **Set options in the PropertyManager.**

   You can set the display style, scale, and dimension type. These options are the same ones covered in the earlier section "Opening a New Drawing Document."

5. **Click OK.**

Detail View

A detail view is a blown-up portion of a small section of an existing view, which you draw a circle around. Figure 7-4 item #11 shows an example of this view type.

To create a detail view:

1. **Click Detail View on the Drawings toolbar, shown in Figure 7-5 item #6.**

   The Detail View PropertyManager appears, and the Circle tool is active. When you pass the pointer over a view, a box appears around the view.

2. **Draw a circle around the area you want to blow up.**

   When you complete the circle, a preview of the view appears next to your pointer, and the PropertyManager for the view appears.

3. **Set options in the PropertyManager.**

   You can set the display style, scale, and dimension type. These options are the same ones covered in the earlier section "Opening a New Drawing Document."

4. **Click OK.**

Crop View

A crop view displays only a portion of an existing view. Cropping a drawing is similar to cropping a photo. If you don't want to look at something in the photo (such as an ex-boyfriend or girlfriend), you crop a rectangle around what you do want and leave out everything else. SolidWorks lets you crop any drawing view except a detail view, a view from which a detail view was made, or an exploded view. Figure 7-4 item #7 shows an example of this view type.

To create a crop view:

1. **Inside one of the drawing views, sketch a closed profile such as a circle or a rectangle.**

   (You can read more on sketching in Chapter 3.)

2. **In the graphics pane, select the sketch profile in the view you want to crop.**

   The box highlights to show the selected view.

3. **Click Crop View on the Drawings toolbar, shown in Figure 7-5 item #8**

   The image crops. Only the area inside the sketch displays. The rest of the view disappears.

Changing View Properties

Setting up drawing views is like arranging your living room. Once you get everything in place, it's time to re-cover the sofa and move things around. Luckily, changing drawing views is easier than moving furniture. To edit a drawing view, double-click the view in the graphic area. The PropertyManager for that drawing view appears, as shown in Figure 7-7.

The PropertyManager for drawing views comes in two versions, and which one you see depends on whether the view is a child or a parent of another view. A child view, such as a detail or section view, references another view that is its parent. The PropertyManager displays only the values that you can change.

One thing that you can change about a view is its display state (Wireframe, Hidden Lines Removed, and so on). You probably have a favorite display state. Mine are Shaded or Shaded with Edges, which make the drawing more readable. When you pick a display state, consider who is reading the drawing and the type of printer you're outputting on. Shaded views, for example, look better on higher definition plotters.

Figure 7-7:
The
Drawing
View
Property-
Manager.

Another thing you can change is the scale of a model. In the view's Property-Manager, you can select Use sheet scale, Use parent scale, or Use custom scale and then select a default scale or enter in your own value.

You can move a view by double-clicking the view in the graphic area and dragging it to a new location. Some limitations exist. If a view is aligned to a parent view, you cannot move it out of alignment.

You also can change the size of a drawing sheet. Right-click the sheet in the FeatureManager design tree and choose Properties. In the Properties dialog box, select a standard size or select a custom sheet size and type the height and width values.

The yellow message box at the top of the PropertyManager and the status window on the bottom left corner of the screen give clues as to what is required for the current command.

If a view has a parent, the boundary box of the parent view also highlights when you select the child view.

Creating Drawing Dimensions

Dimensions are important in your drawings because they indicate how big a part or an assembly is and list other critical measurements that the supplier needs to know in order to make the product. Without dimensions, you don't know if you're building a model airplane or something people fly around in.

SolidWorks offers two types of dimensions: driving dimensions and driven dimensions. *Driving dimensions,* or model dimensions, control the size and shape of the model. *Driven dimension* are reference dimensions, meaning that they don't drive the size or location of features but instead help clarify the drawing.

You can change the display of any dimension type in the Dimension PropertyManager (see Figure 7-8), which appears when you insert a dimension. You can set the following options:

- ✔ **Favorites:** You can create and save your favorite dimension styles in this section. Dimension styles save as .sldfvt files, and you can add them to your design library. (See Chapter 8 for more info on favorites.)

- ✔ **Tolerance/Precision:** You can change the number of decimal places in the dimension value, tolerance type, and value in this field. Tolerance values determine how precise a manufacturer makes the parts.

- ✔ **Dimension Text:** You can place text and symbols around the dimension value, which is noted as <DIM>. Simply type the text. You can align left, center, and justify the text by clicking the buttons below the text field.

- ✔ **Primary Value:** In this field, you can override the value of driving dimensions. Changes to a driving dimension update in the model.

- ✔ **Display Options:** You can select whether to show the values with parenthesis (reference dimensions), dual dimension (inch/metric), and inspection dimension (oval around dimension text).

- ✔ **Layer:** You can select a drawing layer for the dimensions.

You can insert model dimensions and annotations automatically by choosing Insert➪Insert Model Items in the main menu. (You can find out more about Insert Model Items and other drawing automations in Chapter 8.)

Smart Dimensions

You can add dimensions to drawings in several ways. One way is by using Smart Dimensions on the Annotations toolbar. The Annotations toolbar appears by default in the CommandManager when you work on a drawing. You also find Smart Dimensions on the Dimension/Relations toolbar.

Figure 7-8:
You can
set the
appearance
of and add
symbols and
text to
dimensions
in the
Dimension
Property-
Manager.

You can add toolbar buttons to the CommandManager. Right-click anywhere in the CommandManager and choose Customize CommandManager. In the list of toolbar buttons that appear, select or deselect the check boxes to add or remove toolbars. Click outside the list to close the menu.

Smart Dimensions knows what type of dimension to add based on the entity you select. If you select a line, Smart Dimension creates a dimension for the length of the line. Likewise, if you select an arc or a circle, Smart Dimensions creates a radial or diameter dimension.

To insert a model dimension in a drawing:

 1. **Click Smart Dimension on the Annotations toolbar.**

    The pointer changes to a dimensioning tool icon to let you know that Smart Dimensions is active.

2. **Click the object to dimension.**

   You may need to zoom in on the view first. An object turns red as the pointer moves over it and green when you select it. When you click an entity, the dimension values appear above it in gray.

3. **Drag the dimension text for placement.**

   The dimension text follows the pointer, as shown in Figure 7-9.

Figure 7-9: Text placement can change the dimension type.

4. **Click to place the dimension.**

   The dimension is fixed in place, and the Dimension PropertyManager appears.

5. **Set display options in the PropertyManager.**

   The Smart Dimension tool stays active so that you can continue inserting dimensions.

6. **Repeat Steps 2 through 5 to insert more dimensions.**

7. **Click OK.**

Ordinate and baseline dimensions

Driven dimensions are strictly reference geometry and appear as gray in parentheses by default. You cannot edit the values in reference dimensions.

Two types of driven dimensions that may come in handy as you delve further into the world of drawings are ordinate and baseline dimensions. *Ordinate dimensions* are a set of dimensions measured from a zero ordinate. *Baseline dimensions* are a set of dimensions measured from an edge or a vertex.

Both ordinate and baseline dimensions are sets of entities that are grouped. When you drag any member of the group, all the members move together. To disconnect a dimension from the alignment group, right-click the dimension, and select Break Alignment.

To create an ordinate dimensions:

1. **Choose Tools⇨Dimensions⇨Ordinate.**

   The pointer changes to indicate the command is active.

2. **Click the first item (edge, vertex, and so on) from which all others will be measured to be the base (the 0.0 dimension).**

3. **Click again to place the dimension outside the model.**

4. **Click the edges, vertices, or arcs you want to dimension using the same ordinate.**

   As you click each item, the dimension is placed in the view and aligned to the zero ordinate, as shown in Figure 7-10. The Dimension PropertyManager appears.

5. **Set display options in the PropertyManager.**

6. **Press Esc to exit from the ordinate mode.**

   Newly placed ordinate dimensions automatically jog to avoid overlapping text. The size of the jog is determined by the size of the text and the potentially overlapping area of the text.

Figure 7-10:
Ordinate dimensions are measured from a zero ordinate.

TAG	X LOC	Y LOC	SIZE
A1	1.70	2.94	Ø .63 THRU ALL
B1	3.45	1.27	
B2	3.45	2.57	
B3	4.75	1.27	
B4	4.75	2.57	Ø .38 THRU ALL
B5	6.05	1.27	
B6	6.05	2.57	
C1	4.52	3.55	Ø.19

To create a baseline dimension:

1. **Choose Tools⇨Dimensions⇨Baseline.**

   The pointer changes to let you know that the command is active.

2. **Click the edge or vertex you want to use as a baseline.**

   The edge or vertex turns green when you select it.

3. **Click each of the edges or vertices you want to dimension.**

   Those items turn green as well.

4. **Click to place the dimensions.**

   If you select an edge, dimensions are measured parallel to the selected edge. If you select a vertex, dimensions are measured point-to-point from the selected vertex.

   The Dimension PropertyManager appears.

5. **Set display options in the PropertyManager.**

6. **Click OK.**

Adding Reference Annotations

When you finish adding and inserting dimensions into your drawing views, you want to add annotations. *Annotations* are notes, symbols, and text that define engineering characteristics and parameters in your model and in your drawings (see Figure 7-11).

Annotations behave like dimensions in each type of SolidWorks document. You can add annotations in a part or assembly document and then insert them to the drawing views, or you can create annotations in the drawing. (You insert model annotations into the drawing using the Insert Model Items command, covered in Chapter 8.)

In the following sections, I tell you how to add each type of annotation to any SolidWorks document, not just the drawing.

Notes

Notes are virtual sticky notes with a little extra feature. A note can contain text, symbols, a border, parametric text, and hyperlinks (that's the extra). You can include or omit leaders in your notes. *Leaders* point to items in the drawing. Notes can include multiple lines of text and multiple text styles (font type, bold, and so on) in case you want to fancy them up.

Figure 7-11:
You can add
annotations
to the model
and insert
them in the
drawing
automat-
ically.

De Burr O-Ring Surface

To insert a note:

1. Click Note on the Annotation toolbar, shown in Figure 7-12.

The Note PropertyManager appears, and a small rectangle appears near your pointer. If you move the pointer over an object, the object turns red, and a leader extends from the note to the object.

Figure 7-12:
You can
use the
Annotation
toolbar to
add notes
to your
models.

2. If you want a note with no leader, click in the graphic area to place the note. If you want a note with a leader, click an object and then click again in the graphic area to place the note.

The Formatting dialog box appears, with tools that allow you to change the font and style of the text.

3. **Type your text.**

   Text doesn't wrap automatically. To add multiple lines, press Return.

4. **Adjust text properties.**

   You can change the appearance (font, size, and color) of the text by selecting text and then clicking the format tool in the Formatting dialog box (see Figure 7-13).

Figure 7-13:
Tools in the
Formatting
dialog box
let you
change the
appearance
of text in
a note.

5. **Click the right corner of the Formatting dialog box to close the box.**

   The dialog box closes so that you can see more of the graphic area.

6. **Add symbols or links to the note using the buttons in the Text Format box of the Note PropertyManager.**

   For symbols, place the pointer in the note text box where you want the item to appear and then click a symbol. Hyperlinks and custom properties link to the entire note.

   Your choices include the following:

   - **Insert Hyperlink:** Click to include a Hyperlink in the note. The text and characters in the Note turn blue.

   - **Link to Property:** Click to link to a custom property. Linking to custom properties ensures that if the model changes, the note updates.

   - **Add Symbol:** Inserts a standard symbol from a symbol library. In the Symbols dialog box, select a library from the Symbol library list, then select a symbol name from the list, and click OK. The symbol's name is displayed in the text box, and the actual symbol appears in the note.

- **Geometric Tolerance:** Inserts a geometric tolerance symbol into the note. The Geometric Tolerance PropertyManager and the Properties dialog box open so that you can define the symbol.

- **Surface Finish:** Inserts a surface finish symbol into the note. The Surface Finish PropertyManager opens so that you can define the symbol.

- **Datum Feature:** Inserts a datum feature symbol into the note. The Datum Feature PropertyManager opens so that you can define the symbol.

7. **Set other options in the PropertyManager.**

- **Leader:** Allows you to change the style and appearance of the leader.

- **Border:** Click the options under border to change the border around the note.

- **Layer:** Indicate what drawing layer you want to attach the note to.

8. **Click OK.**

You can edit notes. Click a note to bring up the Note PropertyManager. Double-click a note to bring up the Formatting dialog box and the Note PropertyManager.

Balloons

You can create balloons in a drawing document. The balloons label the parts in the assembly and relate them to item numbers on the bill of materials. (You can find out how to insert a bill of materials into a drawing by reading the "Bill of materials" section, later in this chapter.)

However, you don't have to insert a bill of materials table into a drawing in order to add balloons. If the drawing has no bill of materials, the item numbers are the default values that SolidWorks would use if you did insert a bill of materials. If there is no bill of materials on the active drawing sheet but there is a bill of materials on another sheet, SolidWorks uses the numbers from that bill of materials.

You can also add balloons in assembly documents and then import those balloons from an assembly document into a drawing view. (Chapter 8 explains more on how this process works.)

To insert a balloon:

1. **Click Balloon in Annotation toolbar.**

   The Balloon PropertyManager appears, and a small circle follows your pointer around in the graphic area. If you move your pointer over an object, the object turns red.

2. **In the PropertyManager, under Balloon Settings, set the following:**

   • **Style:** Select a style for the shape and border of the balloon from the list. The style None displays the balloon text with no border.

   • **Size:** Select a size from the list — either a specified number of characters or Tight fit, which adjusts automatically to the text.

   • **Balloon text:** Select the type of text for the balloon. Custom allows you to type the text. Item number puts the Item Number in the bill of materials. Quantity adds the number of this part needed for the entire assembly.

3. **In the PropertyManager, under In Layers, select a named drawing layer to add the balloon to.**

   The default is none. This option doesn't appear if you're adding balloons to an assembly.

4. **Click a part and then click to place the balloon.**

   A leader extends from the balloon to the part.

5. **To add balloons, repeat Steps 2 through 4.**

6. **Click OK.**

   The Balloon PropertyManager closes.

You can edit any balloon by clicking it to bring up the Balloon PropertyManager or pressing Delete on the keyboard.

Auto Balloon

You can speed the process of adding balloons to drawing views by using the Auto Balloon command. The Auto Balloon command automatically inserts balloons for all the components in a selected drawing view. SolidWorks inserts the balloons into the appropriate views without duplicates.

To insert balloons into a drawing view:

1. **Click Auto Balloon on the Annotation toolbar.**

   The Auto Balloon PropertyManager appears.

2. **Click the drawing view that you want to add balloons to.**

   You see a preview of the balloons appears around the view.

3. **In the PropertyManager, under Balloon Layout, select how you want the balloons to align around the view.**

   You can choose a square pattern, on the top, to the left, and so on. The balloons are placed outside the view border, and the leaders do not intersect.

4. **In Balloon Layout, select the check box for Ignore multiple instances.**

   By selecting this option, balloons do not appear on multiple instances of a part.

5. **In the PropertyManager, under Balloon Settings, set the following:**

   • **Style:** Select a style for the shape and border of the balloon from the list. The style None displays the balloon text with no border.

   • **Size:** Select a size from the list — either a specified number of characters or Tight fit, which adjusts automatically to the text.

   • **Balloon text:** Select the type of text for the balloon. Custom allows you to type the text. Item number puts the Item Number in the bill of materials. Quantity adds the number of this part needed for the entire assembly.

6. **In the PropertyManager, under In Layers, select a named drawing layer to add the balloon to.**

   The default is none. This option doesn't appear if you're adding balloons to an assembly.

7. **Click OK.**

   Once you close the PropertyManager, you cannot open it again to change the orientation of the balloons. You can delete the balloons or undo the Auto Balloon command and then reinsert the balloons. You can drag a group of balloons or a single balloon.

Surface Finish

You can specify the surface finish and texture of a part face by using a surface finish symbol. You can select the face in a part, an assembly, or a drawing document.

To insert a surface finish symbol:

1. **Click Surface Finish on the Annotation toolbar.**

   The Surface Finish PropertyManager appears.

2. **Click a button for a symbol type in the PropertyManager.**

3. **Enter a symbol layout value.**

   Different symbol types require different codes to specify manufacturing method, texture requirements, and so on. You can enter these values, and they appear with the symbol in the graphic area.

4. **Set other options in PropertyManager.**

- **Format:** Use the document font or choose another font.

- **Angle:** Set the angle or rotation for the symbol.

- **Leader:** Select a leader style.

- **Layer:** Select a named layer (or none) if you're adding symbols to a drawing.

5. **Click the graphic area to add a symbol.**

- **Multi-jog Leader:** A *multi-jog leader* adds bends to the normally straight leader line. Before placing the symbol, right-click and choose Use Multi-jog Leader to add a multi-jog leader. Click in the graphics area to place the arrow end of the leader and then move the pointer and click to add each jog point. To complete the leader and place the symbol, either double-click or right-click and choose End Leader.

- **Multiple instances:** Click as many times as necessary to place multiple copies.

- **Editing each instance:** You can change text and other items in the dialog box for each instance of the symbol.

- **Leaders:** If the symbol has a leader, click once to place the leader and then click a second time to place the symbol.

- **Multiple leaders:** While dragging the symbol and before placing it, press Ctrl. The note stops moving, and a second leader is added. While still holding Ctrl, click to place the leader. Click as many times as necessary to place additional leaders. Release Ctrl and click to place the symbol.

6. **Click OK.**

To edit a surface finish symbol, click the symbol, and the PropertyManager appears.

Geometric Tolerance

There is always a slight variation in manufacturing process. *Tolerancing symbols* indicate how precisely the manufacturer needs to make a part. You can place geometric tolerancing symbols, with or without leaders, anywhere in a drawing, part, assembly, or sketch, and you can attach a symbol anywhere on a dimension line. The Properties dialog box for geometric tolerance symbols offers selections based on the symbol you choose. Only the attributes that are appropriate for the selected symbol are available.

To add a geometric tolerance symbol:

1. **Select the face or edge of a part for the tolerance symbol.**

   Preselecting the location makes placement easier.

2. **Click Geometric Tolerance on the Annotation toolbar.**

   The Geometric Tolerance PropertyManager appears, and the Properties dialog box appears in the graphic area, where you can create a symbol.

3. **In the Properties dialog box, create a symbol.**

   Select any symbol, tolerance, datum references, and material conditions for the geometric tolerance.

4. **Set the display properties in the PropertyManager.**

   Choose the leader type, font, and a named drawing layer (if you're working on a drawing) to apply the symbol to.

5. **Click OK.**

Datum Target

Datum targets are used in conjunction with and define the location and area for geometric tolerance datum symbols. These annotations indicate how to set up the datums to inspect for accuracy after the part is manufactured. You can attach a datum target and symbol to a model face or an edge of any document. To create a datum target and symbol:

1. **Click Datum Target on the Annotation toolbar.**

   The Datum Target PropertyManager appears.

2. **Set the following properties in the PropertyManager:**

   - **Settings:** Select a target symbol style.

   - **Target area:** Select the target area display. You can choose an x, circular, or rectangle target area, or none.

   - **Target area size:** Enter width and height for rectangles or diameter for Xs and circles.

   - **Leader:** Select a leader style and an arrow style.

   - **Layer:** In drawings with named layers, select a layer.

3. **Click in the graphics area to place the target and then click again to place the symbol. If you clicked No target Symbol in the PropertyManager, click only once to place the annotation.**

   The datum target appears in the drawing. The command stays active so you can place as many as you like.

4. **Continue inserting as many symbols as needed.**

5. **Click OK.**

    The PropertyManager closes.

You can move a datum target symbol by selecting the symbol and dragging the item. To edit the datum target symbol, select the symbol.

Datum Symbol

Datum features are used in conjunction with geometric tolerance symbols. These annotations indicate how inspection machines should check a part for accuracy after the part is manufactured. You can attach a datum symbol to the following items:

✔ In a part or assembly, on a planar model surface or on a reference plane

✔ In a drawing view, on a surface that appears as an edge (not a silhouette) or on a section view surface

✔ A geometric tolerance symbol frame

✔ In a note

To add a datum feature:

1. **Click Datum Symbol on the Annotation toolbar.**

    The Datum Symbol PropertyManager appears.

2. **Edit the options in the Datum Symbol PropertyManager.**

    - **Label:** Enter character to appear in the datum feature box.

    - **Use document style:** Select this check box if you want to use the document style, which follows the standard (ANSI, ISO, and so on) specified in Document Properties. (Choose Tools⇨Options. In the Document Properties tab, select Detailing and set options.) If you deselect this box, you can select a different style of box and attachment. Each box has a different set of attachment styles.

    - **Layer:** In drawings with named layers, select a layer.

3. **Click in the graphic area to place the leader and then click again to place the symbol.**

4. **Continue inserting as many symbols as needed.**

    SolidWorks automatically increments the label in the datum feature box (A, B, C and so on).

5. **Click OK.**

Cosmetic Threads

A *cosmetic thread* represents the inner diameter of a thread on a boss (a bolt is an example of a boss) or the outer diameter of a thread on a hole and can include a hole callout. If you add a cosmetic thread while working in a drawing view, the part or assembly is updated to include a cosmetic thread feature.

To add a cosmetic thread:

1. **Choose Insert⇨Annotations⇨Cosmetic Thread.**

   The Cosmetic Thread PropertyManager appears.

2. **Select the holes to add cosmetic threads.**

   On a cylindrical feature (a boss, a cut, or a hole), select the circular edge where the thread begins. If the feature is a conical hole, select the major diameter. If the feature is a conical boss, select the minor diameter.

3. **Set the options in the PropertyManager for the end conditions (how deep) and enter the outer thread diameter.**

4. **Click OK.**

Center Mark

You can place center marks in circles or arcs in drawings, and use them as references for dimensioning. Center marks are available as single marks, in linear patterns, or in circular patterns.

To add a center mark to a drawing:

1. **Click Center Mark on the Annotation toolbar.**

   The Center Mark PropertyManager appears.

2. **Set Options in the PropertyManager.**

   - **Single Center Mark:** Insert a center mark into a single circle or arc. You can change the Display Attributes and Angle of the center mark.

   - **Linear Center Mark:** Insert center marks into a linear pattern of circles or arcs. You can select Connection lines and Display Attributes for linear patterns.

   - **Circular Center Mark:** Insert center marks into a circular pattern of circles or arcs. You can select Circular lines, Radial lines, Base center mark, and Display Attributes for circular patterns.

3. Select a circular edge or an arc for center mark insertion.

You have three options, shown in Figure 7-14. Pick the single, linear, or radial centerline. The example shows all three types. A preview of the center mark appears.

4. Click OK.

Figure 7-14: Centerlines and center marks serve as references for dimensioning.

Centerlines

Centerline annotations in drawings mark the center of a feature, such as when you see a hole viewed on an edge. The center marks are shown within the right side view in Figure 7-14.

1. Click Centerline on the Annotation toolbar.

The Centerline PropertyManager appears.

2. Select one of the following:

- Two edges (parallel or nonparallel)
- Two sketch segments (except splines)
- A face (cylindrical, conical, toroidal, or swept)
- A drawing view in the graphics area (except isometric orientation)
- A feature, component, or drawing view in the FeatureManager design tree
- Insert Component Centerline in the component shortcut menu or in the graphics area (assembly drawings only)

3. Click OK.

Centerlines appear in all appropriate segments of the selected entities.

To repeat any command, just press the Enter key, which restarts the last used command.

The display of annotations is controlled through the FeatureManager Annotations folder. To turn the display of annotations on or off, click the Annotations folder on the FeatureManager, right-click, and select or deselect Display Annotations. To display only certain types of annotations, repeat the process but select Details and then choose the annotations types to display.

You can define standard annotations once and then reuse them by storing them in the Design Library. For example, you can create a standard note that you use often and save the annotation to the design library. To save the note (or any annotation) to the design library, right-click the item and choose Add to Design Library. When the Save As dialog box opens, type a name for the annotation, navigate to the proper folder, and click Save.

You can automatically insert centerlines and center marks when you create views by choosing Tools⇨Options. Then click the Document Properties tab. In the Detailing section, under the Auto Insert On View Creation field, check Centerlines and Center marks.

Checking Spelling

A new feature in SolidWorks 2006 that works on drawings is the Spelling Check tool. It is one of my favorite tools (just ask my editors). This tool spell checks notes, dimensions that include text, and drawing title blocks (when you're in Edit Sheet format mode). Spelling Check operates similar to the spell checker in Microsoft Office applications. SolidWorks identifies words that may be misspelled and provides suggested corrections based on a built-in dictionary. You can select correction, ignore the word, or add it to the dictionary. In fact, this function uses the Microsoft Word dictionary, so you need to have Microsoft Words 2000 or higher loaded on your computer to use it. The tool also has a special user dictionary (swengineering.dic) that picks up on SolidWorks terminology, and you can add custom dictionaries as well.

To check the spelling on a drawing:

1. **Choose Tools⇨Spelling.**

   The Spelling Check PropertyManager appears, and Spelling Check begins to scan your drawing. If it finds a misspelled word, the word appears in the PropertyManager. Under Suggestions, a list of possible alternate spellings appears.

2. **If you want to change the spelling, select an alternate and click Change. Otherwise, click Ignore or Add to Dictionary.**

    Spelling Check continues to scan your document, picking up on any curiously spelled words.

3. **Continue until all misspellings are corrected.**

4. **Click OK.**

Defining Drawing Tables

Tables are a wonderful way to keep track of things, and they prove useful in SolidWorks drawings for a number of purposes. This section covers the bill of materials, Revision, and Hole tables.

When you insert a table, there is a section in the PropertyManager for that table that asks you to select a template. You can find standard templates for these items in <install_dir>\lang\<language>.

You can define many of the properties for tables described herein in the Tables sections of the Document Properties tab. Choose Tools⇨Options. In the Document Properties tab, select Detailing and then Tables.

Bill of materials

A *bill of materials,* generally referred to as simply BOM, lists all the parts and subassemblies in an assembly. The BOM is an important piece of literature. Suppliers use the bill of materials to quote jobs and to order parts.

Anchors away!

Anchors make tables easier to place in the drawing. You can define anchors in the drawing format by editing the drawing format. Right-click a sheet in the FeatureManager design tree and choose Edit Sheet Format. Right-click the corner of the existing geometry within the drawing format to use as an anchor in the graphics area and choose the table type from the Set as Anchor menu.

When you insert a table, set the Table Anchor corner to use for the table. If you have a predefined anchor, select the Attach To Anchor check box to attach the table to the anchor within the table's PropertyManager.

Every company has its own BOM format that they like to use. In this section, I focus on creating a simple bill of materials table. The section "Changing and Customizing Tables," at the end of this chapter, explains how to change and customize the different types of tables.

SolidWorks maintains a list of items that go into an assembly and tracks the part numbers, quantity, and other attributes. A drawing can contain a table-based BOM or a Microsoft Excel based bill of materials but not both. In this chapter, I cover the table-based BOM.

You can use custom properties defined in the individual part and assembly documents to fill in the BOM table so that you don't have to input values in the BOM table manually. You can make formatting changes to the table after you save it to a template. This little bit of extra work up front makes inserting a BOM, shown in Figure 7-15, into a drawing simple and straightforward.

Figure 7-15:
A bill of materials lists all the parts in an assembly, along with part numbers and quantity.

To insert a BOM table:

1. **Choose Insert⇨Table⇨Bill of Materials.**

   The Bill of Materials Table PropertyManager appears, and a message prompts you to select a view.

2. **Click a drawing view to identify the assembly from which to extract the BOM.**

   The PropertyManager expands to show several other options.

3. **In Table Template, click the Open table template for Bill of Materials button.**

   The Select BOM Template dialog box appears.

4. **Select a table template and click Open.**

   The name of the template appears in the Table Template field.

5. **In Table Anchor, select the check box for Attach To Anchor and click an option for the anchored corner.**

   This option determines which corner of the table is fixed to the drawing.

6. **In BOM type, select a check box next to one of the following:**

   • **Top-level only:** Lists parts and subassemblies, but not subassembly components.

   • **Parts only:** Doesn't list subassemblies. Lists subassembly components as individual items.

   • **Indented assemblies:** Lists subassemblies. Indents subassembly components below their subassemblies without item numbers.

7. **In Configurations, manually select the configurations to include quantities in the bill of materials or click Select all configurations or Unselect all configurations.**

8. **Click OK and, if you did not select Attach To Anchor in Step 5, click the graphics area to place the table.**

   The table appears in the drawing and in the FeatureManager design tree.

Revision table

Drawings can go through a lot of changes, and it's important to track the who, what, when, and whys of every revision the document goes through and to track approvals, too. SolidWorks allows you to insert a revision table into a drawing. Figure 7-15 (see preceding section) denotes the revisions with five-sided flags (my personal preference). The Revision table gives you a place to track changes and revision numbers by date. You can type a description of the change, and there's a column for approvals as well.

TIP

The latest revision of a document also appears under REV in the lower right hand corner of a sheet format.

In Figure 7-15, you can take advantage of drawing layers for your revision symbols. Before you insert the revision table, define the layer for revision marks with a different color, which does two things. It highlights the revision marks in another color, and it lets you turn off the revision marks by turning off the layer. When creating the Revision symbol, select the layer used for revision symbols.

If the layer doesn't exist, open the layer dialog box by selecting the Layer toolbar. Click New, enter the layer name in the Name field, and click OK within the Layer dialog box. If the Layer toolbar isn't active, turn it on by choosing View⇨Toolbars⇨Layer Form. (See Chapter 8 for more details on layers.)

To insert a Revision table into your open drawing:

1. **Choose Insert⇨Tables⇨Revision Table.**

   The Revision Table PropertyManager appears.

2. **Set the following properties in the PropertyManager:**

   • **Table Template:** Browse for a template to choose a standard or custom revision template.

   • **Table Anchor:** Set the anchored corner.

   • **Attach to Anchor:** Attach the specified corner to the table anchor.

   • **Revision Symbol Shapes:** Select a border shape for a revision symbol.

   • **Options:** Select a check box for the Enable symbol when adding a new revision. Allows you to click in the graphic area to place revision symbols when you add a revision table. If you clear this option or you add a symbol later, right-click in a row of the revision table and choose Revisions, Add Symbol and then click in the graphics are to place symbols. If you edit revision text, the symbols update.

3. **Click OK and, if you did not select the Attach to Anchor option, click the graphics area to place the table.**

   The table appears in the drawing and in the FeatureManager design tree.

To add a revision to the table:

1. **Right-click in the revision table and choose Revisions⇨Add Revision.**

2. **Double-click inside a revision field.**

   The field highlights, and the text inside the box is selected. The Note PropertyManager appears in the left pane.

3. **Type the new text.**

4. **To change the style or justification of the text, highlight the text and enter in the new style in the Note PropertyManager.**

   The text updates in the revision table.

5. **To add a revision symbol, click where you want to add the symbol and click Add Symbol in the Note PropertyManager.**

   The Symbols dialog box opens.

6. **In the dialog box, select a symbol library using the pull-down arrow.**

   A list of available symbols appears in the box below the library field. If you select a symbol, a preview appears in the dialog box.

7. **Choose a symbol and click OK.**

   The symbol appears in the revision table.

8. **Click OK in the Note PropertyManager.**

The DrawCompare command compares all the entities between two documents. The differences between the drawings are displayed in color codes. When you use this command to compare two versions of a drawing, you can check for any design changes that went unmarked in the Revision table. Choose Tools➪DrawCompare. In the DrawCompare dialog box, browse to select a drawing for Drawing 1 and Drawing 2. In each of the fields, select a color. The two drawings appear side by side. In the Differences field, you can see what was removed and what was added.

Hole tables

Hole tables in drawings measure the positions of selected holes from a specified origin. SolidWorks labels each hole with a tag that corresponds to a row in the hole table (see Figure 7-16).

The Hole Table command creates a table that shows the XY coordinates and hole size for each hole you select. If you make a change to the model, the change is reflected in the hole table.

Figure 7-16:
Hole tables
in drawings
track holes
and update
with the
model.

To insert a hole table in an open drawing:

1. **Choose Insert⇨Tables⇨Hole Table.**

   The Hole Table PropertyManager appears with the Origin field active.

2. **In the graphics area, select a vertex to specify the origin datum.**

   You can select an X axis and a Y axis to define a vertex for the datum. You can also drag the origin into position after you place the table. The Edges/Faces field becomes active.

3. **Select hole edges or select a model face.**

   The holes are added to the Edges/Faces field. If you select a face,

4. **In the PropertyManager, select a template or anchor.**

5. **Click OK and, if you did not select Attach to Anchor option, click the graphics area to place the table.**

   The Hole table appears in the drawing and in the FeatureManager design tree.

Changing and customizing tables

You're not stuck with the standard table templates. You can customize them to fit your requirements. The table types have similar formats, but there are some differences — for example, BOM format for bill of materials, Revisions for Revision tables, and so on).

To edit values of the table, click once inside the table to summon the Cell PropertyManager, as shown in Figure 7-17. You can change the values or select another area to change. When editing a table, an additional grid appears around the table showing row and column labels.

Figure 7-17: If you right-click in the Revision Table Property-Manager, you see this drop-down menu.

The Cell PropertyManager appears with its own properties and links to Column Properties, Table Properties, and Table Format.

- ✔ **Cell Properties:** Allows you to specify the justification and orientation of text in the cells and the font style. You can select the table font (as specified in the Table Format PropertyManager) or specify a new font. In the Bill of materials table, you can use Cell Properties to add up rows or columns.

- ✔ **Column Properties:** Click to access table column properties. In Column PropertyManager, you can select a column type — for example Revision and Approved — and change its header in the table.

- ✔ **Table Properties:** Takes you to the Revision Table PropertyManager, where you can choose a corner for anchoring the table. For the Revision table, you can also select Revision symbol shapes.

- ✔ **Table Format:** Allows you to specify a heading for a table, a border, the text format and font, and a named drawing layer to associate the table to.

You can move an entire table to a new position on your drawing sheet. Put your pointer around the upper right or left corner of a table. When the

pointer changes to a set of four arrows pointing in each direction, click and
drag the table. Releasing the mouse sets the final position of the table.

You can customize your favorite table formats and save them as templates.
Right-click a table and choose Save As Template. In the Save As dialog box,
type a name for the template and browse to its saved location. Make sure
that you store these templates in a common location for all users to access.
To set the location for storing templates, choose Tool➪Options. In the
Systems Options tab, select File Locations. Show folders for the template you
want to save, click Add, and browse for the folder location.

Chapter 8

Speeding It Up: Automating the Drawing

In This Chapter

▶ Marking dimension in the model for import into the drawing

▶ Organizing drawing information with layers

▶ Picking favorites to speed drawing creation

▶ Linking the sheet format to custom properties

*I*n this chapter, I give you hints, tips, and shortcuts that you can use to speed up the drawing creation process. You discover how to import dimensions, annotations, and reference geometry directly from the model. You also find out how to make the most of custom properties and how to create templates to jumpstart your drawings. (For information on creating a drawing, see Chapter 7.)

Planning for the Drawing

The devil's in the details, and this saying is especially true when you're creating manufacturing drawings. The person who designs a product is the one who knows the most about it. As the designer, you need to communicate that wealth of information in your head to the person making the product by including the right amount of detail (not too much, and not too little) in your drawings.

SolidWorks lets you incorporate manufacturing details into your model. You can mark dimensions and add finishing symbols, geometric tolerances, and other annotations to the model that you want to import into the drawing. Your model should contain all the information you need to create the drawings.

Here are the basic steps to follow as you design:

1. When you design the model, create the sketches the way you want them to show up in the drawing. Add annotations to the model and mark dimensions in the Modify dialog box that you want to import to the drawing. (The next section explains how to do so.)

2. Set up your sheet formats and drawing templates in advance and put them where they're readily available to the design team. Include links to custom properties and the drawing symbols that you use most often.

3. After you place the drawing views, use the Model Items command to insert dimensions, annotations, and reference geometry automatically. (See the next section for more on this command.)

Inserting Model Items

In Chapter 7, I tell you ways to insert dimensions and annotations manually in both the model and the drawing. I also want to introduce you to Model Items, a powerful command in SolidWorks that allows you to insert dimensions, annotations, and reference geometry into the drawing views automatically.

Here's how it works. When you create a dimension in a model, you can mark it for import into the drawing. This option is usually on by default, but if not, inside the Modify dialog box, which appears when you add a dimension to a model, click Mark Dimension to Be Imported into Drawing. (To deselect a dimension for import, click the option again.) Be sure to add any annotations and symbols in the model that are important to the manufacturing process.

After you place all of the drawing views, you can use the Model Items command to automatically insert the dimensions, annotations, and reference geometry from the model. Model Items gives you the option to import all the dimensions or only those marked for import. You can also select the specific types of annotations and reference geometry you want to import.

Model Items imports model dimensions, also known as *driving dimensions* because they drive changes in the model geometry. SolidWorks shows model dimensions in black. You can read more about dimension types in Chapter 7.

There are several advantages to using Model Items:

> ✔ **You save time inserting items automatically.** If you couldn't insert dimensions automatically, you'd have to first dimension the sketches to create the part features and then recreate those dimensions again in the drawing, creating twice the work.

✔ **You can capture design intent in the part, not as an afterthought when creating a drawing.** Why not spend a little extra time when you create the part features adding the information that you need in your drawings?

✔ **If tolerance or dimension values change in the drawing, your part updates automatically.** Conversely, any change to the model updates in the drawing. You don't need to redo work on either side.

The example shown in Figure 8-1 shows how I used Insert Model for the profile feature and the holes. Model Items requires no extra cleanup. Simply define the placement and other dimension attributes in the sketch and mark the dimension for import. I also used Model Items to import surface-finish annotations.

Figure 8-1: The Model Items command lets you select the dimension types to import to the drawing.

Before using the Model Items command, you should place all of your drawing views. To insert Model Items into an open drawing:

1. **Choose Insert⇨Model Items.**

   The Model Item PropertyManager appears. You want to go through and carefully set all the options in the PropertyManager.

2. **In Import From, select one of the following:**

   • **Entire Model:** Model Item inserts entities (dimensions, annotations, and reference geometry) from the entire model.

   • **Selected feature:** Model Item inserts entities only from the features or components that you select in the graphic area.

3. **In Dimensions, click the dimension type you want to insert:**

   - **Select all:** If you click the check box for this option, inserts all the dimensions in the model (with the exception of Hole wizard profile sketches).

   - **Marked for drawing:** Inserts only the dimensions marked for drawing in the Modify dialog box.

   - **Instance/Revolution counts:** Inserts only the number of instances for linear or circular patterns.

   - **Hole Wizard Profiles:** Inserts only dimensions for Hole Wizard Profiles.

   - **Hole Wizard locations:** Inserts only dimensions for Hole Wizard locations.

   - **Hole callout:** Inserts only dimensions for hole callouts.

   - **Eliminate duplicates:** Check this option if you want to eliminate duplicate dimensions from appearing in the different drawing views.

4. **In Annotations, click Select All if you want to import all the annotations in the model. Otherwise, click the specific types.**

   You can import notes, surface finish, geometric tolerances, datums, datum targets, welds, or cosmetic threads assembly drawings only.

5. **In Reference Geometry, click the check box for Select All if you want to import all the reference geometry in the model. Otherwise, click the specific types.**

   Selection options include planes, axis, points, origins, surfaces, curves, and routing points.

6. **In Import Into Drawing Views, if you want to import items into all the views, click the check box for Import Items Into All Views. Otherwise, deselect the option and select a single model view.**

   If you select a model view, the items appear in that view.

7. **In Options, select the check box for the following:**

   - **Include items from hidden features:** Imports items that are in features or parts that are hidden.

   - **Use dimension placement in sketch:** Inserts model dimensions from the part in the same locations in the drawing.

8. **In Layer, if the drawing has named layers, select one to add the items to.**

9. **Click OK.**

   The Model Item PropertyManager closes, and the dimensions and annotations appear in the drawing view(s).

If your drawing view is cluttered with dimensions after using Model Items, you can hide some dimensions so that they're no longer visible. Right-click a dimension and choose Hide. You can click and drag to move a selected dimension.

You can see how I used Model Items in Figure 8-2. I imported dimensions that were marked for import in the model, as well as hole callouts and hole wizard locations, all of the annotations, and some reference geometry (centerlines).

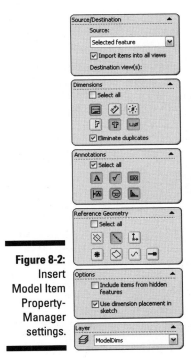

Figure 8-2:
Insert
Model Item
Property-
Manager
settings.

Managing Drawing Clutter with Layers

Layers are a clever way to organize information in your drawings. *Layers* are like transparent sheets that stack up to form the final drawing. You can create as many layers as you want, depending on how complex the drawing is, and group information on the various layers. One layer may contain all the holes in an assembly, and another may contain only dimensions and annotations.

You can turn layers on and off, depending on what you want to display or print, and you can move entities from one layer to another. And, so that you can find your way around, SolidWorks lets you assign a line color, thickness, and style for the entities on the different layers.

TIP

To make sure that you apply layers consistently in all your drawings, define layers within the document templates for drawings. Create the standard layer names and then assign the 2D sketch entities to the appropriate layer. To move a selected entity to a new layer, click the Move button within the Layer dialog box.

To create a new drawing layer in a drawing:

1. Click Layer Properties on the Line Format toolbar.

You may have to add the Line Format toolbar to the CommandManager. (Read Chapter 2 for how to customize the CommandManager.)

The Layers dialog box, shown in Figure 8-3, has column headings for Name, Description, On/Off, Color, Style, and Thickness. If you can't read a column heading, you can expand the heading by clicking the vertical line between the headings and dragging it one way or the other.

Figure 8-3:
The Layers
dialog box is
where you
define line
color and
style for the
different
layers.

2. Click New.

Layer1 appears under Name for the first new layer. The text is highlighted so that you can type a new name over it.

3. Enter a name for your new layer.

The new layer name appears in the Name column. A yellow arrow before the name indicates that this layer is active. (The layer named FORMAT is included within a drawing and is not selected.)

4. To add a description for the new layer, double-click the Description column and enter the text.

The description appears in the Description column.

5. To specify the line color, click the Color box, select a color in the Color dialog box, and then click OK.

The box is set to the new color. There is also a Define Custom Colors option in the Color dialog box. You can use it to define and add custom color options.

6. **To specify a line style, click in the Style column and select the desired line style from the list.**

   Style types include Solid, Dashed, Phantom, and so on.

7. **To specify a line thickness, click in the Thickness column and select the desired line thickness from the list.**

8. **Repeat Steps 2 thru 7 to add any other layers that you need.**

9. **Click OK.**

   The Layers dialog box closes, and your new layers are created. When you add new entities to a drawing, they appear on the active layer.

You can activate a layer, move layers, and maneuver between layers from inside the layers dialog box. To activate or edit layers, click Layer Properties on the Line Format toolbar. You can do the following:

- **Active:** An arrow indicates which layer is active. To activate a layer, click next to the layer name, and an arrow appears.

- **On/Off:** A yellow light bulb appears when a layer is visible. To hide a layer, click its light bulb. The light bulb turns gray, and all the entities on the layer are hidden. To turn on the layer again, click the light bulb.

- **Move:** To move entities to the active layer, select the entities in the drawing and click Move. You can select multiple items by holding down the Ctrl key when you click them.

- **Delete:** To delete a layer, select the layer name and press Delete on your keyboard.

Automating Drawing Creation

Unless you like repetition, you can work smarter when you're creating drawings. This section covers various SolidWorks features that allow you to reuse information and churn out drawings faster.

Using custom properties

Custom properties are metadata about a part or assembly document. *Metadata* is data about data. Think of a book. The book has pages full of information but also contains information about the book itself, such as the author, publisher, copyright, and so on. This detailed information is metadata.

Information that SolidWorks stores about the model includes the who, what, why, and when of file creation, as well as material, vendor information, approvals, and so on. You can create custom properties in a model that carry over to drawings. The title block, notes, and bill of materials include links to custom properties. Other downstream applications (such as analysis and product data management software) also use custom properties from the model. COSMOSWorks, for example, reads the material type and weight of a model to perform its finite element analysis calculations.

You can add custom properties to any active drawing, part, or assembly document. To access custom properties, open a SolidWorks document and choose File⇨Properties. The Summary Information dialog box, shown in Figure 8-4, appears.

The dialog box contains three tabs for part and assemblies; for drawings, you see only two tabs (drawings don't include the Configuration Specific tab):

- ✔ **Summary tab:** This tab includes a basic summary of the document, such as the author, keywords, comments, title, and subject. It also contains a statistics box that tells you when the document was created and last saved, as well as who saved it last.

- ✔ **Custom tab:** In this tab, you can enter custom properties that apply to the entire document. These properties are document specific, which means they're controlled by the SolidWorks document (part, assembly, and drawing) templates and apply to all part and assembly configurations.

- ✔ **Configuration Specific tab:** This tab allows you to define custom properties that vary from one configuration to another. Configurations are variations of a model stored in the same document. The table in the configurations Specific tab has the same heading as the Custom tab, but you can specify which configuration in the document it applies to.

Figure 8-4:
In the Custom tab on the Summary Information dialog box, you can set custom properties for the entire document.

To add custom or configuration properties to an open part or assembly document:

1. **Choose File➪Properties.**

   The Summary Information dialog box appears. The dialog box has three tabs: Summary, Custom, and Configuration Specific.

2. **Select the Custom or Configuration Specific tab.**

   A table appears with the following headings: Property Name, Type, Value/Text Expression, and Evaluated Value. The Configuration Specific tab has a field above where you can select the configuration to apply the property to.

3. **If you are defining a property in the Configuration Specific tab, in the Applies To field, select a configuration from the pull-down list.**

   Now any custom properties you set in the table will only apply to the configuration that appears in the Applies To field.

4. **Click the first blank cell under Property Name and then type a name or choose one from the list.**

   To move between cells in the table, press Tab or Enter, or click in the cell you want to move to.

    To add custom properties to the pull-down list, click Edit List in the Summary Information dialog box, type a new name in the Edit Custom Property List dialog box, and click Add. Select a property and click Delete, Move Up, or Move Down to delete or move a custom property in the list.

5. **Select a type from the drop-down list.**

   Type describes the value that you can enter in the Value/Text Expression cell. Type options include text, date, number, or yes or no.

6. **Under Value/Text Expression, enter a value for the custom property that is compatible with the selection in the Type cell.**

   You can type a value, or you can select a value from a drop-down list if they're available. For example, if you select yes or no for type, yes or no appears in the drop-down list in the Value/Text Expression cell. You must enter a valid type.

7. **Press Tab or Enter.**

   The value of the property appears under Evaluated Value.

8. **Repeat Steps 2 through 7 to add any additional custom properties.**

9. **Click OK.**

   The Summary Information dialog box closes, and custom properties are added to the model.

If you enter a date in custom properties, it must be a valid date. Don't enter a date that is valid but inaccurate.

To ensure that custom properties are available on each document, you should define the custom properties in the drawing, part, and assembly document templates. (Chapter 2 explains how to create templates.)

Setting up a drawing sheet format

A *drawing sheet* is a page in a drawing document. A *sheet format* is the background for your drawing, and typically includes page size, orientation, standard text, borders, title block, and so on. Sheets in a drawing can use different formats. You select a sheet format when you open a new drawing.

Standard sheet formats in SolidWorks include links to custom properties. You can edit a title block in a sheet format using the steps I outline in Chapter 7. You can use the Note PropertyManager, which appears when you edit text in the title block, to edit or add links to custom properties in the drawing document or in the model. For example, you can include links to the model that include the author, comments, and name of the file. The links are populated if the information exists in the custom properties of the model.

One advantage to using custom properties to define the information in the title block is that after you set up the title block, you can use custom properties to edit all the values, and you don't have to use the Edit Sheet function. Figure 8-5 shows the custom properties used to automatically annotate the drawing format.

Figure 8-5:
You can link to custom properties in the title block.

The text notes link to the custom properties. The notes shown (with labels) link to custom properties defined in the drawing. These notes link to values using the following formats:

✔ **($PRP:<value>):** Links to the custom properties in the model used to create the drawing views.

✔ **($PRPSHEET:<value>):** Links to custom properties from the current drawing document.

✔ **($PRP: "SW-Total Sheets"):** Lists special SolidWorks system values (for example, total sheets, sheet number, filename, and so on).

The Link to Property feature links the contents of the text note to a custom property, as shown in Figure 8-6.

Figure 8-6:
You can
create and
edit links to
custom
properties.

SolidWorks lets you customize sheet formats and save them for future use as files with an .slddrt extension. You can store these files in the Design Library. You can also create drawing templates that use custom sheet formats.

Chapter 7 explains how to edit a drawing sheet format. The following steps tell you how to save a drawing sheet format for use in other drawings.

To save a new format as the standard A-Landscape format:

1. **Choose File⇨Save Sheet Format.**

   The Save Sheet Format dialog box opens. Save as Type defaults to Sheet format (*.slddrt).

2. **In the Save In box, use the pull-down menu to navigate to the folder *<install_dir>*\data\.**

   You see the saved format for various sheet sizes.

3. **Click a-landscape.**

   a-landscape appears in File name.

4. **Click Save.**

   SolidWorks prompts you that the file already exists and asks you whether you want to replace it.

5. **Click Yes to confirm that you want to overwrite the existing sheet format.**

   The new format saves. And now when you open a new drawing, those changes appear anytime you select that size drawing sheet.

Using predefined views to start drawings

After you start a drawing, you need to insert and position the drawing views. You also may need to adjust the scale of the drawing views. (SolidWorks formats are a 1:1 size ratio, no scaling required.)

But wait; there is a simpler way. When you start a drawing, use a drawing template with predefined views.

You can create templates with the drawing sheet size and types of views commonly used (top, front, right, and isometric). Figure 8-7 shows an example of four predefined views saved within a drawing template. Predefined drawing views are similar to the multiple view option.

Figure 8-7:
You can speed drawing creation with Predefined Views.

To insert a predefined view into a drawing:

1. **Click Predefined View on the Drawings toolbar.**

   A box appears near the pointer.

2. **Click in the graphic area to place the view.**

   The Drawing View PropertyManager appears in the left pane.

3. **In the PropertyManager, leave Insert Model blank.**

   By leaving this blank, the views automatically propagate when you make a drawing from a part or model and choose this template.

4. **Set remaining options in the PropertyManager.**

   • **Orientation:** Select a standard view.

   • **Scale:** Select Use Sheet Scale or Use Custom Scale and select or enter a scale ratio.

   • **Dimension type:** Select Projected or True.

5. **Click Project View from the Views toolbar to add more views to the drawing.**

6. **Click in the graphic area to place the view.**

   The Drawing View PropertyManager appears in the left pane.

7. **Repeat Steps 5 and 6 to create any other views.**

8. **Click OK.**

   The PropertyManager closes.

9. **Click Save As and save the drawing as a template.**

   Chapter 2 offers more detail on how to save templates.

You can populate predefined views in a few ways. For example, you can drag a model from the FeatureManager design tree of an open part or assembly document into the drawing document. All available predefined views are populated.

Working with Dimension Favorites

Dimension favorites is another feature that saves you time on drawing creation and makes the styles more consistent. It lets you define standard dimension styles (decimal precision, line style, and so on) that you can use throughout a drawing and is similar to styles in Microsoft Word.

You define dimension favorites in the Dimension PropertyManager, which appears when you insert or select a dimension to edit in a drawing view. The Favorites section (see Figure 8-8) is at the top of the PropertyManager. Any properties that you can define within the dimension PropertyManager, you can save as a dimension favorite.

Figure 8-8:
The dimen-
sion favorite
Property-
Manager
field.

Here are the options in the Dimension PropertyManager that you can use to add, edit, or delete a favorite:

✔ **Apply the Default Attribute to Selected Dimensions:** Resets the selected dimension(s) to the document defaults.

✔ **Add or Update a Favorite:** Opens the Favorite dialog box, where you can type a name to add a new favorite to the current document or choose a Favorite from the list to

  • Update all annotations linked to this favorite. All annotations using the selected favorite style update with the changes to the selected annotation.

  • Break all links to this favorite. All links between the selected favorite and annotations are broken. The annotations retain the attributes previously applied by the favorite unless the annotations are subsequently reset to the document default.

✔ **Delete a Favorite:** Deletes the selected favorite in the document.

✔ **Save a Favorite:** Opens the Save As dialog box with Favorite (.sldfvt) as the default file type to save an existing favorite.

✔ **Load Favorites:** Opens the Open dialog box with Favorite (.sldfvt) as the active file type. You can use Ctrl or Shift to select multiple files.

✔ **Set a Current Favorite:** Choose a favorite style from the list to apply to the selected dimension or dimension or to delete or save the favorite.

To ensure that dimension favorites are available in all document types, you should define them within the document templates. You can define them by setting them up from scratch or loading them from another drawing and then saving the new drawing as a template file.

Creating the Drawing Template

Templates are an important tool in creating drawings. You can use templates to capture all your design standards and open one each time you start a new drawing. Here are the basic steps to go through in order to create a drawing template. (See Chapters 7 and the earlier sections in this chapter for all the details.) You may want to think of these steps as a sort of checklist.

1. **Open a new drawing document.**

   This new document is to become your custom template. After you make changes to it, you want to save this document in the template format so that it appears in the Advanced mode of the New SolidWorks Document dialog box. Chapter 2 gives details on how to create a template.

2. **Define the custom properties.**

   Custom properties link to the sheet format. Read the section "Using custom properties," earlier in this chapter, for details.

3. **Edit the sheet format.**

   The sheet format is the background for your drawing and contains the title block. You can link text in the title block to custom properties in the model, such as the author's name, revision date, and so on. (See Chapter 7 for steps on how to edit a title block.)

4. **Put the drawing format on its own layer.**

   This step allows you to easily turn on or off the drawing format so that you can see it.

5. **Set options in Document Properties.**

   With a document active in SolidWorks, choose Tools⇨Options and select the Document Properties tab. You can set all the standards for how you want things in the document to look, from the font style for dimensions to the units of measurement to use throughout the document. (You can read more about document properties in Chapter 2.)

6. **Save the drawing as a document template.**

   In the Save As dialog box, select Save as Type .drwdot.

Chapter 9

Changes, Changes, Changes

*I*n the wonderful world of design, nothing stays the same. New information rolls in, people change their minds, and the CAD model continually evolves. Unfortunately, you either get used to it or find a new line of work.

The good news is that SolidWorks makes it easy to update designs. Because SolidWorks is a *parametric* software, changes you make in one area ripple through all the other areas of your design automatically. You don't have to manually update all the related geometry, assemblies, or drawings. If you did, you'd probably consider a new line of work.

An added benefit to all this is that you can use SolidWorks to tinker with numerous what-if design scenarios, such as "What if I add five inches to this fan blade?" or "What if I make a bicycle with three wheels?"

In this chapter, I show you how to update SolidWorks documents so that you're always working with the current document. I also show you how to query a design for information, such as measurements, mass properties, and rebuild statistics.

Changing the Design

No matter how hard you try to be clairvoyant and figure out what a design ultimately is going to look like, it just doesn't happen. In the design world, change is the name of the game. The three areas you can change in a design include part features, visual properties, and document references.

Changing dimensions and features

You change features in SolidWorks by modifying dimensions. *Dimensions* define the size and the shape of a part.

Typically, you create dimensions as you create each part feature and then insert those dimensions into drawing views. In SolidWorks, when you change a dimension in the model, the drawing updates. By the same token, when you change a dimension in a drawing, the model updates.

The way to change a part feature (a cut, an extrusion, and so on) is to change the model dimensions associated with that feature. You can change model dimensions in the part, the sketch, or in the drawing.

Driving dimensions are sometimes called model dimensions. *Driven dimensions* are another type of dimension used only for reference. In SolidWorks, driving dimensions are black, and driven dimensions are gray. (You can find out more about dimensions in Chapter 3.)

When you double-click a dimension to change it, the Modify dialog box appears (see Figure 9-1). The following list describes the Modify dialog box functions.

Figure 9-1: The Modify dialog box appears when you double-click a dimension.

1 **OK:** Saves the current value and exits the dialog box.

2 **Cancel:** Restores the original value and exits the dialog box.

3 **Rebuild:** Regenerates the model (shows the changes) with the current value. You can use Rebuild to evaluate different values before closing the Modify dialog box.

4 **Spin box value:** Sets the value for the spin increment (up/down arrows). To define the spin default value, choose Tools⇨Options. In the System Options tab, select Spin Box Increments. Set the values in the Spin Box Increments dialog box.

5 **Mark dimension to be imported into a drawing:** Marks the dimensions in part or assembly documents that you want to import into a drawing when you use the Model Insert command. (Read more about this command in Chapter 8.)

6 Dimension value: Displays the current value, which you can change by typing a new one. The default units (inches) are shown after the value.

7 Spin box: Increases or decreases the dimension value by a specified increment when you click the up or down arrows.

8 Close: Closes the dialog box without saving changes.

When you change the value of a dimension within the Modify dialog box, the size or shape of a part doesn't automatically update. You need to rebuild the model with any changes you made. To do so, simply click the Rebuild button in the Modify dialog box. Rebuilding a change while you're still in the Modify dialog box allows you to play with a number of what-if scenarios and make additional adjustments, if necessary.

When you add a brand-new dimension, you typically go back and double-click it to bring up the Modify dialog box, where you enter an exact value. If you want to save a bit of time, choose Tools⇨Options. In the General section of the Systems Options tab, select the check box for Input Dimension Value. When you check this option, the Modify dialog box appears automatically each time you insert a new dimension.

You can change a driving dimension in a part, a sketch, an assembly, or a drawing by completing the following steps:

1. **Open a drawing, part, or assembly document.**

2. **Double-click the part feature you want to change in the FeatureManager design tree or within the graphics area.**

   The dimensions appear as lines with the values next to them. You can only edit driving dimensions, which appear in black. You can't edit reference dimensions, which appear in gray.

3. **Double-click the dimension you want to change.**

   The Modify dialog box appears.

4. **Enter a new value in the dialog box.**

5. **Click Rebuild in the Modify dialog box.**

   The model updates to reflect any changes.

6. **Click OK.**

   The changes save, and the Modify dialog box closes.

You can also change the way you define a feature (extrusion, fillet, and so on). When you modify a feature, the original PropertyManager that you used to define the feature appears. You can change the values in the PropertyManager in order to change or redefine the feature.

To change the way an existing feature was defined:

1. **Open a drawing, a part, or an assembly document.**

2. **In the FeatureManager design tree, right-click the feature you want to change and choose Edit Feature.**

   The feature's PropertyManager appears.

3. **Change the values and definition of the feature in the PropertyManager.**

   Each feature has a different PropertyManager. (Chapter 5 explains the different types of features and how they're defined.)

4. **Click OK.**

   The value and property changes appear within the part.

Changing visual properties

SolidWorks lets you create models that look and act like the real thing. You can assign materials, such as aluminum or cast iron, to parts. Each material has its own associated characteristics, such as density, color, and texture. In parts and assemblies, you can adjust the direction, intensity, and color of light in the shaded view of the model to create more realistic lighting effects.

Material properties stay with the model. Downstream applications, such as the SolidWorks add-ins COSMOSWorks for analysis and PhotoWorks photo-rendering software, use these material properties to calculate their results. At times, however, you may need to edit the material properties.

You can create custom document templates with predefined materials and lighting and store these templates on a shared server for others to use. To find out more about how to create and save templates, see Chapter 2.

Setting materials properties

SolidWorks lets you assign material properties to parts. This process isn't automatic; a part only gets a material property if you assign it one or if you preset the material property in the document template. What's more, only individual parts can have material properties. You cannot assign a single material property to an entire assembly, for example.

To find what material (if any) is assigned to a part, open the document and look in the FeatureManager design tree. You see the material name and type that is listed. If the part has no material, you see Materials <not selected>.

To assign or change the material of a part:

1. **Right-click the part in the FeatureManager design tree and choose Appearance➪Edit Material.**

   The Material Editor PropertyManager, shown in Figure 9-2, appears.

Figure 9-2:
You can assign a material property to a part using the Material Editor PropertyManager.

2. **Select a materials library in the Materials section.**

   SolidWorks Materials is the main library. Any custom libraries may appear here as well. Once you select a library, the library contents display. You see a list of material classes (Steel, Alloy Steel, and so on).

3. **Select a material from the library contents.**

   Click the plus sign next to a material class to find the material type you want.

4. **Click OK.**

   The Materials Editor PropertyManager closes. The material is assigned to your part and shows up in the FeatureManager design tree. The visual appearance of the model updates to reflect its material properties.

Let there be light

Another way to change the visual appearance of a SolidWorks model is with lighting. Lighting applies to both part and assembly documents. Think of lighting like this: When a professional photographer prepares to take a portrait of your child, he tinkers with the lighting. He adds, directs, and adjusts the light to create an overall good picture. You can make similar lighting adjustments in SolidWorks.

SolidWorks offers different lighting types that you can choose for your model. The properties of the light sources work together with the material properties of the model. If you change material properties of the model, you can enhance or reduce the effect of the light properties.

You can choose several light sources in the same document. Here's what SolidWorks gives you to work with:

- **Ambient light:** Illuminates the model evenly from all directions. In a room with white walls, the level of ambient light is high, because the light reflects off the walls and other objects.

- **Directional light:** Comes from a source that is infinitely far away from the model. It's a columned light source consisting of parallel rays from a single direction, like the sun.

- **Point light:** Comes from a very small light source located at a specific coordinate in the model space. This type of light source emits light in all directions. The effect is like a tiny light bulb floating in space.

- **Spot light:** Comes from a restricted, focused light with a cone-shaped beam that is brightest at its center. You can aim a spot light at a specific area of the model. You can adjust the position and distance of the light source relative to the model, and you can adjust the angle through which the beam spreads.

You can define the following properties for a light source inside its PropertyManager:

- **On/Off:** Turns the light source on or off.

- **Color:** You can also choose the color of light. The default is a white light, but you can use a different color to give the model more warmth.

- **Ambient:** Controls the intensity of the light source using a value between 0 and 1.

- **Brightness:** Controls the brightness of the light using a value between 0 and 1.

- **Specularity:** Controls the extent to which shiny surfaces exhibit bright highlights where the light strikes them using a value between 0 and 1.

- **Light position:** Controls the position of the light relative to the model.

To see the lights types in your model, open a part or assembly document in SolidWorks and double-click the Lighting folder in the FeatureManager design tree. The default lights are Ambient and Directional, but you can adjust them or add other lights. A few rules apply:

✔ You can turn the Ambient light on or off, but you can't delete it or add other Ambient lights.

✔ You can turn the Directional light on or off or delete it.

✔ You can add additional Directional light sources.

✔ You can add Point light and Spot light sources.

✔ In any document, you can have up to nine light sources (the Ambient light and eight others in any combination).

To add a light source:

1. **Right-click the Lighting folder in the FeatureManager design tree.**

   A menu appears with the following choices:

   • Add Directional Light

   • Add Point Light

   • Add Spot Light

2. **Choose the type of light you want to add.**

   Once you make a selection, the lighting type appears in the Lighting folder immediately, as shown in Figure 9-3. You can add up to nine light sources to the model.

Figure 9-3:
You can add up to nine light sources for any model.

You can also modify a light source. To modify the lighting properties:

1. **Expand the Lighting folder in the FeatureManager design tree by clicking the plus sign next to the folder.**

   The contents of the Lighting folder appear.

2. **Right-click a light source and choose Properties.**

   The PropertyManager for that light source appears.

3. **Edit the properties to change light qualities.**

   The available light properties depend on the type of light source. You can move the slider on the bar to change the Ambient, Brightness, and Specularity properties from a value of 0 to 1.

   As you edit, a graphical representation of the light source appears in the graphics area to show the color and direction of the light.

4. **Click OK.**

To delete a light source:

1. **Click the plus sign to expand the Lighting folder in the FeatureManager design tree.**

2. **Select the light source to delete and press the Delete key.**

To turn off a light without deleting it:

1. **Click + to expand the Lighting folder in the FeatureManager design tree.**

2. **Right-click the light source and choose Off.**

   This option toggles. If the light source is on, you turn it off, and visa versa.

Changing document references

An assembly may go through many revisions in its design life. Changes are especially common in a multi-user environment where several users are working on the individual parts and subassemblies. You can change assembly components using three methods:

- ✔ **Add:** You can add a new component to an assembly using the methods I cover in Chapter 6 of this book. You can drag a component from File Explorer or use the Insert Component PropertyManager (choose Insert⇨ Component).

- ✔ **Delete:** Deleting a component is as easy as 1-2-3. Open the assembly, select the component you want to delete in the FeatureManager design tree, and press the Delete key. SolidWorks asks you for confirmation prior to deleting the component.

- ✔ **Replace:** A safe, efficient way to update an assembly is to replace the components or subassemblies when you need to.

To replace parts or components in an assembly:

1. **Choose File⇨Replace.**

   The Replace PropertyManager, shown in Figure 9-4, appears.

Figure 9-4:
You can replace an assembly component with the Replace Property-Manager.

2. **In the graphics area, click the component(s) to replace.**

   The component you select appears in the Replace These Component(s) section of the Replace dialog box.

3. **If you want to replace all copies of the part, select the All Instances check box.**

   This feature allows you to automatically replace all occurrences of a part within an assembly, without having to manually select every one.

4. **Click Browse to locate the replacement component for the With This One section.**

   The Open dialog box appears.

5. **Locate the replacement part on your computer and click Open.**

   The Open dialog box closes, and a link to the replacement part appears in the With This One section of the Replace dialog box.

6. **Under Configuration, select Match Name to allow the software to try to match the configuration name of the old component with a configuration in the replacement component.**

   If you're the do-it-yourself type, select Manually Select so that you can choose the matching configuration in the replacement component.

7. **Select Re-attach Mates to allow the software to try to re-attach existing mates to the existing components.**

8. **Click OK.**

The selected component instances are replaced. If you chose Manually Select, choose the configuration to open in the Configurations dialog box. If you selected the Re-attach Mates check box, the Mated Entities PropertyManager appears. (You can read about mates in Chapter 6.)

Mates position a component in an assembly precisely with respect to each other. Mates defines how the components move and rotate together.

The Replace feature works well when you're replacing a component with a similar component. But if the assembly components aren't similar to one another, you're better off deleting the existing component and adding the new one manually.

Getting Information from Your Design

Another advantage to having a 3D design is the wealth of information in the design once it's complete. And that is a good thing, because there is always someone wanting to know how big a model is, how much it weighs, or what it's made out of.

You can query the SolidWorks model in three ways:

- ✔ By measuring your design
- ✔ By calculating mass properties
- ✔ By reviewing your document's statistics

Measuring your design

There are a few ways to measure entities in a SolidWorks design. One way is to extract the dimensions. You can make dimensions of a part visible in the default view. With your part document open, in the FeatureManager design tree, right-click Annotations and choose Show Feature Dimensions. (A check mark next to Show Feature Dimensions indicates that the feature is already selected.) Your dimensions should already appear in your drawing, so you don't need to do anything to see drawing dimensions.

Dimensions are easier to see when you view the part as Shaded. (Click Shaded in the View toolbar.) Some dimensions become more readable when you rotate the part. If you want to display dimensions for a feature, double-click the feature in the FeatureManager design tree.

An easy way to measure entities is with the SolidWorks Measure tool. To open the Measure tool, choose Tools⇨Measure. The Measure dialog box, which is really more like a toolbar (see Figure 9-5), appears. You have the following options:

Figure 9-5:
The
Measure
tool is the
easiest way
to take
measure-
ments.

1   2   3   4

1 Arc/Circle Measurements: Select to specify the distance to display when arcs or circles are selected to measure.

- **Center to center:** Measures the distance between the centers of the circles (the default).

- **Minimum distance:** Measures the distance between the closest points on the circles.

- **Maximum distance:** Measures the distance between the farthest points on the circles.

2 Units/Precision: Select to display the measure units/Precision dialog box, where you can display the custom measurement units and precision.

3 Show XYZ Measurements: Select to display *dX, dY,* and *dZ* measurements between selected entities in the graphics area. Clear to display only the minimum distance between selected entities.

4 Expand or contract the information window: Use when you want to copy the information to a Clipboard.

In most cases, the Measurement tool is straightforward to use. Simply select an entity to measure. To select more than one entity, just keep clicking. To unselect an item, click it again.

As long as you select a valid measurement, SolidWorks displays the values in the Measure dialog box and in the graphics area. If SolidWorks can't take a measurement, a message in the Measure dialog box appears that says, "Invalid combination of selected entities."

TIP

If you select too many items at one time, the Measure tool displays nothing, and you need to restart the Measure tool. One way to restart and clear the selections is to either click in an area of the graphics window where no geometry appears or hit the Enter key twice.

If you look at Figure 9-6, you see three examples of entities that I selected in a gasket part and used the Measure tool to measure:

- ✔ **Arc selected:** Displays the radius and center *(X, Y, Z)* values.
- ✔ **Line selected:** Displays the length of a line.
- ✔ **Two circles selected:** Displays the center distance, or the distance between the holes, *dX,* and *dY* values. The *dX, dY,* and *dZ* values are the change (delta) in the distance along the *X, Y,* and *Z* axes.

Figure 9-6:
The best way to extract measurements is with the Measure tool.

Working with mass properties

SolidWorks calculates mass properties and section properties (density, mass, volume, surface area, and so on) for parts and assemblies.

Mass properties look at the entire part or assembly and *section properties* look at multiple faces that are in parallel planes. You can assign values for mass and center of gravity to override the calculated values. The ability to assign values is useful, for example, when you want to assign the correct mass and center of gravity to a simplified representation of a component.

When either mass or section property is calculated, a tricolored reference 3D triad displays at the origin of the part or assembly along with the mass properties or section properties.

To display mass properties:

1. **Choose Tools⇨Mass Properties.**

   The Mass Properties dialog box appears, as shown in Figure 9-7.

Figure 9-7:
The Mass
Properties
dialog box
gives the
density of
this gasket.

2. **Click a part or assembly in the FeatureManager design tree.**

   The part or assembly name appears under Selected Items. If you choose more than one entity, you get the calculated mass properties for the combination of those entities.

3. **Select from the following options.**

   - **Include Hidden Bodies/Components:** Select to include hidden bodies and components in the calculations.

   - **Show output coordinate system in corner of window:** Select to display the tricolored reference 3D triad in the corner of the graphics area, or clear to show the triad at the origin.

   - **Assigned Mass Properties.** Select to assign values for mass and center of gravity to override the calculated values. You can assign properties only to a single entity, not a combination.

4. **Choose Recalculate in the Mass Properties dialog box.**

   The mass properties display in the dialog box. If you chose an assembly file, you see the mass properties for the assembly as a whole.

5. **To clear an entity, select the entity and press Delete on the keyboard.**

   The items clear from Selected Items. You can then select another item for a new mass properties calculation.

6. **Click Close to close the dialog box.**

 If you want mass properties to display in different units (feet instead of meters, for instance), select Options in the Mass Properties dialog box. In the Mass Property Options dialog box that appears, select a different unit of measure, and click OK.

 Mass property calculations are based on the physical properties of a part. To change a part's physical properties (aluminum to iron ore, for instance), right-click on the material name or Material <not selected> in the FeatureManager design tree, and select Edit Material. In the Materials Editor PropertyManager, select a new material, and click OK.

 The unit of measure for the mass property calculation is set in the document template. You can change the unit of measure by choosing Tools⇨Options⇨ Document Properties⇨Units in an open document. You can also define material properties in the template.

You can use the Section Property feature to display the area, centroid (sketch and part origin), and other information for a 2D sketch.

To display section properties for multiple entities:

1. **Edit or create a sketch.**

   To edit an existing sketch, select the feature, right-click, and choose Edit Sketch.

2. **Choose Tools⇨Section Properties.**

   The results appear in the Section Properties dialog box.

3. **Click Close to close the dialog box.**

Getting the stats on your documents

Understanding what makes up a document from a feature, size, and complexity standpoint is useful information when you're reviewing a design or working on a new design. Each SolidWorks document type has statistics. No, the document statistics are not a description on how your drawing likes to take long walks on the beach and is looking for a caring, sensitive partner to spend free time with. I'm talking about rebuild statistics.

When you make changes to a SolidWorks document, you need to rebuild the model to check for geometry errors. In a large assembly, rebuilds can take a lot of time. Feature Statistics is a tool that tells you how much time it takes to rebuild each feature in a part, or each part in an assembly.

Depending on the document type you have open, the Feature Statistics dialog box displays different information and a different user interface. The following information appears for:

- **Drawing statistics:** The number of drawing sheets, number and types of drawing views, and the number and types of drawing annotations (such as notes, dimensions, and symbols).

- **Feature statistics:** In a part file, the Feature Statistics dialog box lists all features in the part with their rebuild and their rebuild times in descending order (see Figure 9-8). In the case of an unusually long rebuild time, you may consider reworking the geometry (so that the feature takes less time to rebuild) or suppressing the feature in a rebuild. A feature that takes up 60 percent of the rebuild time for a part isn't always a bad thing. It's just good to know in case you're heading to Happy Hour in 15 minutes.

  In Figure 9-8, the counter bored hole is the key contributor to the rebuild time in the gasket model. In this case, that's okay. The idea is to use the information as a reference and not to get too worked up on how to remodel the feature to save time. Some features have longer build times than others. Get an idea for what they are and if something doesn't pass the smell test (smells fishy), then further investigation may be warranted.

- **Assembly statistics:** Displays the total number of components, number of unique parts and subassemblies, how many mates exist, and the number of top-level mates and components. When you're taking assembly performance into consideration, a large number of top-level components and mates can be a performance drag.

Figure 9-8:
You can find out what features take the most time to rebuild in the Feature Statistics dialog box.

To get feature statistics (or drawing or assembly statistics):

1. **Open a part document (or a drawing or assembly document).**

2. **Choose Tools⇨Feature Statistics.**

   If you're working on an assembly document, it's Part Statistics; on a drawing, it's Drawing Statistics.

   The Feature Statistics dialog box appears with a list of all the features and their rebuild times in descending order.

3. **Click Feature Order to sort the features to match the FeatureManager design tree.**

4. **Click one of the following:**

   • **Print:** Prints the statistics.

   • **Copy:** Copies the statistics so that you can paste them into another file.

   • **Refresh:** Refreshes the feature statistics.

5. **Click Close.**

When displaying Feature Statistics for a part, the features (by default) appear in order of their rebuild times. You can reorder the list by clicking one of the category headings; for example, if you click Feature Order, the features appear in alphabetical order.

Chapter 10

Leveraging Your Existing Designs

SolidWorks offers several tools that let you get extra mileage out of existing designs. For example, many engineers have a stockpile of product designs that exist as old *(legacy)* drawing files. With SolidWorks, you don't have to throw that 2D data in the trash and start from scratch. You can maintain those files in their native formats or import them into SolidWorks and use them as a basis for 3D models.

Multiple configurations are another way to get more play out of designs. *Configurations* are variations of an existing design. Think of a screw that comes in different lengths. Instead of having to create 50 different files, SolidWorks lets you create those variations in a single document. This way, you can manage files more easily and edit all configurations consistently.

You also can use SolidWorks to create exploded views of an assembly that you can use in technical documentation. The views show the assembly with the components separated so that you can see how things fit together.

Maintaining Old Drawing Files

Few new products are totally new. More often, they're built on existing designs. Many of these existing designs are in DWG or DXF drawing formats. These formats generally mean that someone created the drawings in AutoCAD, a 2D design program that was popular before 3D modeling programs such as SolidWorks existed. Engineers often refer to DWG and DXF files as *legacy,* even if the documents were created in recent versions of AutoCAD. Many SolidWorks users come from an AutoCAD background, and they still have a lot of AutoCAD files that they want to maintain.

SolidWorks offers tools that allow you to work with these drawing files. You can import a DWG or DXF file into SolidWorks using an import wizard so that you can use the file as the basis of a 3D design. If you need to make only a minor change, a SolidWorks tool called DWGEditor allows you to work with AutoCAD DWG and DXF files in their native format. DWGEditor lets you open and save any file created in AutoCAD Version 2.5 through 2005 without file conversions. DWGEditor has an AutoCAD-like interface (see Figure 10-1), so it's familiar to use if you're from an AutoCAD background.

DWGEditor also allows you to save a file back to an earlier version of AutoCAD. If you work with a vendor that has AutoCAD 2000, you can save drawing files in that version's format to work on the vendor's system.

Figure 10-1:
SolidWorks
DWGEditor
offers an
AutoCAD-
like
interface.

You can use DWGEditor independent of SolidWorks. To access DWGEditor, in Windows choose Start⇨All Programs⇨SolidWorks 2006⇨DWGEditor. If you import a DWG or DXF file into SolidWorks, the DXF/DWG Import dialog box appears, as shown in Figure 10-2.

You can use DWGEditor in several ways:

- ✔ **Perform a quick change to a DWG or DXF file in its native format, without going through any file conversions.** When you're finished making the change, you can save the file in its native format so AutoCAD can open it again.

- ✔ **Import a DWG or DXF file and use it as the basis of a SolidWorks part.** There a few ways to do this, but my preference is to open a DWG or DXF file in DWGEditor and use Windows copy (Ctrl+C) and paste (Ctrl+V) functions to paste the DWG geometry you want to use directly into the SolidWorks sketcher.

- ✔ **Import a DWG or DXF file and use it as the basis of a SolidWorks drawing.** In SolidWorks, choose File➪Open. When the Open dialog box appears, change the Files of Type to DWG or DXF and browse to the file you want to open. Click on the file to select and then click Open. When the DXF/DWG Import dialog box appears, select the Create New Solid-Works Drawing option and the Embed As a Sheet in Native DXF/DWG Format option, as shown in Figure 10-2. The file imports into a new SolidWorks drawing sheet.

Figure 10-2:
The DXF/ DWG Import dialog box lets you use an AutoCAD drawing file as the basis of a SolidWorks drawing.

During install, SolidWorks gives you the option to associate DWG and DXF files with the SolidWorks DWGEditor. If you select this option, the DWGEditor DXF/DWG Import dialog box opens automatically when you double-click a DWG or a DXF file in SolidWorks Explorer or Design Library or when you check a DWG or a DXF file out of the PDMWorks vault.

To edit a DWG or DXF file in its native format using DWGEditor:

1. **In SolidWorks, choose File⇨Open (or you can run the program independently).**

   The Open dialog box appears.

2. **Select DWG or DXF for Files of Type. Browse to the location of the file you want to open, click it, and select Open.**

   The DXF/DWG Import dialog box appears.

3. **Check the option Edit/View in DWGEditor and click Finish.**

4. **In the DWGEditor, make whatever changes to the drawing that you need to make.**

5. **Choose File⇨Save As.**

   The Save As dialog box appears. In the Save As Type box, you can select to save the file in the current version of AutoCAD or an earlier version.

6. **Click Save to close the dialog box and save the file.**

Managing Configurations

At times, you need to create several variations of a design. For example, you may want to create a family of screws, or you may want to create multiple configurations of a carburetor. After all, a single carburetor isn't going to fit all vehicle types. If you have to create a different file for each design scenario, it's going to take a lot of time — and patience. Even a simple geometry change may make for a long day at the office.

Fortunately, there's a better way. The ConfigurationManager in SolidWorks manages multiple configurations of a part or an assembly in the same document to save you time and reduce errors. And you don't have to recreate the wheel each time you create a smaller one. ConfigurationManager lets you create various design scenarios by simply suppressing part or assembly components and features, or in the case of that screw family, by varying dimensions and parameters.

You can create design variants in two ways, manually or with Design Tables. A *Design Table* allows you to build multiple configurations of parts or assemblies by applying the values in the table to the dimensions in the part. Design Tables are the best way to create a family of screws that vary in width, length, and number of threads. If you want to show a door in open and close positions, it's easier to create those variations manually.

Some of the purposes of configurations are as follows:

- Produce multiple versions of a model or display optional features in a part or optional components in an assembly.

- Create a simplified part configuration to use in a large assembly so that the assembly loads into memory faster. Smaller parts and assemblies rebuild quicker when you use simplified configurations. Also, editing a document is easier when you have less visual clutter.

- Create additional drawing views. A single drawing can display multiple configurations of a part or assembly in the different views.

- Create exploded views of assemblies. You can use different design configurations to document a multistep installation process.

- Define multiple positions of a part for motion studies. For example, you can show how a car door looks open and closed by creating one configuration of the door at 0 degrees and another at 90 degrees.

- Define custom properties per configuration. A *custom property* is a file attribute (such as the revision date, part number, or a description of the document) defined within the original document template. You can define these properties by choosing File⇨Properties. In the Summary Information dialog box, click the Custom tab for properties that apply to the entire document, or the Configuration Specific tab for properties that vary from one configuration to another.

To view the different configurations in your document, click the Configuration-Manager tab at the top of the FeatureManager design tree and double-click the configuration names.

Varying the design

When you create variations of a design, the idea is to simply make your changes to the model and save those changes as a different configuration, rather than a different document. The next two sections explain how to do that. For the moment, here's a list of ways that you can vary a part or an assembly design in order to create new configurations.

You can vary a part configuration as follows:

- Modify feature dimensions.
- Suppress features, equations, and end conditions.
- Define configuration-specific properties.

You can vary an assembly configuration as follows:

- ✔ Change the suppression state (Suppressed/Unsuppressed) or visibility (Hide/ Show) to highlight different components. You can have multiple display states per configuration.

- ✔ Change the referenced configuration of components.

- ✔ Change the dimensions of distance or angle mates or the suppression state of mates.

- ✔ Modify dimensions or other parameters of features that belong to the assembly (not to other components), including cuts and holes, component patterns, reference geometry, and sketches.

- ✔ Define configuration-specific properties, such as end conditions and sketch relations.

You can *hide* features or components to highlight other items in a document. When you hide an item, it's like making the item invisible. The item is still there, you just can't see it.

You can use the *suppressed* state to temporarily remove a feature from a part or a component from an assembly, without deleting it. The item is no longer a functional member of the part or assembly, so you can't select, reference, or edit its children. And because SolidWorks removes the suppressed item from memory, the document loads, rebuilds, and displays faster.

To access the Hide/Show and Suppress/Resolved commands, in the FeatureManager design tree, right-click a feature in a part or component in an assembly and choose the command. If a component is hidden, Show appears in the menu. If a component is suppressed, Unsuppressed appears.

Creating a configuration manually

There are two ways to create a configuration in SolidWorks, manually and with Design Tables. If you want to make a few variations on a complex assembly, you're best off doing it manually.

Here is how to manually make a new configuration of a part or an assembly:

1. **Open a part or assembly file in SolidWorks.**

2. **Click the ConfigurationManager tab at the top of the FeatureManager design tree.**

   In the place of the FeatureManager, you now see the ConfigurationManager.

3. **In the ConfigurationManager, right-click the part or assembly name and choose Add Configuration.**

   The Add Configuration PropertyManager appears (see Figure 10-3).

4. **In the Add Configuration PropertyManager, type a Configuration Name and specify properties for the new configuration.**

   In the PropertyManager, you have room to add a descriptive name and a comment. These fields make it easier for someone who goes to review or modify your design to understand what you were trying to do.

   Advanced Options properties control what happens when you add new features and components to other configurations and then activate this configuration again. By default, SolidWorks suppresses in this configuration any new components or features that you add to another.

5. **Click OK.**

Once you create the new configuration, you can make overall changes to the design. The reason to create the configuration first and make changes later is so that you know what configuration you're making changes to.

Figure 10-3:
You can name your configuration and add a description and comments in the Configuration Property-Manager.

To change an existing configuration, in the ConfigurationManager, double-click the configuration you want to change to make it active. Any changes you make apply only to that configuration.

When you double-click on a driving dimension to change it, a Modify dialog box appears, as shown in Figure 10-4. In the Modify dialog box, you can indicate which configuration you want to apply your change to by selecting All Configurations, This Configuration, or Specify Configuration(s).

A *driving dimension* is one that changes the size of a model when you update it. *Driven dimensions* are for information only. You can only modify driving dimensions.

Figure 10-4:
Specify the configura-
tions you
want to
apply a
change to
inside the
Modify
dialog box.

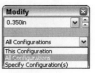

To open a document to a predefined configuration:

1. **Choose File⇨Open.**

   The Open dialog box, shown in Figure 10-5, appears.

2. **Click the configuration name to open within the Configurations field.**

   The preview window updates. If you have not recently saved the document, the preview window may be blank. The current preview updates when you save the document again.

3. **Click Open.**

Always give your configurations meaningful names so that you can recognize them easily.

Figure 10-5:
The Open
dialog box
shows
derived
configu-
rations.

Creating configurations with Design Tables

Design Tables allow you to create an infinite number of variations on a single design. SolidWorks uses Microsoft Excel to create the Design Table, so you need to have a copy of the program on your computer to use this feature.

To create a Design Table, you insert a new empty Design Table in the model and enter the Design Table information directly in the worksheet. You enter the names of the configurations you want to create, specify the parameters you want to control, and assign values for each parameter. Parameters can be dimensions, features, or parts. When you finish entering information, SolidWorks creates the new configurations for you. And if your configuration data already exists, you can add it to the table automatically.

The first column of the worksheet lists the different configuration names. Parameters go in the first row of cells, and dimensions and suppression values go beneath each parameter. When you change a dimension value in a Design Table, the configuration updates with the specified value. In addition to changing dimension values, you can also change the suppression state of a feature in Design Tables. You can suppress or unsuppress a feature.

Figure 10-6 displays row values (4–40 x .500) and column headings (Head Dia@Profile) that define the configuration name (row name) and the driving value (column name).

The *SolidWorks 2006 Online Users Guide* contains a list of valid Design Table parameters. For example, proper parameter syntax for a feature dimension is *dimension@feature_name*. Legal values under this parameter heading include any decimal number. You can find the *SolidWorks 2006 Online Users Guide* under Help in the main menu of SolidWorks.

Figure 10-6:
Row column
format for
a Design
Table.

	Head Dia@Profile	Head Thickness@Profile	Length@Profile
4-40 x .500	0.125	0.055	0.5
6-32 x .125	0.14	0.066	0.125
6-32 x .250	0.14	0.066	0.25
6-32 x .375	0.14	0.066	0.375
6-32 x .500	0.14	0.066	0.5
6-32 x .625	0.14	0.066	0.625
6-32 x .750	0.14	0.066	0.75

A Design Table that uses named features and comments is easy to understand and to modify. It's a waste of time to have to continually exit the spreadsheet to review features and dimension names in the model. The example in Figure 10-6 uses decipherable names for the dimension values.

To create a Design Table:

1. **Open a part or assembly document in SolidWorks.**

2. **Choose Insert⇨Design Table.**

   The Design Table PropertyManager appears, as shown in Figure 10-7.

Figure 10-7:
You can
choose
options for
how you
want to
handle
changes to
the Design
Table
Property-
Manager.

3. **In the PropertyManager, under Source, select Auto-create.**

   Auto-create extracts data from the model that is valid in the design table, such as a list of dimensions.

4. **In the PropertyManager, select options for Edit Control and Options.**

   Check one of these options in Edit Control.

   - **Allow model edits to update the design table.** Any changes you make to the model update in the Design Table.

   - **Block model edits that would update the design table.** Any changes you make to the models do not update in the Design Table. You cannot makes changes in the model that affect the Design Table's parameters.

   Select from the following options in Options.

   - **New parameters.** Adds a new column to the Design Table if you add a new parameter in the model.

   - **New configurations.** Adds a new row to the Design Table if you manually add a new configuration to the model.

   - **Warn when updating design table.** Warns you that the Design Table will change based on the parameters you updated in the model.

5. **Click OK.**

   The PropertyManager disappears, and an embedded worksheet appears in the window, and Excel toolbars replace the SolidWorks toolbars.

6. **Enter Configuration names in the first column.**

   Cell A1 contains the Design Table name, and cell A2 is blank. So the first column includes cells A3, A4, and so on. If configurations already exist in the document, they appear in these columns. Any new configurations you add here update in the model according to your selections in the PropertyManager (see Step 4).

   To add a new configuration, enter a new name in column A under the last configuration.

7. **Enter parameter names in first row columns.**

   You want to enter your parameter names in cells B2, C2, and so on. (The Design Table name is in the first row.) Parameter names should reflect the feature or dimension in the model that you want to vary. To add a parameter name to the Design Table, place your pointer in a cell and then double-click the feature or dimension you want to add in the FeatureManager design tree.

8. **Enter dimension and suppression values in the appropriate cells.**

   You can enter dimension and suppression values beneath the parameter name in the row of the corresponding configuration. Dimension values are decimal numbers. Suppression values are S (Suppressed) or U (Unsuppressed).

9. **Click outside of the Design Table window to close the Design Table.**

Working with configurations

Here are some more useful notes and tips on configurations:

✔ You can't delete an active configuration. To delete a configuration, make another configuration active and then delete the configuration.

✔ The comment field is a good place to include a description on the reasons for and the function of the configuration. Comments

help document the intent and the purpose of the configuration.

✔ To activate a configuration, double-click the configuration name within the Configuration-Manager.

✔ The FeatureManager displays the active configuration to the right of the part name in the ConfigurationManager.

Here are a few tips to keep in mind when working with a Design Table:

✔ To edit a Design Table, in the FeatureManager design tree, right-click the Design Table icon and choose Edit Table.

✔ Microsoft Excel lets you add comments. To add a comment in Excel, right-click the cell you want to comment on and choose Insert Comment. In the box, type the comment text.

✔ If you make an entry in a cell within the Design Table that doesn't have a corresponding row (leftmost cell in the row) and column (topmost cell in column) heading, Design Table treats the cell contents as a comment.

Using configurations to create exploded views

Once you design a product, manufacturing needs to know how to assemble it, and maintenance needs to know how to take it apart. Another way to get more mileage from your SolidWorks assembly design is to create exploded views. *Exploded views* show the assembly components separated so the viewer can visualize how parts fit together. You can use configurations to show a series of exploded views to create product documentation.

An exploded view consists of one or more explode steps. You create these steps by selecting and dragging parts in the graphics area. When you're done, SolidWorks stores the exploded view with the assembly configuration that you created it with. Each configuration can have only one exploded view.

Figure 10-8 shows an exploded view of a Sea Scooter. SolidWorks lets you toggle between the exploded and collapsed views.

Figure 10-8:
This exploded view of a Sea Scooter shows how parts fit together.

To create an exploded view of an assembly:

1. **Open an assembly file.**

2. **Click the ConfigurationManager tab at the top of the FeatureManager design tree.**

   In the place of the FeatureManager, you now see the ConfigurationManager, which lists the configurations in the design.

3. **Double-click the configuration you want to explode.**

   This makes the configuration active.

4. **Click the Explode View icon on the Assembly toolbar.**

   The Explode PropertyManager appears.

5. **In the graphics area, select one or more components to include in the first explode step.**

   A manipulator with three handles (red, green, and blue) appears in the graphics area. In the PropertyManager, the components appear in Component(s) of the explode step under Settings.

6. **Move the pointer over the manipulator handle that points in the direction that you want to explode the part.**

   The pointer changes to a blue drag handle.

7. **Drag a manipulator handle to explode the components, as shown in Figure 10-9.**

   The explode step appears under Explode Steps.

8. **Under Settings, click Done.**

   The PropertyManager clears and is ready for the next explode step.

9. **Create more explode steps until you are done.**

10. **Click OK.**

    The assembly appears in the exploded state and saves with the active configuration.

Figure 10-9:
You can drag a component to create an explode step.

To change an exploded view, open the ConfigurationManager and click the Explode Step that you want to edit. For example, to change the location of the nose cone in the Sea Scooter assembly, click the Exploded View icon, below the configuration name and, in the graphics area, move the blue arrow handle to reposition the component.

Animating the explode or collapse sequence

You can do more than just explode or collapse the assembly. You can animate the explode or collapse sequence to show the assembly components come apart and back together again. Figure 10-10 shows the animation controller toolbar. The Save As AVI button on the toolbar lets you save the explode sequence as an AVI file that you can send or include in an eDrawings file.

Figure 10-10:
The Animation control toolbar lets you create video files of the assembly explode and collapse sequence.

To animate the explode or collapse of an exploded view of an assembly:

1. **Open an assembly file.**

2. **Click the ConfigurationManager tab on the top of the FeatureManager design tree.**

   In the place of the FeatureManager, you now see the ConfigurationManager, which lists the configurations in the design.

3. **Click the + sign beside the configuration that contains the exploded view you want to animate.**

   You see the Exp⎥View feature, which contains each step in the explode.

4. **Right-click the Exp⎥View feature and choose Animate Collapse or Animate Explode.**

   The assembly explodes or collapses, and the Animation Controller toolbar appears.

You can use the playback controls to animate the explode or collapse. The two controls on the rightmost side of Figure 10-10 allow you to slow it down (x1/2) or speed it up (x2).

Adding exploded views to a drawing sheet

You can add exploded views to a drawing sheet. To change a drawing view to the exploded state, open a drawing file, right-click a view, and choose Properties. The Drawing View Properties dialog box appears. In the Configuration Information section of the dialog box, check Show in Exploded State, as shown in Figure 10-11, and click OK.

Figure 10-11:
You can check the exploded state option in the Drawing View Properties dialog box to display the drawing view in the exploded state.

Drawing View Properties

View Properties | Show Hidden Edges | Hide/Show Components

View information
Name: Drawing View5   Type: Named View

Model information
View of: ZS06 SEASCOOTER FINAL
Document: C:\DataSW\SeaScooter_ZS06 SEASCOOTER FINAL.SLDA

Configuration information
○ Use model's "in-use" or last saved configuration
⦿ Use named configuration:
   Default
☑ Show in exploded state

Display State
   Display State-1

Bill of Materials (BOM)
☐ Keep linked to BOM   ☐ Align breaks with parent
   <None>   ☐ Display sheet metal bend notes

OK   Cancel   Help

Chapter 11

Printing and Plotting

· ·

In This Chapter

▶ Adding a printer to the network

▶ Defining the SolidWorks document settings

▶ Printing SolidWorks parts, assemblies, and drawings

▶ Understanding the different printing methods

· ·

*N*o matter what people say about a paperless workplace, sometimes nothing can replace a physical copy of a SolidWorks document. Hard copies of large engineering drawings are easier to read than electronic copies on tiny computer screens. Some companies require printed copies for reviews and record-keeping. Other folks might not have the means to view an electronic copy. And while CAD files contain proprietary information, a hard copy protects your interests.

In this chapter, I take you through the steps of setting up your printer in Windows and show you the best ways to print SolidWorks documents.

Delving into Printing and Plotting

You can print flat images of parts and assembly models using a regular office printer, but for high-quality large-scale engineering drawings, a *plotter* is best. While printers simulate lines by printing a closely spaced series of dots, plotters draw continuous lines using a pen. *Multicolored plotters* use different colored pens to draw different colored lines. Plotters are considerably more expensive than printers, but they're called for when precision is mandatory.

You can access any printer or plotter, local or remote, using the standard Windows operating system. Printing from SolidWorks is similar to printing from any Microsoft Office application, so if you know how to do that, you're halfway there.

You can print SolidWorks documents directly from SolidWorks or from the eDrawings Viewer or the SolidWorks Viewer, two free programs that let you view SolidWorks documents without the SolidWorks software. (Chapter 14 offers more information on viewers.) You can download both viewers at www.solidworks.com/pages/products/designtools.html.

Installing a Printer in Windows

In a larger organization, the job of adding a printer to a network is one that generally belongs to the IT group. But in the case of a small business or home office, that IT person may be you.

The good news is that most new printers and plotters support Plug and Play in Windows. If you have a plug-and-play printer (look for Plug and Play on the printer's list of features), you just need to plug the printer into your computer, and Windows takes care of the setup.

If you have an older printer or if you're connecting your printer to a network, you need to take a few extra steps. First, make sure that you have the CDs that came with your printer handy. The Add Printer Wizard installs the printer drivers from the CDs. If you don't have the CDs, you can get the driver from the Web site of the printer manufacturer.

To install an older printer without plug-and-play technology on Windows 2000/XP (the Windows operating system currently supported by SolidWorks):

1. **Choose Start➪Settings➪Printers and Faxes or choose Start➪Printers and Faxes, depending on how your Start menu is configured.**

   A list of currently defined printers and faxes appears.

2. **Choose File➪Add Printer.**

   The Add Printer Wizard appears to walk you through installing a printer or making a printer connection.

3. **Click Next.**

   The next frame of the wizard asks whether you have a local or network printer.

4. **Check whether you have a local printer or a network printer.**

   Click the local printer option if the printer is attached to your computer or if it's a network printer not attached to a print server.

   If the printer is on a network, click the network printer option.

5. **Click Next.**

   The Specify a Printer dialog box appears.

6. **Specify a printer by checking one of three options:**

    • **Find a printer in the directory:** Click this option to locate the
      printer on your computer.

    • **Connect to this printer:** Click this option and type the name of the
      printer below it.

    • **Connect to a printer on the Internet or on a home or office net-
      work:** Click this option if the computer is on a network and type
      the URL for the printer.

7. **Click Next.**

    The Browse for Printer dialog box appears.

8. **Set the printer as the Windows default.**

    Check Yes or No as to whether the printer should be the system default.

    The default printer is the printer your documents print to automatically
    unless you select another output device. To set a printer as a default
    printer at any time, in the Windows Start menu, choose Settings➪Printers
    and Faxes. Right-click on a printer and select Set As Default. A check
    mark appears next to the default printer icon in Printers and Faxes.

9. **Click Next.**

10. **Click Finish.**

    The new printer is added to the system and is available for printing.

Setting printer and document preferences

After you've added the printer to your network (see preceding section),
Windows allows you to change print preferences. Keep in mind that the preferences you set for a printer become the default settings for any user who
connects to the printer. Some of the following commands may not be available on every printer. If an option you want is not selectable (it appears in
gray), see your system administrator.

To access the following commands in Windows, choose Start➪Settings➪
Printers and Faxes. Then right-click your printer and choose from the following commands:

✔ **Open** opens the print queue for the printer, which shows active print
  jobs. Use this option to cancel, reprint, or pause a print job.

✔ **Set as Default Printer** sets the printer as the default printer for all
  applications.

✔ **Printing Preferences** defines the default print quality, the number of
  pages per sheet, the input and output paper trays, paper orientation,
  and so on.

✔ **Pause Printing** pauses any current print job. To resume, right-click the printer icon again and choose Resume Printing.

✔ **Sharing** allows other users on the network to use the printer. When this option isn't enabled, only you can use the printer.

✔ **Rename, Delete, or create a Shortcut** allows you to rename the printer, to delete it, or to create a shortcut on the desktop.

✔ **Properties** include the printer's name, port, sharing, security, and so on.

You can also set many print properties within the SolidWorks document. And if you have a consistent way of printing — for example, you always print part documents in a landscape orientation scaled to 90 percent — you can set these preferences directly in the SolidWorks document template.

To save time, you can save a SolidWorks document (for example, a part, assembly, or drawing) as a template document for reuse. A *template* forms the basis of a new SolidWorks document. SolidWorks saves these files using a different file extension, much like Microsoft Word templates. SolidWorks assigns the extension .prtdot to a part template, .asmdot to an assembly template, and .drwdot to a drawing template.

You can make a new template by saving any SolidWorks document as a template. To do so, select the appropriate file format in the Files As Type section of the Save As dialog box. (See Chapter 2 for more details on document templates in SolidWorks.)

Defining printer page setup properties

The Page Setup dialog box is where you can change printer settings such as resolution, scale, paper size, and so on. The preferences are set automatically to those of the default printer. You can keep those preferences or override them. Either way, these preferences are saved with the document.

To define the printer page setup properties in an open document:

1. **Choose File⇨Page Setup.**

   The Page Setup dialog box, shown in Figure 11-1, appears. This dialog box contains the default printer settings.

2. **Select the setting defaults and other options.**

   Select whether to use the system printer settings or the document settings. You can also define resolution and scale, paper size and source, drawing color, and orientation using this option.

3. **Click OK to accept the changes.**

   SolidWorks saves Page Setup changes with the document so that the document prints the same way next time. If you don't want the changes to Page Setup to be permanent, do not click OK and simply close the document after printing.

Figure 11-1:
You can use the Page Setup dialog box to adjust printer settings.

Setting options within the Print dialog box

You can set a number of options within the SolidWorks document using the Print dialog box, shown in Figure 11-2. Similar to the page setup options (see the preceding section), SolidWorks saves these values within the document templates. SolidWorks saves any changes you make to these printer setup values with the document.

To access the Print dialog box in an open SolidWorks document, choose File➪Print. The dialog box contains six areas:

✔ **Document Printer** specifies the following printer options:

- **Name** specifies the printer. The system provides read-only status about the printer's status, type, and location.

- **Properties** sets options specific to the selected printer.

- **Page Setup** specifies page setup options and advanced printer options, such as scale, orientation, resolution, and so on.

Figure 11-2:
You can choose a printer in the Print dialog box.

✔ **System Options** defines the line weights (see Figure 11-3) and printer margins. By default, the margin default values are set to the printer margin and rarely need to change. The line weights correspond to the thickness value that you set for line fonts. (To access Line Fonts in the open document, choose Tools⇨Options. Look for Line Font in the Document Properties tab.)

Figure 11-3:
You can set line weights for a plotter under System Options in the Print dialog box.

Line Weights			
Thin:	0.00708661in	Thick(3):	0.02755906in
Normal:	0.00984252in	Thick(4):	0.03937008in
Thick:	0.01377953in	Thick(5):	0.05511811in
Thick(2):	0.01968504in	Thick(6):	0.07874016in

OK   Cancel   Help

• **Line weights** specifies the line weights that work best with your printer or plotter.

• **Margins** specifies values for the top, bottom, left, and right margins for the document.

✔ **Document Options** defines Header/Footer values (see Figure 11-4).

• **Header/Footer** specifies headers and footers for the active document only. You can select a predefined header or footer or create new ones. Headers and footers can include information such as page number, total pages, date, filename, and so on.

Figure 11-4:
You can create a header and footer with a page number, the date, and filename in Document Options under Page Setup.

Header/Footer

Header preview
UNCONTROLLED DOCUMENT

Header: ,UNCONTROLLED DOCUMENT,   Custom Header...

Footer: Page 1 of 1,revolve.SLDPRT,4/28/2   Custom Footer...

Footer preview
Page 1 of 1   revolve.SLDPRT   4/28/2005

OK   Cancel   Help

✔ **Print Range** allows you to select the sheets you want to print in a drawing.

- **All** prints all pages in the document.
- **Pages** prints the sheets you specify (drawings only).
- **Selection** prints a selected area of a drawing sheet at a scale you specify (drawings only).

✔ **Other options.**

- **Number of copies** sets the number of copies to print.
- **Print background** prints the window background in addition to the model or drawing.
- **Print to file** prints to a file instead of the printer. If you check this item, you're prompted to type a name for the file in the Print to File dialog box.
- **Convert draft quality drawing views to high quality** (drawings only) converts the current draft quality view into high quality for printing purposes only.

After setting the options, click OK to close the dialog box. The next time you print the document, it uses the new settings.

Printing a Document

After you configure the printing, you're ready to print a document. The first thing you should know is that not all SolidWorks documents print the same, and the way a document prints is based on its type:

✔ **Parts:** SolidWorks prints the active document on the screen, using the current setting for zoom, view orientation (front, back, isometric, and so on), and display mode (wire frame, hidden lines visible, hidden line removed).

✔ **Assemblies:** SolidWorks prints assemblies as it does parts, in the active display setting, using the current zoom, orientation, and display mode.

✔ **Drawings:** SolidWorks print a full-size copy of the active sheet, regardless of the current zoom scale. You can print individual sheets or all the sheets in a multiple sheet drawing using the Print range function in the Print menu.

You can print a document in SolidWorks in one of three ways: from the Print Preview screen, from the Print dialog box, and from the Print icon at the top of the menu bar.

Printing from the Print Preview screen is my favorite method. The Print Preview feature shows you how a document will look when it prints. You can use this preview to judge any necessary adjustments to the header, footer, and margins. A quick look at the print preview saves paper and time.

To preview the printed image of an active document:

1. **Click the Print Preview icon.**

   A preview of the document appears. Command buttons at the top of the window allow you to scan different pages of a multipage document, zoom in and out, and print the document. If you want to make changes to what you see, click Cancel to close the window. Otherwise, continue to Step 2.

2. **Click Print.**

   The Print dialog box appears.

3. **Review and set the printing options, if necessary.**

   If you're not sure what these options are, see the earlier section "Setting options within the Print dialog box." If you're satisfied with the default settings, continue to Step 4. Otherwise, make changes to the print properties and page setup.

4. **Click OK to print.**

To print quickly within SolidWorks, open a document in View-Only mode and print. To do so, choose File➪Open and check View-Only in the Open dialog box, as shown in Figure 11-5. In View-Only mode, the document loads faster for viewing and printing, but you can't edit the document or see features in the FeatureManager design tree.

Figure 11-5: If you want to print quickly, open a document using the View-Only option in the Open dialog box.

The quickest means to print is to click the Print icon. Your document prints to the default printer using the current options.

Part IV

Playing Nicely with Others (And Picking Up Your Toys)

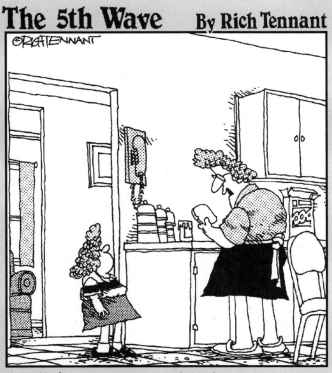

The 5th Wave   By Rich Tennant

"I don't care what your friends at school say. You are not redrawing plans for the house with Solidworks so that you can have a bigger room."

In this part . . .

Working well with others in the design process is a key to success. Your job of collaborating with team members, vendors, customers, and so on is easier and more effective when you know what data they need and how they need it formatted. In this part, I tell you everything you need to know about working with others, as well as introduce eDrawings and the SolidWorks Viewer.

Chapter 12

Managing the Clutter

Data is one of your company's most valuable assets. In an engineering company, that data includes not just CAD files, but project specifications, design review information, finite element analysis results, engineering change orders, and so on. This data constitutes the basis of your products, so managing it properly is important.

You can manage design data in two ways: automatically using product data management (PDM) software, or manually by setting up a system of file structures. This chapter tells you what to look for when you set up a PDM system and how to set up file directories to manage data manually in SolidWorks.

Managing Data with or without a Net

One of the most important decisions to make when you implement SolidWorks is how to manage the data. The safest bet (what I call managing with a net) is to implement product data management (PDM) software, which manages and tracks product data automatically. PDMWorks is the PDM software made to work with SolidWorks, but others on the market also work with SolidWorks.

However, if your design team is small, you can opt to organize your data manually with a system of file folders that you organize on a shared network server. You can also take advantage of SolidWorks collaboration settings, which allow you to control who has access to what data so that you can be sure that one person doesn't overwrite another's changes. (See Chapter 13 for more details on collaborating with others.)

Checking your list

Whether you choose to implement a PDM system or you decide to manage your data manually, consider this important checklist:

- **Ease of use:** I'm a firm believer that any system you want others to use should follow this rule of automation: It needs to be easy, offer value, and save time. Otherwise, no one is going to use it, or if they do use it, they'll use it so inconsistently that the value of the investment is lost.

- **Data security:** As anyone who has experienced a computer hard drive crash knows, data is never as valuable as when it's gone. In a multi-user environment, you want to put all your design data on a network server, develop a good backup plan, and stick to it.

- **Performance:** Working with large files over a network server can be slow. PDMWorks copies data onto a local workspace (on the user's computer) and updates the information to the server periodically. Do you have a similar plan for your manual system?

- **Search capabilities:** The ability to quickly find data is one of the most important features in a data management system. PDMWorks has search tools built in. With a manual approach, the best way to find data is to do a Windows Search by custom properties and filename.

- **Product life cycle:** Designs go through several revisions and changes throughout their life cycle (sort of like software). You need a system for tracking various versions and for storing documents that are in different development phases, such as in-progress, released, or obsolete.

- **Document access:** When working with other users on the same design project, you need to know who is working on what and when a new revision of a document is available. You also need a way to communicate that information back to other team members.

- **Meta data:** These custom properties, used in drawing title blocks, are stored in the document. Choose File⇨Properties and then click the Custom tab in the Summary Information dialog box to see which values are defined within each type of document.

- **File manipulation:** How does the system copy, rename, archive, and delete documents and projects?

- **Versioning:** How does the system handle old or legacy versions of documents? Does the system allow others to access old versions of drawings after a new change?

Deciding which way to go

The ways that you can manage your CAD data can be broken into three categories:

✔ **Manual,** such as a system of file folders that contain project data. It's best to keep such folders on a shared network server.

✔ **Workgroup-level PDM,** such as PDMWorks, is a simple, inexpensive, easy-to-deploy data management system.

✔ **Enterprise-level PDM,** such as SMARTeam from Dassault Systemes, provides advanced data management tools, such as work flow, integration into other corporate computer systems, and so on.

Each of these categories have pros and cons, which I list in Table 12-1.

Table 12-1   Pros and Cons of the Different Data Management Tools

Category	Pros	Cons
Manual	Simple. No additional software required.	Manual, error-prone process. Lack of search capabilities. Difficult to version (Rev A, B, and so on) and keep old design history.
Workgroup-level PDM	Easy to install. Less expensive application. Has a vault, or central database.	Limited advanced capabilities, API, and integration support.
Enterprise-level PDM	Scalable (size of installation and scope of application). Has more advanced features.	More expensive. Difficult to implement.

The rest of this chapter covers manual data management. While you don't need a PDM system to create great designs in SolidWorks, the process is easier and more straightforward when you do have one.

Personally, I think managing your data manually is time-consuming and can be like running around with sharp sticks. You take the risk of falling and jabbing yourself. Similarly, at some point, trying to manage multiple documents manually is a problem.

For more information about PDMWorks, visit www.solidworks.com/pages/products/solutions/pdmworks.html.

For more information about SMARTEAM, visit www.3ds.com/products-solutions/brands/SMARTEAM/.

Managing Your Data Manually

Whether you work alone or with a team of designers, if you don't have a PDM system, you need to manage files manually. In order for a manual system to be even remotely workable, you need to define some meaningful directory structure for storing projects and their related documents.

Here's an example of a directory structure setup in Windows:

- ✔ **Main-level directories:** Use these top-level directories to organize your data. You could have two top-level directories, one named Released (for documents that have been checked and approved) and one called WIP (for works in progress, copies of files being changed). When you're looking for released files, you know to look in the Released directory. Likewise, files that are being worked on are in the WIP directory.

- ✔ **Standard part directories:** If a lot of your work entails the use of standard parts, put the standard part models in a shared network drive so that others can access the files and use them in designs. You may want to make the directory read-only so that only the CAD administrator can make changes or additions.

- ✔ **Project-level directories:** Below the main directories could be another level of directory folders used to further organize the data. Examples of second-level directories include Standard (for standard parts), Projects (name project number), Part Numbers (setup directories based on part numbers), and Part Type (motors, brackets, and so on).

Having too many levels of directories can make documents hard to find. Try to keep it simple so that everyone can find what they're looking for fast.

When you name SolidWorks documents, it's best not to include the revision number in the filename. For example, don't name a plate model plate-RevA because any changes in plate-RevB will not reflect in any drawing or assembly file that references that part. You have broken the reference.

Copying Files

When you start a new project or revise an existing project, you need to copy files. You're better off making copies using SolidWorks Explorer, not Windows Explorer. Windows Explorer is not SolidWorks "aware," which means it can't identify document references. If you copy a SolidWorks drawing using Windows Explorer, the next time you open the drawing, you'll get a message telling you that the file cannot locate its references.

SolidWorks Explorer has the following advantages over Windows Explorer:

✔ You can copy, replace, and rename SolidWorks documents without breaking links to external reference documents. When you copy a drawing, for example, SolidWorks Explorer gives you the option to copy any part or assembly files that the drawing references.

✔ You can view and change the custom properties of a document.

✔ You can find out which other SolidWorks documents reference or use the file. If the file is a model of a standard component, you can find out what assembly designs are using the component. The limitation is that you can only search one directory at a time. You may need to change the directory and run the search again several times.

✔ You can operate the aforementioned functions without opening a SolidWorks document. This feature offers a performance advantage, especially when dealing with massive assembly files that take a long time to load.

You can run SolidWorks Explorer independent of SolidWorks. To copy a file in SolidWorks Explorer:

1. **Choose Start➪All Programs➪SolidWorks <version and service pack>.**

   The SolidWorks Explorer dialog box appears.

2. **Click the Browse button at the top-right corner of the dialog box and then browse to and choose the document you want to copy.**

3. **In the dialog box, choose Tools➪Edit➪Copy.**

   The Copy Document interface appears, as shown in Figure 12-1.

Figure 12-1: The best way to copy files is with SolidWorks Explorer.

4. **Select the Copy To (Folder:) Location and Copy To Name (To:).**

   To change the name of the document, enter a new name in the To: field. To change the copy to location, click the Browse button (right side of the Folder: field) and select the location to copy the files. To copy related documents, check Copy Children.

   Check Copy Children to locate documents that the drawing or assembly references. SolidWorks Explorer finds the child documents and adds them to the list automatically. Use Find Where Used to locate drawings associated with the document. To copy to a new location, browse to the desired location from the To: field.

5. **Click Apply.**

By default, the Copy To Name (To: field) defaults to the current directory with a new filename. To copy to a new location, use the Browse button in either the To: field or the Folder: field when Copy Children is selected. Either of these buttons will change the default directory. To use the same document names, remove the revision number at the end of the filename (file2.SLDPRT).

Always remember to leave the Prefix/Suffix text field blank when copying files with SolidWorks Explorer. Otherwise, the filenames are changed.

When it comes to manual data management, remember two things: First, back up your data regularly. In fact, you may want to back up data to another building location in case your office disappears in a flood, fire, or earthquake and you need to go to work the next day.

Second, when you need to make a change to a document, make sure that you don't edit the production copy. You should have a separate directory where you keep original copies for later reference. It's a bad day when your boss asks for revision B, and all you have to show is revision E.

Keep non-SolidWorks copies (such as eDrawings or PDF files) of all your released drawings. This way, you have a simple backup and additional .references for all released drawings.

Chapter 13

Collaborating with Team Members

- -

In This Chapter

▶ Setting up SolidWorks for a multi-user environment

▶ Working with standard components

▶ Swapping data with other CAD systems

▶ Fixing models with import errors

- -

As a designer, rarely will you find yourself working on a design alone. More likely, you'll be part of an extended design team, with members spread out across the country or around the world. In a multi-user environment, keeping projects on a network server allows everyone to access the files. At the same time, you need to control who is working on what so that one person doesn't overwrite another's changes. You also want to store common design elements in a design library to save time and rework.

This chapter introduces SolidWorks tools that allow you to collaborate and work with other designers in a multi-user environment.

Keeping Everyone on the Same Page when Collaborating

In a *multi-user environment,* multiple designers are accessing and revising assembly files at the same time. One of the biggest issues in such a situation is figuring out how to manage the data. A SolidWorks assembly can include hundreds of part and subassembly documents, manufacturing drawings, and other engineering material. And to complicate things even more, many of the documents reference other documents, so one change can ripple through thousands of other documents. For this reason, you need to keep a close watch on who modifies what and when, or an entire project can go down the gurgler.

Many people use *project data management* (PDM) software to manage data in a multi-user environment. PDMWorks is a PDM software that runs inside the

SolidWorks environment. PDMWorks stores documents in project directories in a vault (usually on a server). And it controls projects with procedures for check out, check in, revision control, and other administrative tasks.

Not everyone feels the pull to go the PDM route. If your design team includes only a few members and you're not yet ready for the additional software investment, you can opt to manage your data manually by placing the data on a server (or otherwise making it available on a network) and setting up Windows folders for different projects.

SolidWorks offers tools to manage access to data in a multi-user environment where there is no PDM system. One of those tools is the *Collaboration Mode* option.

When enabled, Collaboration Mode offers several advantages:

- **Allows you to mark parts and subassemblies for read and write access.** *Read-only* means that users can review the parts and subassemblies but cannot make changes to them. If someone tries to make a change, a message warns that the document is read-only. Users can modify only documents marked write-access.

- **Identifies who is working on what.** With the assembly open, a ToolTip in the FeatureManager design tree informs you, via visual clues on the component icons, whether a part or subassembly is write-access or read-only. If another user with write-access has a document open, a ToolTip names the user.

- **Notifies when items are modified.** In File Explorer, modified files appear in bold, read-only files appear in orange, and write-access documents appear in black. Icons for files open in SolidWorks are solid. Icons for referenced components that are in memory but not open are transparent. The File Explorer tab (see Figure 13-1) is in the SolidWorks Resource Task Pane located to the right of the graphics display.

Figure 13-1: In File Explorer, icons for files open in SolidWorks appear solid.

Setting the Collaboration Mode options

Okay, so you've decided to manage your data manually. You'll be fine as long as your design team is relatively small, and you set up a system that others can follow. First, be sure to put project data in a central location, such as a networked server, so that others can access it. Next, organize your projects in Windows folders. (Read more about organizing projects in file directories in Chapter 12.) Finally, turn on Collaboration Mode in SolidWorks to ensure that one person doesn't inadvertently overwrite another's changes when you're working on the same assembly. Collaboration Mode allows you to set documents as read-only or write-access.

Here's how to set up Collaboration Mode:

1. **Choose Tools⇨Options.**

   A dialog box appears. If you have a document open, it contains two tabs (see Figure 13-2). If no document is open, only the Systems Option tab appears.

2. **In the System Option tab, click Collaboration.**

   The Collaboration Mode options appear in the right panel.

3. **Select the check box for Enable Multi-User Environment.**

   After you select this option, other options become available.

4. **Select the check boxes for these two other options:**

   - **Add shortcut menu items for multi-user environment.** Checking this option adds menu items for Make Read-Only and Get Write Access that are accessible when you right-click an assembly component in the FeatureManager design tree. You can now switch the read and write access of any document with a single right-click.

   - **Check if files opened read-only have been modified by other users:** When this option is enabled, at a time interval you specify (the default is every 20 minutes), SolidWorks checks files that you've opened as read-only to see whether they'be been modified in one of the following ways: Another user saves a file that you have open in SolidWorks, making your file out of date or another user relinquishes write access to the file that you have open in SolidWorks by making the file read-only, allowing you to take write access. If the system detects a change, a tooltip in the lower right graphics area points to an icon on the status bar. Click the icon to access the Reload dialog box.

5. **Click OK.**

Figure 13-2:
Collabora-
tion Mode
allows you
to manage
access to
documents.

Switching read/write access

Collaboration Mode allows you to make any assembly component read-only or write access. Here's how to weld your power:

1. **Open the assembly document.**

   A list of components appears in the FeatureManager design tree.

2. **Right-click a component in the FeatureManager design tree.**

   A pull-down menu appears.

3. **Choose Get Write Access or Make Read-Only.**

   The part changes to write-access or read-only.

If you want to check whether anyone has updated one of the documents in your current assembly, click Check Read-Only Files on the Standard toolbar, as shown in Figure 13-3. If the files haven't changed, a message appears. If any files have changed, the Reload dialog box appears. This dialog box gives you the choice of reloading modified items into your current session or reloading the original version of a document without exiting SolidWorks.

Figure 13-3:
Read-only
files appear
on the
Standard
toolbar.

Covering the bases (external references)

In SolidWorks, many documents reference others. For example, an assembly may reference dozens of part and subassembly documents. Any change to one of those external references may affect the assembly. The External Reference option in SolidWorks automatically marks as read-only any documents that an assembly references while you have that assembly open. Here's how you activate this feature in SolidWorks.

1. **Choose Tools⇨Options.**

   A dialog box appears with one or two tabs, depending on whether or not you have a document open.

2. **In the dialog box that appears, select the System Options tab.**

   The System Options options appear.

3. **Select External References.**

   The External References options appear in the right pane, as shown in Figure 13-4.

4. **Select the check boxes for the following options:**

   - **Open referenced documents with read-only access.** When you check this option, SolidWorks makes all referenced documents read-only by default.

   - **Don't prompt to save read-only referenced documents (discard changes).** Specifies that when you save or close a parent document, SolidWorks doesn't prompt you to save its read-only reference documents. (Otherwise, the multitude of prompts can get really annoying.)

5. **Click OK.**

Figure 13-4:
You can set External References options so that SolidWorks doesn't prompt to save any read-only references of an assembly.

Exploring Standard Design Elements

Whenever possible, re-use information. Redesigning standard components is a waste of time, especially if the supplier makes component models available through online supplier catalogs. Likewise with features that your design team uses over and over again. Find or build the components once and then put them somewhere where everyone can grab a copy. Inside the SolidWorks Design Library tab of the SolidWorks task pane (see Figure 13-5) are three folders where you can store standard components and design elements for use by your entire design team. Here's a brief description of each:

✔ **SolidWorks Design Library:** Located in a separate folder (of the same name) inside the Design Library tab, where you can store company-standard features, annotations, and components.

✔ **SolidWorks Toolbox:** Contains a library of standard hardware (bolts, nuts, washers, standoffs, and so on) that integrate with the SolidWorks software.

✔ **3D ContentCentral:** Has links to component supplier Web sites and a library where SolidWorks users can share CAD models that they design.

Figure 13-5:
The SolidWorks Design Library stores standard design elements.

Inside the Design Library

The Design Library (which you should put on a shared network server if you work in a multi-user environment) is a place for you to store the design components and elements that you use most often. It contains separate folders for parts, assemblies, features, and so on. SolidWorks supplies content for these folders, but you can add new folders and customize existing ones by adding your own content over time.

One criteria I use to decide whether a part belongs in the Design Library or in the PDM vault (if you use PDM software) is whether your organization has design control over the part. If you designed the part and need to maintain a design history of it, then put the part in the PDM vault. If the component is a purchased part, it's a good candidate for the Design Library.

Finding your way around in the Design Library is pretty straightforward. The following command buttons are available in the Design Library tab:

- ✔ **Add File Location:** Adds an existing folder to the Design Library.
- ✔ **Create New Folder:** Creates a new folder in the Design Library.
- ✔ **Refresh:** Refreshes the view of the Design Library tab.
- ✔ **Search:** Searches the Design Library local view or 3D ContentCentral.

If you want to use an item in the Design Library, simply select the item and drag it onto your design. Similarly, you can also drag items from your design into folders in the Design Library. When you drag an item into a folder, the Save As dialog box appears with the item's default file type. You only need to type an optional part description and click Save.

Design Library folders accept all document types. You can save a part file in a folder marked "assemblies" just as you can put socks in your underwear drawer. The folder names are only there to keep you organized.

Here are a few other ways to copy design elements into the Design Library:

- ✔ **To copy an assembly or part into the Design Library:** Select the item in the FeatureManager design tree and drag it to an appropriate folder in the lower pane of the Design Library tab.
- ✔ **To copy annotations or blocks into the Design Library:** Hold down the Shift key on your keyboard and drag the annotation or block from the graphics area to the lower plane of the Design Library.
- ✔ **To copy a feature into the Design Library:** Drag the feature from the FeatureManager design tree or the graphics area. Features are saved as library feature parts with the extension `.sldlfp`.

By default, SolidWorks installs the Design Library in C:\Program Files\ SolidWorks\data\design library. If you plan to use SolidWorks in a multi-user environment, copy the Design Library to a network directory and make it read-only so that only the system administrator can make changes.

Using SolidWorks Toolbox

If you're like me, you keep a box of nails, screws, and other parts that you can reach into whenever you need to fix or build something at home. You don't want to run to the hardware store each time you need a nut or a bolt. SolidWorks has something similar: a virtual toolbox.

SolidWorks Toolbox includes a library of standard fasteners (bolts, nuts, chain sprockets, timing belts, and so on) that you can add to your SolidWorks assembly. Here's how Toolbox works: Say that you want to attach a hinge to a door or fasten a waste pipe to a sink. Simply select the standard screws and washers included in SolidWorks Toolbox and drag them into your design. This way, you don't have to make additional parts to complete your assembly.

Searching for a bolt or a nut in Toolbox is like thumbing through the pages of a part catalog. Similar to a catalog, SolidWorks Toolbox folders are broken down into standards (ANSI, BSI, CISC, and so on), categories (washers, pins, screws), and types (lag screws, machine screws, miniature screws).

SolidWorks fills Toolbox folders with some standard items, but you can customize Toolbox to include those parts that you refer to most frequently. You can also make a copy of any Toolbox part and edit it as needed.

SolidWorks Toolbox is a SolidWorks add-in, which means it isn't available with the standard SolidWorks program. You have to buy it separately or as part of the SolidWorks Professional and SolidWorks Premium bundles. Once you install Toolbox, open SolidWorks and choose Tools⇨Add Ins. In the Add-Ins dialog box, check the SolidWorks Toolbox and the SolidWorks Toolbox Browser. Click OK.

Inserting the hardware

You can easily add fasteners to your assembly by dragging them out of Toolbox and dropping them into your model. You can also configure fasteners to your exact needs. Here's how to edit a Toolbox fastener and insert it into your open assembly:

1. **Click the Design Library icon on the SolidWorks task pane.**

   The task pane displays the contents of the Design Library.

2. **Click the Toolbox folder.**

   The Toolbox folder expands to reveal several folders that represent standard part catalogs.

3. **Click the + sign to the right of a standard folder.**

   The folder expands to reveal more folders. Instead of thumbing through catalogs, you drill down through the folders (standards, categories, types, fasteners) until you find the fastener you need.

4. **Drill down through the folders to find the fastener you need.**

5. **Right-click the part you want and choose Create Part.**

   A dialog box for the part you selected appears (see Figure 13-6). You can use this dialog box to set the property values for the part or to change the part number or to add a description before adding the part to the assembly.

6. **Find the Property you want to update and then select a value from the pull-down list next to it.**

   For parts included with SolidWorks Toolbox, the values in the list are valid standards-based values for the selected part.

7. **Continue to update the remaining properties and values until the size is correct.**

8. **Click OK.**

   The part appears in the assembly.

Figure 13-6:
You can use Toolbox to insert standard fasteners into an assembly.

SolidWorks marks a Toolbox file with an attribute (IsFastener) that identifies the file as a fastener. If you add new components to Toolbox, you can run a utility to mark the new files as Toolbox content. You can find this utility at *<SolidWorks install directory>*\Toolbox\data utilities\sldsetdocprop.exe. Open the utility and select the Toolbox directory that you want to update using the Add Files or Add Directories button. Browse to the directory and click OK. Select Update Status to update the document property.

Adding fasteners the smart way

Toolbox allows for the use of SmartFasteners, a SolidWorks feature that automatically inserts bolts and screws into your assembly where there is a hole, hole series, or pattern of holes (see Figure 13-7) sized to accept the standard hardware. SmartFasteners use fasteners that come from the Toolbox library, but you can also add your own custom designs to the Toolbox database and use them within SmartFasteners.

SmartFasteners can also add nuts and washers to your fasteners. Bolts and screws can have an associated Top Stack (washers under the head of the fastener) and Bottom Stack (washers and nuts added to the end of the fastener).

You can use SmartFasteners to insert bolts, screws, nuts, and washers to your assembly in a few simple steps, as shown in Figure 13-7.

Figure 13-7: Smart-Fasteners add fasten-ers to an assembly automat-ically.

To add SmartFasteners to an open assembly:

1. **Choose Insert⇨SmartFasteners.**

   The SmartFastener PropertyManager appears.

2. **If you want to add fasteners to all holes in the assembly, under Selections, click Populate All.**

   SmartFasteners fills the holes in your assembly with fasteners.

   If you're working on a very large assembly, SolidWorks may prompt you with the message: "This operation may take a long time. Do you want to continue?" If you have time on your hands, click Yes and skip to **Step 5**. Otherwise, click No and proceed to Step 3.

3. **If you want to add fasteners to only certain areas of your assembly, select a hole (or holes), a face, or a component.**

   The selected items appear under Selection. If you want to remove an item, select the item and press the Delete key.

4. **To add fasteners to the items, select Add under Selections.**

   Fasteners are added to the items you selected. If you selected a compo-nent, SmartFasteners finds all available holes in that component. If you selected a face, SmartFasteners finds all available holes that pass through the surface. Fastener types appear under Fastener.

5. **If you want to change a fastener type or the top or bottom stacks, under Fasteners, right-click the item and select Change Fastener Type.**

The SmartFastener dialog box for the fastener type displays.

6. **Select a replacement fastener by using the pull-down menus in the Standard, Category, Type, and Fastener boxes.**

7. **Click OK.**

The Smart Fastener dialog box closes, and the model updates with the new fastener types.

8. **Click OK (the green checkmark).**

The Smart Fastener PropertyManager closes.

A place for sharing: 3D ContentCentral

It's a waste of time to design standard parts when you can find ready-made CAD models online. 3D ContentCentral helps you find the part models you need in a format you can use. It's an online resource that offers direct access to time-saving CAD models from leading suppliers and from individual SolidWorks users worldwide. 3D ContentCentral has two main areas:

✔ **Supplier content:** The Supplier Content folder provides links to the Web sites of suppliers who use SolidWorks 3DPartStream.net to create their online part catalogs. Some of the part models in the catalogs are configurable so that you can tailor them to suit your needs.

✔ **User library:** In this section, you can share parts with other designers. You can download a ready-made part model to use in your design or post one of your own for others to access. When you post a component, your name appears on the download page of that part.

Anyone can access 3D ContentCentral at www.3dcontentcentral.com. The benefit of getting there directly from the inside of SolidWorks is that you don't have to register to use the site. (Some individual supplier sites, however, do require a separate registration to download the models.)

To use a component from 3D ContentCentral:

1. **In the SolidWorks task pane, click the Design Library tab (see Figure 13-8).**

2. **Click the + to expand the 3D Content Central folder.**

Icons appear for Supplier Content and User Library.

Figure 13-8:
You can access 3D Content-Central from the Design Library.

3. **Select Supplier Content or User Library.**

   In the lower pane, folders appear for part categories, such as Air Filters, Ball Screws, Conveyors, and so on.

4. **Click a folder for the part category you want.**

   If you're looking under Supplier Content, after you click a category in the lower pane, you see icons with Supplier Names on them. These icons are links to the supplier Web sites.

   If you're looking in the User Library, in the lower pane, you see additional part categories. These categories are actually links to Web pages that contain the user parts that you can download.

5. **Click a supplier name or a subcategory.**

   If you click a supplier name, a Web browser opens in SolidWorks and you're taken to the supplier's online part catalog, where you see a selection of parts to peruse. Supplier sites vary slightly, and some allow you to configure components to your specifications (see Figure 13-9).

   If you select a subcategory in the User Library, you see a Web page that contains a list of parts. Under Contributed By, you see the name of the user who designed that part. Some users include their e-mail address. You also see a detailed description of the part and an image of the model. Click a model to download it.

6. **Locate a part and click the Download tab.**

   After you click the Download tab, you can choose the file format that you want to download. In the User Library, the models are generally offered in only the SolidWorks format.

7. **When the part is ready, click and drag the file into your assembly.**

8. **Close the Internet Browser window.**

If you want to submit a model to the 3D ContentCentral User Library, right-click 3D ContentCentral and choose Share a Model. Follow the directions on-screen to enter your profile information and upload your model. SolidWorks Corporation reviews your model and informs you whether the model has been accepted for sharing.

The SolidWorks Resources task pane includes an engineering search engine that you can use to locate engineering-related topics that you want to read about. The search is conducted by the GLOBALSPEC search engine.

Figure 13-9: Some supplier sites allow you to configure components before you download them.

Working with Different File Formats

At times, you may need to exchange files with people who use other CAD systems or no CAD system at all. For example, you may need to communicate with a vendor who doesn't accept native SolidWorks files or to show a design to a customer (or someone in your own internal marketing department) who doesn't have access to a CAD system.

It pays to become familiar with the different translation formats so that you can send and receive information easily, without the extra work of having to verify and clean up imported documents.

In general, you need to be familiar with four important topics, which I cover in the following sections:

✔ **Types of formats:** Knowing the different types of CAD and image formats that you can use makes life easier when transferring SolidWorks documents.

✔ **Exporting files:** Understanding how to send documents to other systems *(exporting)*.

✔ **Importing files:** Understanding how to work with documents sent from other systems *(importing)*.

✔ **Fixing import and export issues:** Discovering how to fix issues with imported data if the need arises.

Types and uses of data formats

During your career as a designer, whether you work on a team or as a lone contractor out of your home, you may run across many occasions to swap files with other people. Here are a few reasons that I've encountered:

✔ A supplier wants to send you a CAD model of a standard component so that you can check it for fit and clearance within your assembly.

✔ You need to export a file to a customer for review and approval.

✔ Your internal marketing department wants a graphic image of the model to create advertising materials for print products and the Web site.

✔ A supplier needs 3D data of the product to program his computer-aided manufacturing (CAM) software with.

✔ The shop floor wants a manufacturing drawing of the product so that it can see how to assemble the product.

✔ A customer sends you an existing DWG or DXF sketch of the product that you need to import into SolidWorks and base a model on.

Lucky for you, SolidWorks can import and export in several different file formats so that you can share files with other users. Table 13-1 describes the categories that data formats fall into.

Table 13-1	Data File Format Categories
Name	*Description*
SolidWorks	Native SolidWorks documents (parts, assemblies, drawings, library features, templates, and so on).
eDrawings	A lightweight 2D and 3D viewing format. You can publish an eDrawings file from inside of SolidWorks or any major CAD system.

Name	Description
Neutral	Neutral 2D and 3D file formats are nonsystem specific and include DXF, DWG, IGES, STEP, ACIS, and Parasolid.
Vendor specific	Formats native to other systems (AutoDesk Inventor, Unigraphics, Solid Edge, and so on).
Graphical	Image formats (JPEG, TIFF, and so on).

How you save your SolidWorks document depends on the recipient's plans for the document and his type of system. If the recipient uses SolidWorks, you can send him a native SolidWorks file. But if you only want him to get a general idea of the model, you might send an eDrawings file. While SolidWorks supports many different files formats, keep in mind the following:

- Use SolidWorks native files whenever possible.

- If the other system is Parasolid-based (Unigraphics NX and SolidEdge), use the Parasolid format. Because SolidWorks is also built on the Parasolid kernel, it makes sense to send in the neutral Parasolid format.

- Consider sending more than one neutral format (IGES and STEP) when working with a new supplier to allow for troubleshooting in case one file doesn't convert properly.

Exporting SolidWorks files

When you export a SolidWorks document, all you're really doing is saving it in a different format using the Save As dialog box. To export a file for use in another program:

1. **Open the file to export and choose File⇨Save As.**

   The Save As Document dialog box appears.

2. **From the Save As Type drop-down list, choose the format you want to save the file in.**

   If you're not sure of the best format to use, refer to Table 13-1.

3. **Click Save.**

   Your document saves in the new format. The actual "exporting" is up to you. Depending on the size of the file and your time constraints, you can send the file via e-mail or snail mail, post it on an FTP site, or hand the job over to an overnight courier service.

Importing non-SolidWorks files

When you're working with other members of your design team, importing files is no problem because they all use SolidWorks. Trouble arises when you receive *non-native files,* which are files created in another system, such as Mechanical Desktop, Pro/Engineer or SolidEdge, or when you receive intermediary 3D file types, such as IGES or STEP.

CAD files can be large and complicated. It isn't uncommon for a CAD program to have difficulty interpreting information that arrives in a different format. Most problems occur because a CAD system has trouble recreating faces or edges on the model when importing the file. (The next section on problem-solving covers how to correct this type of issues.)

To import a file from another application:

1. **Choose File⇨Open.**

   The Open Document dialog box appears.

2. **In the dialog box, select a file type in Files of Type (for example DWG, IGES, STL, and so on).**

   Check the file extension of the file you're importing. If the filename is Newpart.dwg, use the DWG file format.

3. **Browse to select the file that you want to open and click Open.**

   Your file opens inside of SolidWorks.

   If you're importing a DXF or DWG file, the DXF/DWG Import Wizard appears. You can choose to edit the file in the DWGEditor or to import it to a sheet in a native format (view only) in addition to importing it to a part or drawing document.

   If you import an IGES, STEP, or other 3D file that contains surfaces, SolidWorks reads the surfaces as follows:

   • If the file has surfaces that are hidden, SolidWorks imports the surfaces and adds them to the FeatureManager design tree as surface features.

   • If SolidWorks is able to knit the surfaces into a solid, the solid appears as the base feature (named imported 1) in a new part file. You can add features (bosses, cuts, and so on) to this base feature, but you cannot edit the base feature itself.

- If the surfaces represent multiple closed volumes, then one part is made for each closed volume. An assembly file also is made that includes the imported parts positioned relative to the assembly origin, according to how the surfaces are defined in the imported file. For ACIS files, if the imported ACIS file consists of surfaces only, then SolidWorks creates only surfaces even though the surfaces represent multiple closed volumes, regardless of the import options you choose. If the ACIS file consists of data about multiple solid bodies, SolidWorks creates parts or surfaces, depending on the import option you choose.

- If SolidWorks isn't able to knit the surfaces together, the surfaces are grouped into one or more surface features (named Surface-Imported 1, 2, and so on) in a new part file.

Problem-solving

Things don't always go smooth when importing documents. Errors can occur for a number of reasons. The problem may have to do with the method the other system used to write the document, how SolidWorks reads the file, or an incompatible feature type in the neutral file. When you import from another system and you get a surface body instead of a solid body, it's an indication that SolidWorks had trouble reading the file and turning the surfaces into a solid body. Bad surface geometry, gaps in surfaces, or surfaces that overlap can all cause these problems. Fortunately, SolidWorks has an Import Diagnostics tool that can help you identify and fix problems.

Here's how you can tell that a file hasn't imported properly:

✔ After importing the file, SolidWorks displays a warning and a prompt to open the diagnostic function, as shown in Figure 13-10.

✔ After SolidWorks opens the part, a warning or error appears next to an imported feature in the FeatureManager design tree.

Figure 13-10:
SolidWorks warns you when a file doesn't import properly.

The Diagnosis tool diagnoses and repairs gaps and faces on imported features. To diagnose and fix or simplify faces:

1. **Right-click the imported feature in the FeatureManager design tree and choose Diagnosis.**

2. **In the PropertyManager, under Faces, click Diagnose.**

   Faces that are faulty or that require simplification are highlighted in the graphics area and appear in the Faces to Be Fixed/Removed section.

3. **Move the pointer over a face in the list to display a ToolTip that reports the problem with that face.**

4. **Click Fix to simplify that face.**

   The diagnosis automatically finds faulty faces and spline curves/surfaces that it can simplify to analytical features for operations such as sheet metal creation and assembly mating.

To simplify entities with a tolerance greater than 1.0e-8 meters and less than 1.0e-5 meters, you must manually select the relevant faces and then click Fix.

1. **Select the two faces in the graphics area.**

2. **Click Fix.**

   If the two faces are meant to be one (for example, the two halves of a cylindrical face), the two faces merge. The diagnosis performs an in-depth check on all the entities in a model.

3. **Click OK.**

   If the imported body still shows rebuild error markers even though a body check and the Import Diagnosis PropertyManager report no surface problems, the body is probably valid.

4. **Click Rebuild to clear the rebuild error markers.**

   You can merge multiple edges into a single edge with Heal Edges on the Features toolbar. To view and fix gaps:

   a. Right-click the Imported feature in the FeatureManager design tree and choose Diagnosis.

   b. In the PropertyManager, under Gaps, click Diagnose.

      The PropertyManager reports the number of Gaps found.

   c. View and fix the gaps using the View/Close Gaps tools.

   d. Click OK.

If you run into a dead end and, no matter how hard you try, the methods in this section don't seem to fix the problem, here are some ideas:

- Call the sender and ask him to send you a native format if possible.

- Ask for another file type or another version of the file format.

- Use a direct translator (available through SolidWorks partners).

- Manually identify and clean up the problem areas using the import diagnostics described in this section and then remove and re-create the faces in question.

Chapter 14

Viewing and Reviewing Documents

Sharing your design with others doesn't mean that you have to continually send huge CAD files via overnight courier services. Instead, you can take advantage of CAD viewers to save time and be more efficient. CAD viewers allow people without CAD licenses to view, mark up, and measure your CAD design without having to own or operate any expensive or complex software.

Imagine, for example, that you want to send a model of your stovetop espresso maker to a vendor to see if the vendor can manufacture it. You can e-mail a lightweight version of the model so that the vendor can take measurements, add comments, and e-mail it back to you the next day.

In this chapter, I introduce you to two CAD viewers that let you look at SolidWorks drawings, parts, and assembly documents: eDrawings and the SolidWorks Viewer.

I also briefly touch on graphic files and embedded and linked documents so that you know how to include SolidWorks documents in your presentations.

Viewing with CAD Viewers

When you work with other design team members, vendors, or customers, the ability to communicate design ideas quickly is key. But sometimes you don't want to, need to, or simply can't send someone an entire SolidWorks file.

CAD (computer-aided design) files, for example, tend to be very large (a SolidWorks assembly can easily reach 150MB), which makes them cumbersome and tricky to send. And they contain propriety information, so you don't want to send your CAD files to just anybody. You may want to send someone only enough information to take accurate measurements or to see how an assembly fits together.

CAD viewers help this process. A *CAD viewer* lets you look at 2D and 3D design data in its non-native format, without having to own or operate complicated or expensive CAD software. (Not that SolidWorks is either of those things, but a less technical person may consider it so.)

Two CAD viewers — eDrawings and the SolidWorks Viewer — allow you to review and print SolidWorks documents in a non-native format. Both viewers are free and available at the SolidWorks Web site (`www.solidworks.com`).

Here are a few scenarios where a CAD viewer may come in handy:

- **Requesting quotes from vendors:** You can send a compressed eDrawing file (see "Communicating with eDrawings," later in this chapter) to a vendor who can then use the markup tools in eDrawings to request changes or additions.

- **Virtual design reviews:** What better way to distribute design data than in an e-mail? CAD viewers give you that advantage. Your design team can view a document, mark it up, and send back comments.

- **Customer presentations:** Your customers don't want to invest in SolidWorks just to see your works of art. A CAD viewer lets a customer view a CAD file without having any special knowledge of CAD. And if you send your customer an eDrawings file, a special animation feature plays the design so that it rotates automatically through different orientations.

- **Engineering change notices:** Design engineers spend their entire careers making changes to designs. A CAD viewer can make it easier to check and approve designs and send back comments.

Keep in mind that CAD viewers aren't the only way to present your design brilliance to people. Graphic formats (such as TIF, BMP, and JPEG) are great for sharing, too. The only problem is that they're flat images that contain no real CAD data, so you can't measure them or check for mass properties.

Communicating with eDrawings

eDrawings is a free e-mail-enabled program included with SolidWorks that lets you share designs with the people who need to see them, no matter what CAD program they have — or don't have. eDrawings is easy to use and comes in two parts, a Viewer and a Publisher. A Professional version includes additional capabilities to mark up and measure a model. The standard Viewer and Publisher are free, but you have to pay for the Professional version.

You can download the standard eDrawings Viewer and Publisher or the Professional version of eDrawings at `www.eDrawingsViewer.com`. If you download the Publisher or the Professional version, the Viewer downloads automatically, so you don't have to download it again. You need the Viewer to save any eDrawings files you publish in your CAD system.

eDrawings Publishers are available for SolidWorks and most major CAD systems. Anyone with the eDrawing Viewer can read an eDrawing file.

Using eDrawings offers you many advantages:

✔ The eDrawings Viewer reads and prints any eDrawings file, native SolidWorks drawing, part, and assembly files, and DWG and DXF drawing files.

✔ The eDrawings Publisher produces a lightweight, compressed format, making your CAD design small enough to send in an e-mail.

✔ While an eDrawings file hides proprietary data, it retains external graphical details as well as the dimensions and mass properties of your model. This feature makes eDrawings accurate enough for proper measurements.

✔ You can send an eDrawings file with a built-in viewer in a self-extracting e-mail. The recipient just double-clicks the attachment, and the CAD model or drawing appears.

✔ With the extra collaboration features included in eDrawings Professional, you can measure and mark up files, add comments, and manage markups from other design team members.

✔ eDrawings also offers several tools that give you a better understanding of the design. A Play button moves the model or drawing through different views automatically. You can interrogate the model and examine it up close with Zoom, Rotate, and Pan functions.

eDrawings Viewer has two user interface (UI) modes — Simplified and Complete — and you can toggle between them. The Simplified UI, shown in Figure 14-1, hides the markup, measure, and eDrawings Manager tabs. Unless you're using these features, the Simplified UI is easier to use.

Creating an eDrawings file

With eDrawings Publisher, you can publish native SolidWorks documents as eDrawings files, which anyone can view with the free eDrawings Viewer. Because the eDrawing Publisher is a SolidWorks add-in, a Publish eDrawings 2006 File command icon appears in the SolidWorks main toolbar.

Figure 14-1:
The Simplified UI is an easier way to work with eDrawings files, unless you're using the markup, measure, or eDrawings Manager tabs.

eDrawings 2006 comes standard with SolidWorks, but just like other add-ins, you need to select it in the Add-Ins dialog box so that it appears in the SolidWorks Standard toolbar. In SolidWorks, choose Tools⇨Add-Ins. When the Add-Ins dialog box appears, select eDrawings, and click OK. To publish an eDrawings file from within SolidWorks:

1. **Open the drawing, part, or assembly file that you want to publish.**

2. **Choose File⇨Publish eDrawings 2006 File.**

   The eDrawings Viewer appears, displaying the new eDrawings file you just created.

   Your file doesn't save automatically. You must save it using the eDrawings Viewer (see the next step).

3. **Within the eDrawings Viewer, choose File⇨Save As.**

   The Save As dialog box appears.

4. **In the Save In drop-down list, browse to the location where you want to save the document.**

5. **Enter the name for the file in the File Name field.** The default name is based on the original SolidWorks document. To change the name, type a new name for the file.

6. **In Save As Type, select the file format you want to save the file as.**

   Your choices include Edrw, EPRT, or EASM formats.

7. **Check any other options you want to apply.**

   Depending on the file type you're saving, other options include the following:

   - **Save with simplified UI:** eDrawings lets you toggle between a simplified user interface and a complicated one with more toolbars open. When saving a file as ZIP, EXE, or HTML, you can save the file so that it opens to the simplified UI. You can't check this option when saving in the eDrawing format.

   - **Save with shaded area** (drawings only): This option saves the shaded data from a drawing in the eDrawings file.

   - **Allow STL export** (parts and assemblies only): This option allows the recipient to save the eDrawings file as an STL (stereolithography) file for output on a rapid prototype machine.

   - **Enable measure:** If you have eDrawings Professional, by checking this option you enable the recipient to measure your design.

8. **Click Save.**

Sending an eDrawings file

A benefit that sets eDrawings apart is the ability to send a file with the eDrawings Viewer encapsulated in an e-mail. This way, the receiver has nothing to download. He simply clicks the attachment, and the eDrawings drawing or model appears. Firewalls don't like executable files because they look like virus attachments; however, eDrawings offers several sending options to ensure that your file gets through.

To send an eDrawings file:

1. **Open the eDrawings file in the eDrawings Viewer.**

2. **Choose File⇨Send.**

   The Send As dialog box appears.

3. **Choose how you want to save your file.**

   Your options include the following:

- **eDrawings file (.edrw, .eprt. or .easm):** Allows you to send as an eDrawings file. The recipient needs to install the eDrawings Viewer, but this is the best option for the smallest file size.

- **Zip file (.zip):** Creates a firewall-friendly zip file that contains the self-extracting eDrawings Viewer, but the recipient needs to have the software to unzip the viewer.

- **HTML file (.htm):** Displays the eDrawings file within a firewall-safe HTML Web page that the recipient can view with Internet Explorer. Installs the Viewer automatically.

- **Executable file (.exe).** Creates a self-executable file with the Viewer attached. The least firewall friendly option, it's also the most likely to have the recipient's antivirus program strip it from the e-mail. The file is larger (1.4MB) due to the embedded viewer.

 4. **Click Save.**

    eDrawings generates an outgoing e-mail with the file attached.

 5. **Type the recipient's e-mail address and click Send.**

Measuring and marking up

The standard version of the eDrawings Viewer includes interrogation tools (Spin, Pan, and Zoom) that allow you to get a closer look at a design. But if you want the collaboration tools, including the ability to mark up and measure, you need to get your hands on the Professional version.

A unique feature of eDrawings Professional is that it automatically publishes eDrawings files as *review-enabled.* Anyone who receives a review-enabled file — whether they have the Professional version or not — can use the mark-up and measure functions in the eDrawings Viewer. This feature lets other designers, customers, or vendors use these advanced tools without having to purchase the Professional version.

If you only want the receiver to see certain measurements and not others, you can disable the eDrawings Measure tool (in the eDrawings Save As dialog box, leave the Enable Measure option unchecked) and use basic dimensions to indicate the length, width, diameter, and so on of your model.

Measuring a model

The Measure tool is a handy feature of eDrawings. Vendors often need accurate measurements of your product. For example, a vendor who makes packaging may need to measure your television design to make sure that it fits inside the Styrofoam packaging that he's designing.

In order to measure a model, the eDrawings file that you're viewing must be Measure enabled. Look for a measuring tape icon in the bottom-right corner of the user interface. A red line through it means that measurement is disabled.

To measure an eDrawings file in the eDrawings Viewer:

1. **Choose File⇨Open to open the eDrawings file you want to measure.**

2. **Choose Tools⇨Measure.**

   The Measure tab appears in the eDrawings Manager.

3. **Move the pointer to the graphics area.**

   The pointer changes to a measuring tool. When the pointer detects a potential measurement starting point, that starting point is highlighted. Points are highlighted with an X image, edges and the borders of faces are highlight with thick solid lines, and holes are highlighted with a circle with a plus sign in the middle.

4. **Click to set the measurement starting point.**

   Your starting point appears in the Selected Items box in the Measure tab.

5. **Move the pointer over the second point, edge, or face.**

   A measure line appears as you drag the pointer.

6. **Click again.**

   The measurement appears in the graphics area, as well as under Distance in the Results box of the Measure tab. The second item appears in the Selected Items box. In the Units box, the unit of measurement defaults to the file setting or Millimeters if no file setting exists.

Marking up your eDrawings file

If you want to communicate and collaborate with other members of your design team, you can use Markup tools in eDrawings Professional (see Table 14-1). Using the Markup functions, you can add notes, dimensions, text, and graphic elements to the model (see Figure 14-2). In the Markup tab, you have room to include more lengthy descriptions and comments on the model.

The Markup tools also contain a comment section, shown in Figure 14-3, where you can reply to, accept, or reject comments of others (see Table 14-2). eDrawings automatically saves markup files as threaded comments with the eDrawings file. You can also save markup data separately without the models. Reviewers can add their comments and send only the markup file (*.markup). You can open your version of the model and each individual markup file separately to see the comments. Comments appear in the graphics display and in the Markup tab of the eDrawings Manager.

Figure 14-2:
You can add longer comments in the description box of the Markup tab in the eDrawings Viewer.

New Comment

Reply

Accept

Reject

No status

Options

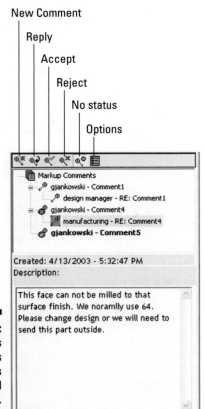

Figure 14-3:
eDrawings saves markup files as threaded comments.

Table 14-1		Markup Tools
	Button	*Purpose*
	Save Markup	Save the markup as a separate file.
	Dimension	Create a markup dimension between two points on the drawing.
	Text with leader	Create a text note with a leader.
	Text	Create a text note.
	Cloud with leader	Create a cloud with text (refer to Figure 14-2) with a leader.
	Cloud with text	Create a cloud with text inside.
	Cloud	Create a cloud.
	Line	Sketch a line by picking the beginning and end points of the line.
	Rectangle	Sketch a rectangle by picking the opposite corners of the rectangle.
	Circle	Sketch a circle by picking the center and radius locations.
	Arc	Sketch an arc by picking the center and radius locations and the start and end points of the arc.
	Spline	Sketch a curve by selecting multiple points to create the spline.

Table 14-2	Markup Comments Functions
Button	*Purpose*
New Comment	Create a new comment.
Reply	Reply to the selected, existing comment.
Accept	Accept the selected, existing comment.
Reject	Reject the selected, existing comment.
No Status	Comment without rejecting or accepting the comment.
Options	Set preferences for username, markup color, and other eDrawing configuration values.

To mark up your eDrawings:

1. **In the eDrawings Viewer, open a document to mark up.**

   When you open a document, several tools appear in the eDrawings interface. The eDrawings Manager, on the left side of the interface, displays tabs that let you manage eDrawings information. A complete set of markup tools (refer to Table 14-1) appears to the right of the interface.

   If you don't see the eDrawings Manager or the markup tools, click the UI Mode button on the main menu to toggle to the Complete UI mode.

2. **Click the Markup tab in the eDrawings Manager.**

   You see the following icons appear in the tab window: New, Reply, Accept, Reject, Clear, and Options (see Figure 14-3).

3. **In the Markup tab, click Options.**

   The Options dialog box appears.

4. **Select the Markup tab in the Options dialog box.**

5. **In the Comment Preferences section, type your name, phone number, and e-mail address and select a color and font for your comments.**

   This information identifies your comments to other reviewers. eDrawings now saves any future comments you make under your name.

6. **Click OK to save the changes.**

   With your user preferences set, you're now ready to mark up your document.

7. **To add a text element, skip to Step 8. To add a geometric element, click one of the following icons and use it as described:**

   • **Line:** To draw multiple lines connected with a vertex, click the graphic to start the line, move the mouse to draw a line, click to create a vertex, and then continue adding lines and vertices. Double-click in the graphics area to exit this tool.

- **Rectangle:** Click the graphic to set a corner of the rectangle and then drag the mouse to create the size rectangle you want. Release the mouse to finish.

- **Circle:** Click to place the centerpoint, drag the mouse outward, and then click again to draw a circle.

- **Arc:** Click to place the arc centerpoint. Move the mouse and click again to set the radius. Move the mouse and click again to draw the arc.

- **Spline:** Click, move the mouse, and then click multiple times to draw a spline. Double-click to exit this tool.

8. **To add a text element, click the icon you want.**

   Your choices are Text, Text with Leader, Cloud, or Cloud with Leader.

9. **Type your comment in the box that appears and click the green check-mark to accept your comment.**

   Clicking the red *x* cancels the comment.

10. **Click in the graphic where you want to insert the text element.**

11. **Add any additional markups by repeating Steps 7 through 10.**

12. **Choose File⇨Save.**

   eDrawings saves your comments automatically with the eDrawings file.

If you want to find out more about a command in eDrawings, try eDrawings Quick Help. This feature displays pop-up messages that point to different functions and features in eDrawings. You can turn Quick Help on or off by choosing Help⇨Quick Help in the eDrawings Viewer.

Using the SolidWorks Viewer

Similar to eDrawings, the SolidWorks Viewer opens native SolidWorks documents and is available free. And like the eDrawings Viewer, the SolidWorks Viewer opens native SolidWorks documents in *read-only mode,* meaning that you cannot modify the document but you can look at it. A benefit of read-only mode is that it enables the file to open faster because only a subset of information is opened. You can download SolidWorks Viewer from the SolidWorks download Web page at `www.solidworks.com/pages/services/downloads.html`.

To view a SolidWorks document using the SolidWorks Viewer, simply open the document as you would in most Microsoft programs.

Including SolidWorks Documents in Your Presentations

You can show off your SolidWorks designs in a few other ways. You can display your model inside a Microsoft application, such as Word, Excel, or PowerPoint, using a clever Microsoft technology known as object linking and embedding. Or you can make a 2D graphic image (JPG, TIF, BMP, or PDF) of your design and paste it in a document, presentation, or a Web page.

The advantages to using OLE are that:

✔ You can edit the object directly from within another application. Double-click the object or link, and the menus change to SolidWorks (as long as you have SolidWorks installed on your computer).

✔ A linked object stays current to the original document.

✔ You can combine different document types and programs into one document. For example, you can embed a SolidWorks document into a Microsoft PowerPoint report.

✔ You can include and show the object without having the actual application for the OLE object for viewing. The application that created the object only launches if you double-click the OLE object.

The advantages to using images are that:

✔ They're simple, typically small file sizes.

✔ They're easy to create as screen captures, edit, and annotate.

✔ You don't need to worry about the location of the actual file.

You can either link or embed an OLE object into a Microsoft document. A *linked object* contains a link to the original file, so any updates to the original appear when you double-click the link. In contrast, an *embedded object* is just like a copy, with no link to the original. The default in most Microsoft applications is to embed the OLE object into the file.

When you insert an OLE object, you can either create a new OLE object or add an existing file.

To embed an existing SolidWorks document into a Microsoft document:

1. **Open the document you want to embed the SolidWorks file into.**

2. **Click in the document where you want to place the embedded object to appear.**

3. **Choose Insert➪Object.**

   The Object dialog box, shown in Figure 14-4, appears.

Figure 14-4:
You can use
the Object
dialog box
to embed an
OLE object
into your
Microsoft
document.

4. **Click the Create from File tab.**

   The Create To create a new file, click Create New, click the application you want, and then create the file.

5. **In the Create from File dialog box, click the Browse button and browse to and select the file you want to embed.**

6. **Click one of these options to indicate how you want the file to display in your document:**

   • **Link to File:** Links the embedded file to the original. Any changes in the original reflect in the link.

   • **Display As Icon:** Inserts an icon that represents the contents of your file.

7. **Click OK.**

You can make edits to OLE objects. To edit an OLE object, double-click on the object and make your changes. To return to the original Microsoft document, click outside the embedded document inside the original document.

You can create a graphic image of your SolidWorks model in several ways. You can save an eDrawings file as a JPEG, TIFF, or BMP by selecting one of those formats in the Save As Type field in the Save As dialog box. The SolidWorks Save As dialog box offers similar options, including PDF.

You can take a snapshot of your SolidWorks model using the Windows screen capture function. Copy the active window onto the Windows Clipboard (Alt+Print Screen) and paste (Ctrl+V) the image into another application.

Part V
The Part of Tens

In this part . . .

No *For Dummies* book is complete without The Part of Tens. In this fun part, I provide information, tips, resources, and links that make your SolidWorks experience more productive and enjoyable. Each of the three chapters in this section lists tens ways (imagine that!) to become more proficient with SolidWorks, extend and reuse your design, and introduce you to the SolidWorks community.

Chapter 15

Ten Tips for Becoming More Proficient with SolidWorks

A craftsman is only as good as his tools, they say. But a tool is only as good as its craftsman, I say. This saying is true of SolidWorks, a brilliant but extensive design tool. To get the most out of SolidWorks, you need to become familiar with the nooks and crannies of the program — and there are a lot of them. Not to mention the dozens of add-on programs, such as PhotoWorks, COSMOS, Toolbox, and so on, that work inside of SolidWorks. The more adept you are at SolidWorks, the more productive and efficient you'll be at design. And the way to hone your SolidWorks skills is through practice and training.

You can follow plenty of other routes in mastering SolidWorks, such as books, online sources, and SolidWorks user groups. The best way to stay on top of it all is to mix and match several training routines and to stay current. SolidWorks issues a new release of its software ever year, and there are always new features and functionality that you'll want to keep up with.

Your efficiency in using SolidWorks translates into the bottom line for you and your company. In this chapter, I cover ten ways that you can make sure that you get the most out of SolidWorks.

Go to Class (Formal Training)

If you're serious about learning SolidWorks, formal training is the first step. Nothing instills discipline and structure like going to class. When you sign up for a SolidWorks course, you're committed to showing up and to learning. On the other hand, when you try to master SolidWorks on your own, you can easily find reasons to put things off. ("Someone has to sweep the garage!")

Through an extensive reseller network, SolidWorks offers a variety of training courses on everything from the basics of part and assembly modeling to advanced processes such as sheet metal design and custom routines.

A word of advice: When you sign up for a class, do some prep work before the class begins. Don't depend on your instructor to download knowledge into your brain. Read some articles on SolidWorks, tinker with the program, and try out the online tutorials located under the SolidWorks Help menu. If you walk into a classroom never having looked at SolidWorks, you'll have a long week, and so will the instructor and the rest of the class. So be prepared. A few warm-up exercises ensure that you get the most out of a course.

You can find an up-to-date list of training courses on the SolidWorks Web site under Training: www.solidworks.com/pages/services/Training/ TrainingCourses.html.

Courses vary by reseller, but here's what's to expect:

- ✔ **SolidWorks Essentials: Parts and Assemblies:** This class takes you through the basics of creating parts, assemblies, and drawings in SolidWorks.

- ✔ **SolidWorks Essentials: Drawings:** Once you've got part and assembly design under your belt, this class teaches you how to create manufacturing drawings based on your 3D design.

- ✔ **Advanced Part Modeling:** In this class, you discover how to use SolidWorks surfacing tools to create swoops, curves, cores/cavities, and other wacky freeform shapes that are popular in today's designs.

- ✔ **Advanced Assembly Modeling:** This class teaches you advanced techniques for building complex assemblies.

- ✔ **Sheet Metal and Weldments:** In this class, you find out how to build standalone sheet metal parts, how to convert parts to sheet metal, and how to model sheet metal parts in the context of an assembly.

- ✔ **Animator:** This course covers the SolidWorks Animator add-in that is part of the SolidWorks Office bundle.

- ✔ **PhotoWorks:** This class covers the PhotoWorks add-in that is part of SolidWorks Office.

✔ **CAD Productivity Tools:** This class teaches you about three add-ins that are part of the SolidWorks Office Professional software package: FeatureWorks, SolidWorks Utilities, and Toolbox.

✔ **API Fundamentals:** In this class, you discover how to create macros that automate tedious manual tasks in SolidWorks using the SolidWorks applications programming interface (API).

✔ **COSMOSWorks Designer:** This class shows you how to use the analysis add-in for SolidWorks to run linear stress analysis, as well as gap and contact analysis on your SolidWorks model.

Be Creative (Nontraditional Training)

You don't have to go to class to become a SolidWorks whiz (see the preceding section). In fact, you can stay in your pajamas if you prefer. You can find a plethora of SolidWorks books and online training materials to satisfy all your home-schooling needs. One caveat: These methods of learning are self-paced, so depending on the sort of person you are, you may want to apply glue to your chair or put a lock on the fridge. (My personal weakness is the espresso machine.)

Several third-party vendors, including Cadpo (www.cadpo.com), can provide computer-based training as well. At the SolidWorks Web site, you can sub-scribe to the online newsletter *SolidWorks Express* to have tips and tricks sent every other month to your e-mail address.

But really, one of the best places for getting up to speed in SolidWorks is the SolidWorks program itself. Open up SolidWorks and choose Help to find the following:

✔ **SolidWorks Help Topics:** It contains the SolidWorks Online User's Guide and What's New Manual. A Search tool allows you to look up information in these two online sources on just about any SolidWorks feature (see Figure 15-1).

✔ **Moving from AutoCAD:** Many new SolidWorks users are switching over from the 2D AutoCAD program. This guide shows you the differences between SolidWorks and AutoCAD and helps make the transition easier.

✔ **Online Tutorials:** SolidWorks includes more than 30 tutorials that are a good launching point for learning the program. These tutorials cover part creation, assembly operations, drawings, and several of the SolidWorks add-in programs.

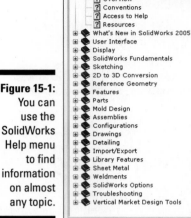

Figure 15-1:
You can
use the
SolidWorks
Help menu
to find
information
on almost
any topic.

TIP

In SolidWorks, when a command is active, a question mark appears in the PropertyManager. Click the question mark to jump to the Help Topic for that command.

Check Local Reseller Events

In addition to formal SolidWorks training courses, SolidWorks Value Added Resellers (VARs) also hold special events to introduce new users to the SolidWorks program. These events include "Night School," "Lunch and Learn," as well as other special programs. At these events, you can find out more about SolidWorks and share your questions and experiences with other users.

Many VARs also hold the SolidWorks Personal Edition Hands-on Test Drive class. Upon completion of this free two- to three-hour seminar, which offers basic instruction on SolidWorks, attendees receive a free copy of the Personal Edition software, a noncommercial version of SolidWorks. Personal Edition offers all the core features of SolidWorks, but any designs you create don't transfer into SolidWorks.

The availability and scheduling of events varies from VAR to VAR. The best way to find out more about these events is to contact your local VAR. SolidWorks has a listing of VARs at www.solidworks.com/pages/news/usergroupsseminars.html.

Join a User Group

Meeting and networking with other SolidWorks users is another great way to learn about SolidWorks and stay current with happenings in the CAD world. Located around the country and internationally, these user groups are independent groups organized by SolidWorks users. You can find user groups for both SolidWorks and the COSMOS line of analysis software that works inside SolidWorks. Visit www.solidworks.com/pages/services/Training/locateTrainingCenter.html.

Groups vary slightly in structure, but usually it costs nothing to join one. Anyone with an interest in SolidWorks is welcome. Groups meet periodically to discuss and share what they know about SolidWorks. Meetings often offer technical presentations, visits from local resellers, and case studies presented by other users. Users also discuss the newest version of SolidWorks and technical tips. In additional to local meetings, user groups also sponsor regional events. The biggest annual user event is SolidWorks World, which is usually held in January somewhere warm with a golf course nearby. At this annual conference, you can attend seminars; meet other users, SolidWorks partners, and SolidWorks personnel; and share ideas and learn more about SolidWorks.

Aspire to Be a Superuser

Within every SolidWorks-using company lurks the superuser, the program guru (or geek, whichever you prefer) to whom everyone goes with their questions on the inner workings of SolidWorks. This person saves you from calling technical support or digging through user manuals to learn about a SolidWorks add-in. Some superusers get formal recognition. Others are quietly acknowledged for the services they provide to coworkers.

You, too, can aspire to be a SolidWorks superuser, or — if you don't have the time to be one — you can cultivate one in your company. To become one, simply do whatever is needed to learn more than anyone else about SolidWorks. In order to cultivate a SolidWorks superuser, make every effort to recognize, encourage, and grow the SolidWorks geniuses in your organization. Encourage them to take the Certified SolidWorks Professional exam. (See the section "Take the CSWP Test," later in this chapter.) Give them a business title that acknowledges their know-it-all status. Issue a certificate, a plaque, or a medal that they can proudly display in their cubical. Send them to the mother of all SolidWorks user group meetings: SolidWorks World. Whatever it is, find some imaginative way to reward them, and they will take root and blossom.

Network Virtually: The Discussion Forum

SolidWorks user groups are a great way to shake hands with other users. But if you're not into shaking hands or rubbing elbows — or your schedule won't permit it — maybe *discussion forums* are the answer.

SolidWorks discussion forums are yet another way to exchange ideas with other users. The SolidWorks *discussion forum* is a threaded message board where you can submit questions (which can include document or image attachments that illustrate your confusion) and wait for others to respond.

Of course, you don't always have to be the one asking questions. You can also submit advice based on your own experiences. SolidWorks forums are moderated. Primarily they're users talking to one another, but occasionally someone from SolidWorks (myself included) chimes in.

SolidWorks discussion forums serve as a place where you can

- Discuss design, drafting, programming, and administration of SolidWorks CAD systems and SolidWorks-related products.
- Share ideas, information, and specific experiences regarding the use of SolidWorks and SolidWorks-related products.
- Discuss third-party add-on products for SolidWorks.
- Discuss enhancements in SolidWorks and SolidWorks-related products.
- Educate and inform others about the strengths, weaknesses, and general usage of SolidWorks and SolidWorks-related products.

Discussion forums are broken down into functional groups, such as parts, assemblies, drawings, installation, sketching, and so on. This structure makes it easier to ask the right people questions.

You can find SolidWorks discussion forums in the Support section of the SolidWorks Web site: www.solidworks.com/pages/services/Community.html.

Take the CSWP Test

If you aspire to become the SolidWorks superuser in your office, how about taking the test? The Certified SolidWorks Professional (CSWP) program provides a standard measure of SolidWorks competency. CSWP recognizes the most qualified and advanced SolidWorks professionals. Certification is a way to get recognition from your company and your peers. Now no one will ever doubt your advanced knowledge again.

The way to become a CSWP is to take a test, which is offered through participating SolidWorks VARs (check the SolidWorks Web site). The test has two parts. The first part is a series of written questions that test your expertise in the different areas of SolidWorks. In the second part, you're asked to create an actual design in SolidWorks. For more information, visit `www.solidworks.com/pages/services/Training/Training.html`.

But really, what's the point of getting certified? Basically, it's like putting four stars across the top of your resume. Certification acknowledges your skill level in SolidWorks. When companies look for new employees or consultants, they look for a CSWP. What's more, employers can use certification to train more advanced users. You have more confidence in the skills of someone who has passed CSWP certification.

Document Your CAD Standards

One of the best ways to ensure productivity in SolidWorks for you and your staff (if you have one) is to create a CAD standard book. Your CAD standard doesn't have to be a tome, just a binder's worth of documentation on how you get your work done in SolidWorks. Documented CAD standards help new employees get up to speed fast and bring projects to completion more quickly.

A well-defined CAD standard should document how you begin new parts and drawings, what layers contain what information in a drawing, how you handle design revisions, where and how you manage standard parts, and so on. All these documents should go into a manual.

Defining a set of CAD standards can be, and should be, a simple process. Hold a couple of meetings with the key SolidWorks users or even bring it up as a topic for an internal user group meeting. One way I have found to be effective in ensuring attendance at a meeting like this is to offer food. It's rare to find an engineer who will turn down free pizza to talk about CAD.

Once the standards have been defined, you need to determine how to share this information. An effective means is to create an HTML or PDF document (that no one can mess with) and place it on a network drive where everyone can reach it. I prefer HTML as it comes up faster in a Web browser.

Here is a checklist of items to cover in your CAD standards:

- ✔ Data management, or how you create, store, and archive files
- ✔ Document templates
- ✔ SolidWorks settings
- ✔ Assembly structure
- ✔ Materials
- ✔ Standard parts
- ✔ Modeling practices, such as feature names and order, in-context references, and so on
- ✔ Drawing practices, such as standards notes, custom properties, title blocks, and so on

Communicate Design Standards

Just as important as creating a set of CAD standards is communicating what they are and how they are used. You can communicate your design standards by adding standards review to your design review or checking process, holding internal user group meetings, or conducting training classes on the standards. You may have a great set of nicely documented and detailed CAD standards, but what good are they if no one follows them?

The other advantage of this review is that the designers get feedback so that they can incorporate it into current and subsequent designs.

Make sure that the standards are located where all the designers can get to the documents easily. Find a common place on the network and store the CAD standards in that location.

Manage SolidWorks Well

A CAD system plays a major role in how your organization designs its products. How well you manage and implement your CAD system has a large impact on your company's productivity and success. A key to this success is how well this technology is managed. So what makes a good CAD manager in a SolidWorks environment, and why is that role important to your company?

Most companies have some form of CAD manager, whether formal or informal, full- or part-time. In a SolidWorks environment, a CAD manager is usually responsible for the following tasks:

- ✔ Implementing SolidWorks
- ✔ Managing SolidWorks
- ✔ Managing CAD data
- ✔ Training
- ✔ Implementing the CAD standards
- ✔ Communication

If you're a CAD manager, your goal should be twofold. The first goal is to find ways to increase your company's efficiency and effectiveness using SolidWorks software. Small productivity gains in these areas can yield significant gains in productivity in the long term, especially when multiplied across all the CAD users in your organization. The second goal is to lower your organization's TCO (total cost of ownership) in regards to using SolidWorks.

Chapter 16

Ten Ways to Extend and Reuse Your Design Information

In This Chapter

▶ Getting the most out of your designs with SolidWorks add-ons

▶ Including SolidWorks designs in Microsoft applications

▶ Allowing others to view and print PDM data

*T*he fun never ends when you design in 3D, even after your product design is complete. You'll be pleased to know that you can take advantage of, literally, dozens of other applications developed by SolidWorks and by other companies that allow you to reuse and show off your designs in many ways. These methods include add-in and downstream applications.

A SolidWorks *add-in* is a separate program that works inside of SolidWorks. An add-in shows up on the SolidWorks main menu, so it looks like it's part of SolidWorks. One example is SolidWorks Animator, which creates AVI movies of parts and assemblies. Another is PhotoWorks, which creates photorealistic images of parts and assemblies. Analysis, simulation, and manufacturing programs are considered *downstream applications*. The downstream programs that I cover in this chapter work directly off the SolidWorks model, so data translation is never an issue.

In this chapter, I introduce you to ten add-ins and downstream applications. Keep in mind that my purpose is simply to make you aware of these programs, not to explain the details of how each program works.

SolidWorks add-in applications are available for purchase separately or as part of a SolidWorks package. Check with your SolidWorks reseller for what is available. After you've installed an add-in program, open SolidWorks and choose Tools⇨Add-Ins to run the program inside SolidWorks.

Microsoft OLE

Next time you want to add zest to a PowerPoint presentation, color to a report, or oomph to a ho-hum presentation, include a SolidWorks design. Your audience can get an instant understanding of the benefits of your two-seated lawnmower if you simply show them the actual model.

You can add a SolidWorks model to a presentation or a document by using *object linking and embedding* (OLE) or by including an image of the model.

OLE technology lets you embed or link an object from another program into a Microsoft document. When you *embed* an object, it's like including a copy of the real thing in the document. The embedded object has no link to the original. In contrast, a *link* is connected to its original and updates whenever the original document updates.

To access an OLE embedded or linked SolidWorks document, simply double-click the link or the object. As long as you have the SolidWorks program installed, the document opens. If the object is a SolidWorks model, you can spin the model around, show different views, or make changes as desired.

Another way to include a SolidWorks model in a report, presentation, or even a Web page is to include an image file of the model. One way to create an image is through a Windows screen capture. To capture the current window on your screen, press Alt+Print Screen, which places the image on the Clipboard. Open an application such as Microsoft Word and choose Edit⇨Paste.

Another option is to save your SolidWorks model as a JPEG, TIFF, or PDF file. These options are available in the SolidWorks Save As dialog box. (Simply choose File⇨Save As to reach this dialog box.)

When you start working with graphic formats, you'll find that some fit your needs better than others. JPEG and GIF are generally safe bets. TIFF and BMP create larger files. My personal favorite is PNG. It's a small size format that allows you to resize images without losing too much quality.

SolidWorks 3D Instant Website

If you want to create as little work as possible for the receiver, SolidWorks 3D Instant Website is a great way to send someone a SolidWorks design. In just one mouse click, this SolidWorks add-in allows you to publish a Web page of your SolidWorks document on a local intranet or — if you don't have an Intranet or Web server to use — on a SolidWorks-hosted Web site. The Web page is based on a template and a style that you can customize with limited HTML programming experience.

By sending an e-mail with a link to the Web page, you can share SolidWorks models or drawings with anyone without requiring them to manually install any viewers or CAD software. An automatic wizard installs the necessary viewing software for them.

Here's an example of how this add-on can work. Say your company makes high-efficiency fan blades, and your suppliers are located around the country. Sending a link to a Web page of your design makes it easy for all your suppliers to inspect your fans (they can rotate, zoom, and pan 3D models), add comments, and so on. They also can print the document from the Web page.

To start the 3D Instant Website Wizard, with your SolidWorks document open, choose Tools⇨3D Instant Website.

PhotoWorks

A 3D model of a toaster looks just like, well, a 3D model of a toaster. But if you really want to sell someone your design idea, show them how the toaster looks sitting on a kitchen counter. PhotoWorks, a SolidWorks add-in, allows you to create photo-realistic images of your SolidWorks model in the model's natural (or unnatural) environment.

PhotoWorks lets you specify model surface properties, such as color, texture, reflectance, and transparency. You can also place the model in the setting you want, as I've done with my toaster in Figure 16-1. Although I could have made my toaster purple, given it the texture of brushed aluminum, and set it inside of a log cabin, I chose something more mainstream instead.

Figure 16-1:
You can use PhotoWorks to specify color, texture, and even setting.

Photo-realistic images lend impact to presentations and to proposals and allow you to present design concepts quickly. Rendering an image in PhotoWorks is much easier than creating a physical prototype of the product and then hiring an expensive photographer to shoot it.

SolidWorks Animator

What better way to demonstrate your SolidWorks assembly than to show how it moves? The SolidWorks Animator add-in generates AVI movies of your SolidWorks part or assembly that play on any Windows-based computer. Animations show the viewer how a product assembles and functions. In conjunction with PhotoWorks, Animator can output photo-realistic animations complete with lights, shadows, materials, and reflections.

Suppose that you want to impress a group of potential customers with your design of a water filter that moves like a jellyfish around a swimming pool sucking up debris with its mechanical tentacles. You can create AVI files that show how your product operates. This way, prospects can see how the pool filter moves and watch its filtering mechanisms.

In SolidWorks Animator, a wizard walks you through the process of recording a fly-around, exploded view, or collapsed view animation. Once you create the basic animation, you can edit or delete animation steps or play the animation a frame at a time using the Animation FeatureManager. The Animation FeatureManager tab is located at the bottom of the graphics window. Click the tab to view the Animation FeatureManager and a timeline, which shows the steps in the animation.

To open an add-in product, choose Tools➪Add-ins and check the box next to the add-in you want to use.

PDMWorks Advanced Server

If, during a large design project, you need to give folks outside your design team access to your SolidWorks data, you may find PDMWorks Advanced Server a handy add-in.

This add-in extends access to the design information stored in your PDMWorks database. PDMWorks is the product data management (PDM) software that works with SolidWorks. (You can read more about PDM software in Chapter 13.)

PDMWorks Advanced Server has three functions:

- ✔ **A Web-based portal** gives the user view and print access to data in the PDM vault (a central database) via a standard Web browser.

- ✔ **Application Program Interface (API)** automates mundane PDMWorks functions to tailor PDMWorks to the specific needs of your organization.

- ✔ **Event triggers** automate the execution of a task per a specific PDMWorks event. For example, you can set it up so that when PDMWorks releases a drawing, PDM Advanced Server creates a PDF file of the drawing and sends the PDF to design team members via an e-mail that notifies them that the drawing is available for use.

COSMOSWorks Analysis

As a designer, you may be asked to do upfront *finite element analysis* (FEA) on your models. FEA shows you how your model holds up under real-world conditions. The results of analysis allow you to make better decisions about the types of material to use, the geometry of parts, and how the parts in an assembly interact. Analysis software helps to improve the quality and function of your design, as well as lower the cost of making it.

COSMOSWorks is a suite of four FEA programs that integrate tightly with SolidWorks and run directly on your SolidWorks model. COSMOSXpress comes standard with SolidWorks. The three other COSMOSWorks bundles are sold as add-ins and work on both parts and assemblies.

- ✔ **COSMOSXpress** is an analysis wizard that comes standard with SolidWorks and allows you to do upfront analysis on parts, as shown in Figure 16-2.

- ✔ **COSMOSWorks Designer** performs stress, displacement, thermal stress, and contact analyses on parts and assemblies.

- ✔ **COSMOSWorks Professional** adds frequency and buckling, heat transfer, and drop-testing.

- ✔ **COSMOSWorks Advanced Professional** goes even further with capabilities to analyze beams and trusses, perform nonlinear stress analysis, and study fatigue and dynamic response.

Figure 16-2:
COSMOS-
Xpress steps
you through
the process
of analyzing
a part.

COSMOSMotion

While COSMOSWorks (see the preceding section) tells you whether or not a part or assembly will break, COSMOSMotion allows you to understand the mechanical motion of your assemblies. This SolidWorks add-in takes into consideration joints and linkages and the actual forces that occur during motion so that you can detect problem areas, such as collisions between parts. COSMOSMotion enables you to size motors, determine power consumption, lay out linkages, develop cams, understand gear drives, and size springs/dampers.

Included in the COSMOSMotion software are tools to simulate displacement, velocity, acceleration, linear and torsion spring and dampers, joints (created from assembly mates), and additional constraints to define how the components in an assembly interact with one another.

The assembly shown in Figure 16-3 illustrates how you can size motors and actuators on a design based on the COSMOSMotion results. The graphical output helps identify key areas and values for the analysis.

Figure 16-3:
COSMOS-
Motion
lets you
determine
what size
and kilowatt
motor you
need for the
job.

SolidWorks API

The SolidWorks *application programming interface* (API) helps you record macros even if you don't have a lot of programming experience. *Macros* are small custom applications that automate a series of steps for a mundane task in SolidWorks. For example, if you export designs for machine tooling, you can create a macro that provides a one-button export with all the options set inside the macro. Macros are also a good way to maintain compliance with company standards. You can create a macro that ensures specific settings are properly set and that a document complies with all the settings. You can even save macros in the SolidWorks Design Library to share with other design team members. (To find out more about the Design Library, see Chapter 13.)

When you record a macro in SolidWorks, the SolidWorks API creates a file that contains a record of all the commands (mouse clicks, menu choices, and key strokes) that take place from the time you start recording to when you stop. The commands are stored in the Microsoft Visual Basic program language. SolidWorks has some limitations to what you can record in a macro, but most of the basic functions are automatic. SolidWorks saves macros with an .swp extension. You can edit the files using Visual Basic editor, so you do need some understanding of Visual Basic.

The commands to record a macro are located on the Macro toolbar, shown in Figure 16-4. To access the Macro toolbar, choose Tools➪Macro.

- ✔ **Run Macro:** Opens the Run Macro dialog box. In the dialog box, browse for the macro you want to run and click OK.

- ✔ **Stop Macro:** Stops the recording of the macro and opens the Save As dialog box. Enter the name of the new macro in the dialog box and click Save. The .swp extension is automatically added to the filename.

- ✔ **Record/Pause Macro:** Pauses the recording of a macro. Click again to begin re-recording.

- ✔ **New Macro:** Creates a new macro. Begin entering the steps you want to record. Click Stop Macro to save the file.

- ✔ **Edit Macro:** Allows you to edit or debug a macro that you've already recorded. Click the Edit Macro button and browse to the macro to edit. The Microsoft Visual Basic editor appears. Edit the macro and close the editor.

For additional reference, the SolidWorks API support site, located at www.solidworks.com/pages/services/APISupport.html, has a wealth of API examples, downloads, and tips.

Figure 16-4:
You can
open the
Macro
toolbar and
access the
Macro
commands
by choosing
Tools⇨
Macro.

Note that many of the VB application examples on the API support Web site have a .bas file extension. To use one of these example files, you need to import it into VBA. To do so, create a new macro and import the file using Import File from the Microsoft Visual Basic File pull-down menu.

SolidWorks Task Scheduler

Labor intensive tasks, such as batch importing, exporting, and plotting, can gobble up hours, if not days. Even though these jobs don't require excessive brain power, they still tie up your mind and computer. But now you can automate these processes. Task Scheduler, a software utility included in the SolidWorks Office and Office Professional packages, puts your system to work while you're off in the Bahamas. It lets you run resource-intensive processes overnight or on weekends, times when the computer is normally idle, freeing you to focus on more creative projects.

Scheduling a task in Task Scheduler takes minutes. The program is a separate utility, so you access it either through Windows program files or a shortcut on the desktop. Once Task Scheduler is up and running, here's how you can schedule a project:

1. **In the Task Scheduler screen, click the task you want from the list on the left side of the screen (see Figure 16-5).**

   Options include Print Files, Create Drawings, Import and Export Files, and so on. You can even run customer scripts.

   Depending on the task, the program queues you for more information.

2. **Provide the necessary information.**

   If you select Print Files, for example, Task Scheduler asks you to enter the paper size, number of copies, and the printer you want to print on.

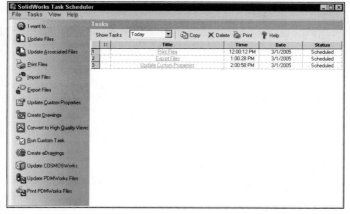

Figure 16-5:
You can
select the
task you
want to run
from a list in
the
SolidWorks
Task
Scheduler
interface.

3. **Select the files you want to run the task on using Add File or Add Folder (see Figure 16-6).**

4. **Select the frequency (once, daily, weekly, or monthly), start time, and start date for the task.**

5. **Click Finish to close the Task Scheduler dialog box.**

   The task is now scheduled to run at the scheduled time and date.

Figure 16-6:
Select the
files or
folders you
want to run
the task
on in the
SolidWorks
Task
Scheduler
Update Files
interface.

SolidWorks Task Scheduler runs tasks at any time, even when you're logged off the computer. The Microsoft Windows service that runs the SolidWorks Task Scheduler is swBOEngine.exe, and it starts automatically whenever SolidWorks Task Scheduler is installed. When you restart the computer, the service appears in the Windows Start program group, and you simply click it to start the service. To remove the automatic activation of this service, remove SolidWorks Task Scheduler from the Windows Start program group.

Various Manufacturing Software

The final stage in product development is to send your SolidWorks design to the manufacturer to have the part or assembly made.

Manufacturers use *computer-aided manufacturing* (CAM) *software* to create parts using a variety of manufacturing methods (stamped, machined, turned, cast, forged, and so on). Some of these manufacturing methods use specialized software for the different processes, but in most cases, they can take information directly from your SolidWorks design.

For more information on SolidWorks CAM software partners, visit the Partner section of the SolidWorks Web site at www.solidworks.com.

Chapter 17

Ten Resources for the SolidWorks Community

As a SolidWorks user, you can relax knowing that you'll never have to go it alone. You can find plenty of places (most of them on the Internet) to meet up with other users, locate training and tech support, and get info on SolidWorks upgrades and add-on products.

In this chapter, you discover ten resources that are available from the SolidWorks community. Each element is a useful resource or reference as you begin or continue your journey with SolidWorks.

SolidWorks and COSMOS User Groups

One of the best ways to find out more about SolidWorks is to network with other users, which you can do by joining a user group. If you can't find a user group in your area, you can always start one. These groups are beneficial because they give you an opportunity to swap stories and share software experiences with other users.

It's all about community

The SolidWorks community is comprised of six groups that work together and complement one another:

- ✔ **Solution Partners:** Companies that offer hardware and software products certified to work with SolidWorks software.

- ✔ **SolidWorks Corporation:** The company that develops the software.

- ✔ **SolidWorks Resellers:** Organizations, sometimes called Value Added Resellers or VARs, that sell SolidWorks products and provide training and technical support.

- ✔ **SolidWorks Manufacturing Network:** A network of manufacturers who accept your native SolidWorks files to build parts with.

- ✔ **Educational Institutions:** Schools that include SolidWorks in their curriculum.

- ✔ **User Groups:** Groups of SolidWorks users who meet to discuss SolidWorks and its products.

User groups are a key component of the SolidWorks community. Figure 17-1 shows how the user groups have links to each of the other major areas of the SolidWorks community.

Figure 17-1: The SolidWorks community offers a cornucopia of resources.

You can find user groups for SolidWorks and for COSMOSWorks, the finite element analysis (FEA) program that works inside of SolidWorks. These user groups have local chapters all over the world. SolidWorks also hosts regional events worldwide and an annual international user group convention, which changes location each year, called SolidWorks World.

To find a group or to discover how to start one, go to www.solidworks.com/ pages/news/usergroups.

SolidWorks Web Site

To get the latest on SolidWorks, your first stop should be the SolidWorks Web site (www.solidworks.com), shown in Figure 17-2. The site has six main sections, which you can access by using the top menu bar:

- ✔ **Products:** Offers information on SolidWorks products, which include CAD, analysis, and data management software.

- ✔ **Services:** Broken into two main categories: Support and Training and Certification. The upcoming section "SolidWorks Online Support" covers Support (as in technical support) in more detail. Training and Certification offers information on software courses available at SolidWorks training centers and on how to become a certified SolidWorks know-it-all. (Read the upcoming "Certified SolidWorks Professional Program" section.)

Figure 17-2:
The SolidWorks Web site offers information on products, services, partners, news and events, and success stories.

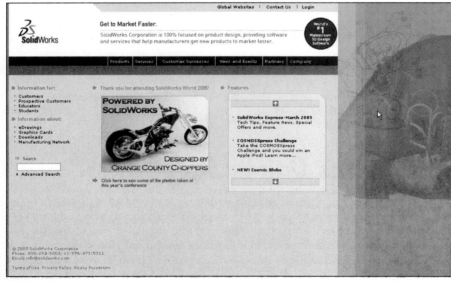

- ✔ **Customer Successes:** Includes links to customer success stories categorized by industry and the SolidWorks add-on used.

- ✔ **News and Events:** Offers the lowdown on what's happening in SolidWorks. Includes press releases, seminars, trade show schedules, user group meetings, and a link to the *SolidWorks Express* newsletter.

- ✔ **Partners:** Includes information on SolidWorks Solution Partners and the Manufacturing Network. (For more on the latter, see the "SolidWorks Manufacturing Network" section, later in this chapter.)

- ✔ **Company:** Lists the latest information on SolidWorks the company, such as who's running the show, directions to the office, and a list of internal employment opportunities (in case you're looking for a job).

SolidWorks Express Newsletter

SolidWorks Express is an online newsletter for SolidWorks customers that comes out once every other month, and sometimes more often. Each issue features technical tips, news on the latest happenings at SolidWorks, and real customer stories.

You can subscribe for free at www.solidworks.com/swexpress. To sign up for e-mail notification for new issues, click Subscribe at the top of the current issue of *SolidWorks Express* and complete the form. After you sign up, e-mails notify you that a new edition of the newsletter is available, and you can click the URL that takes you to the site.

If you happen to miss an issue of *SolidWorks Express,* click Archive at the top of the *SolidWorks Express* home page to view past articles. The archive conveniently sorts Technical Tips by category (Administration, Modeling, Detailing, Assembly, and FEA) so that you can find what you need fast.

You can also search through *SolidWorks Express* technical tips on the SolidWorks support site.

SolidWorks Online Support

One of the most important resources for SolidWorks users is technical support. Everyone needs a hand now and again. The Support section of the SolidWorks Web site is where you find online technical support, software to download, and a slew of additional resources. To access the support area of the SolidWorks Web site, you need to purchase an annual maintenance contract (about $1,200 for SolidWorks). Don't have one? Talk to your local reseller and have them explain the features, benefits, and costs of the subscription service program.

The Support section of www.solidworks.com includes

- ✔ Links to download the latest version or service pack for SolidWorks software, including COSMOSWorks, PDMWorks, and eDrawings.

- ✔ The latest news and technical bulletins.

- ✔ Signups to receive alerts, via e-mail, about new postings in the Support section of the Web site, *SolidWorks Express* online newsletter, and other announcements from SolidWorks.

- ✔ Ability to search for technical information and technical tips.

- ✔ Access to Customer Experience Programs, which allow you to try out prerelease versions of software so that SolidWorks can get your opinions on its products and services.

- ✔ Links to a wealth of reference documents. The References and Guides section has installation, best practices, and other useful technical information.

- ✔ Information on system requirements and graphics card drivers that you need to properly operate SolidWorks software.

- ✔ Online webcasts and archives of previous webcasts.

- ✔ Numerous links to other community pages, including the *SolidWorks Express* newsletter, online discussion forums, user groups, the Manufacturing Network, 3D ContentCentral, the CSWP program, SolidWorks customer experience programs, and a page of links to other CAD industry Web sites.

For more information on this SolidWorks community resource, visit www.solidworks.com/pages/services/subscription.

Certified SolidWorks Professional Program

Another resource is the Certified SolidWorks Professional (CSWP) program. A *CSWP* is a person who knows SolidWorks like the back of his hand. But not just anyone can become a CSWP. You have to first pass a test, which is given at an authorized testing center, such as a reseller office. Being a CSWP entitles you to member-only privileges, including a special logo that you can put on your business card, as well as invitations to exclusive CSWP-only events.

What's more (and this is the best part), your name is put on a searchable Certified Professional directory on the SolidWorks Web site. If anyone in your area needs to hire someone who is quick on her feet with SolidWorks, he may give you a call.

From a company perspective, having a CSWP in the office is an advantage. You become the office guru, someone other SolidWorks users can look up to and go to for software support. And the certification enables you to help your company identify qualified new hires, consultants, or contractors that understand SolidWorks.

For more information on this resource, visit the CSWP section of the SolidWorks Web site at www.solidworks.com/pages/services/training/CSWP.html.

3D ContentCentral

Often, designs call for standard parts. It's a waste of time to model those parts from scratch. 3D ContentCentral (www.3dcontentcentral.com) is a free Web site by SolidWorks that offers millions of supplier certified and user contributed part models in a number of different formats that you can download and drop into your SolidWorks designs.

The site has two sections: Supplier Certified parts and the User Library. The Supplier Certified parts section contains standard part models certified by the vendor to be accurate. The User Library is where designers can upload CAD models to share with other users.

To get started using 3D ContentCentral, all you need to do is register with the site and create an account. The process takes about a minute. Once you're onboard, 3D ContentCentral makes searching for standard components easy. Once you find what you need, you can download the model and request a quote from the vendor. Some online catalogs allow you to configure parts to your unique specifications.

SolidWorks Manufacturing Network

When you need to work with a vendor or a manufacturer, it's a heck of a lot easier if the company can just accept your native SolidWorks data. Otherwise, you end up hassling with intermediary exchange formats, such as STEP and IGES, which can add extra steps to the process and put your data at risk.

If you need to find a company who will take your data straight up, check the SolidWorks Manufacturing Network. It's a free online directory of contract engineering, CNC machining, mold making, industrial design, machine design, rapid prototyping, and other companies that accept native SolidWorks files. When you work with a company in the Manufacturing Network, there's no stressing over file transfer issues.

The Manufacturing Network Web site (see the URL at the end of this section) allows you to search for a designer, manufacturer, or supplier by name or by area of expertise, such as industrial design, metal stamping, rapid prototyping, or even reverse engineering.

If your organization provides services to the SolidWorks Community, consider joining the Manufacturing Network yourself. Sign-up is free, and you get a free listing on the Manufacturing Network Web site.

For more information on this SolidWorks community resource, visit www. solidworks.com/pages/partners/mfgnetwork.html.

SolidWorks Solution Partners

One of the strengths of SolidWorks is its Solution Partner program. Solution Partners are companies that develop best-in-class software and hardware that work with SolidWorks software. Look for logos on products to identify the following certification levels:

- **Research Associate:** A company that has the intent or is in the process of developing a product for the SolidWorks market.

- **Solution Partner:** A company that has successfully released a SolidWorks compatible product and has a minimum of two SolidWorks customers.

- **Certified Gold Product:** A software product that carries the Certified Gold logo and is directly integrated with SolidWorks. Certified Gold products are designed to work well with SolidWorks.

- **Certified CAM Product:** A best-in-class computer-aided manufacturing or CNC (computer numerical controls) machine software that works well with SolidWorks geometry.

For more information on this SolidWorks community resource, visit www. solidworks.com/pages/partners/partners.html.

SolidWorks Resellers

When you're ready to purchase SolidWorks, you can go to your local SolidWorks Value Added Reseller (VAR). SolidWorks has hundreds of VARs throughout the world. You can find one that is near you on the SolidWorks Web site by going to www.solidworks.com/pages/company/solidworks officeworldwide.html.

VARs do more than push a product. They offer a number of other services, including product demonstrations, technical support, and training programs. Among the clever and entertaining training courses they offer are Night Classes, Lunch and Learn Workshops, and SolidWorks Test Drives. Check with your local VAR to see what it has to offer.

SolidWorks Educational Community

If you're in college, keep your eyes peeled for SolidWorks in the classroom. SolidWorks develops a special Educational Edition of its software for use in high schools, colleges, and universities. Students who learn with SolidWorks get practical training and real experience. The Educational Edition also comes with a Teacher's guide, curriculum ideas, courseware, and sample part files.

Maybe you're not a student. You're thinking "What's this got to do with me?" If you're about to hire an intern or college graduate, post your ad at colleges and universities that offer SolidWorks in their curriculum. Students from these schools are ready to start designing tomorrow. You won't have to spend heaps of money training them.

For more information, visit the SolidWorks Education Web site at `www.solid works.com/pages/products/edu`. Also available on the Web site are a list of events, associations, and a newsletter for the educational community.

Appendix

About the CD-ROM

This CD contains demos on how SolidWorks works, information about add-on solutions for SolidWorks, and examples of how other companies use SolidWorks within different industries. The CD is self-running, so all you need to do is stick it in the CD drive.

System Requirements

Make sure that your computer meets the minimum system requirements shown in the following list. If your computer doesn't match up to most of these requirements, you may have problems using the software and files on the CD.

✔ A PC with a Pentium or faster processor

✔ Microsoft Windows 2000 or Windows XP Professional

✔ At least 256MB of total RAM installed on your computer

✔ A CD-ROM drive

✔ A sound card for PCs

✔ A monitor capable of displaying at least 256 colors or grayscale

✔ A Flash compatible web browser

✔ A point device (mouse)

If you need more information on the basics, check out these books published by Wiley Publishing, Inc.: *PCs For Dummies* by Dan Gookin or *Windows 2000 Professional For Dummies* by Andy Rathbone and Sharon Crawford.

Using the CD

To run the Interactive Tour CD, follow these steps.

1. **Insert the CD into your computer's CD-ROM drive.**

   The CD's introduction page appears. You see links to interviews discussing the focus, innovation, and use of SolidWorks.

   Note to Windows users: The interface won't launch if you have Autorun disabled. In that case, choose Start⇨Run. In the dialog box that appears, type

   :\start.exe. (Replace D with the proper letter if your CD-ROM drive uses a different letter. If you don't know the letter, see how your CD-ROM drive is listed under My Computer.) Click OK.

2. **Click the Start Tour button in the lower lefthand corner of the main page to continue.**

   The product demo section appears on the left of the screen.

3. **Select which area to review by clicking the Product Demos, Add-On Solutions, or Case Studies tab at the top of the window.**

   After selecting a tab, the menu on the left of the window changes to reflect the selected area.

4. **Click the topic category to view.**

   For example, when you click Drawing Creation within the product demos, the demos Create Drawings, Revise Drawings, Revision Tables, and so on appear.

5. **Click the specific topic to view.**

   The main screen changes to show the selected demo, solution, or case study.

6. **Click the View button within the main window.**

   The View button is listed as View Demo for product demos, View Add-On Info for add-on solutions, and View Video for case studies.

7. **To exit the tour, choose File⇨Exit.**

What You Find on the CD

I organized the following sections by category and provide a summary of the software and other goodies on the CD. If you need help with installing the items provided on the CD, refer back to the installation instructions in the preceding section.

Shareware programs are fully functional, free, trial versions of copyrighted programs. If you like particular programs, register with their authors for a nominal fee and receive licenses, enhanced versions, and technical support.

Freeware programs are free, copyrighted games, applications, and utilities. You can copy them to as many PCs as you like — for free — but they offer no technical support.

GNU software is governed by its own license, which is included inside the folder of the GNU software. There are no restrictions on distribution of GNU software. See the GNU license at the root of the CD for more details.

Trial, demo, or *evaluation* versions of software are usually limited either by time or functionality (meaning that it may not let you save a project after you create it).

Product Demos tab

The Product Demos tab has links to demonstrations of SolidWorks features and functions. These video demonstrations show you how to use many of the features within SolidWorks.

The Product Demos tab is broken into different categories, such as Time-Saving Innovations, Drawing Creation, Part Modeling, Assembly Design, Product Data Management, Design Communications, and CAD Productivity. The links appear on the left side of the window.

Add-on Solutions tab

One of the strengths of SolidWorks is the breadth and quality of the solution partners that add functionality and extend the reach of SolidWorks into other areas, such as electronic design, computer-aided manufacturing, and optical design.

The Add-on Solutions tab has links and references for a wide variety of SolidWorks add-on products broken into different categories, including Analysis, Communication, Component Libraries, Data Management, Design, Manufacturing, and Mold Making.

Case Studies tab

One way to discover more about SolidWorks is to see how other companies use and apply SolidWorks in their design environment. The Case Studies tab has industry segmented case studies of SolidWorks customers.

Sales and Support tab

If you want more information about SolidWorks, the Sales and Support tab displays contact information for SolidWorks offices worldwide.

Troubleshooting

This CD is self-contained and self-running, so it doesn't need to be installed on your computer.

If the CD doesn't work properly, the two likeliest problems are that you don't have the CD set up to play Macromedia Flash within your browser or the CD doesn't auto-play the tour application.

If you get an error message such as Not enough memory or Setup cannot continue, try one or more of the following suggestions and then try using the software again:

✔ **Make sure that you have a Flash-compatible web browser.** Current Web browsers come with the ability to play Flash content. You can also visit the Macromedia Flash Player Download Web site at www.macromedia. com/shockwave/download/download.cgi?P1_Prod_Version=Shock waveFlash for more details.

✔ **Close all running programs.** The more programs you have running, the less memory is available to other programs. Installation programs typically update files and programs; so if you keep other programs running, installation may not work properly.

✔ **Try running the application on another computer.** This is a simple way to see whether the problem is just a setup issue on your computer. If the CD runs fine on another computer, you may have a CD driver or Flash compatibility issue.

✔ **Reboot your computer.** Restart your computer and see whether the problem clears up.

If you still have trouble with the CD, please call the Customer Care phone number: (800) 762-2974. Outside the United States, call 1 (317) 572-3994. You can also contact Customer Service by visiting our Web site at www.wiley.com/ techsupport. Wiley Publishing Inc. will provide technical support only for installation and other general quality control items; for technical support on the applications themselves, consult the program's vendor or author.

To place additional orders or to request information about other Wiley products, please call (800) 225-5945.

Index

• D •

Notes

BUSINESS, CAREERS & PERSONAL FINANCE

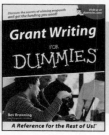

0-7645-5307-0

0-7645-5331-3 *†

Also available:

- Accounting For Dummies †
0-7645-5314-3
- Business Plans Kit For Dummies †
0-7645-5365-8
- Cover Letters For Dummies
0-7645-5224-4
- Frugal Living For Dummies
0-7645-5403-4
- Leadership For Dummies
0-7645-5176-0
- Managing For Dummies
0-7645-1771-6

- Marketing For Dummies
0-7645-5600-2
- Personal Finance For Dummies *
0-7645-2590-5
- Project Management For Dummies
0-7645-5283-X
- Resumes For Dummies †
0-7645-5471-9
- Selling For Dummies
0-7645-5363-1
- Small Business Kit For Dummies *†
0-7645-5093-4

HOME & BUSINESS COMPUTER BASICS

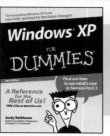

0-7645-4074-2

0-7645-3758-X

Also available:

- ACT! 6 For Dummies
0-7645-2645-6
- iLife '04 All-in-One Desk Reference For Dummies
0-7645-7347-0
- iPAQ For Dummies
0-7645-6769-1
- Mac OS X Panther Timesaving Techniques For Dummies
0-7645-5812-9
- Macs For Dummies
0-7645-5656-8

- Microsoft Money 2004 For Dummies
0-7645-4195-1
- Office 2003 All-in-One Desk Reference For Dummies
0-7645-3883-7
- Outlook 2003 For Dummies
0-7645-3759-8
- PCs For Dummies
0-7645-4074-2
- TiVo For Dummies
0-7645-6923-6
- Upgrading and Fixing PCs For Dummies
0-7645-1665-5
- Windows XP Timesaving Techniques For Dummies
0-7645-3748-2

FOOD, HOME, GARDEN, HOBBIES, MUSIC & PETS

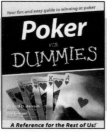

0-7645-5295-3

0-7645-5232-5

Also available:

- Bass Guitar For Dummies
0-7645-2487-9
- Diabetes Cookbook For Dummies
0-7645-5230-9
- Gardening For Dummies *
0-7645-5130-2
- Guitar For Dummies
0-7645-5106-X
- Holiday Decorating For Dummies
0-7645-2570-0
- Home Improvement All-in-One For Dummies
0-7645-5680-0

- Knitting For Dummies
0-7645-5395-X
- Piano For Dummies
0-7645-5105-1
- Puppies For Dummies
0-7645-5255-4
- Scrapbooking For Dummies
0-7645-7208-3
- Senior Dogs For Dummies
0-7645-5818-8
- Singing For Dummies
0-7645-2475-5
- 30-Minute Meals For Dummies
0-7645-2589-1

INTERNET & DIGITAL MEDIA

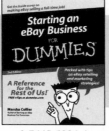

0-7645-1664-7

0-7645-6924-4

Also available:

- 2005 Online Shopping Directory For Dummies
0-7645-7495-7
- CD & DVD Recording For Dummies
0-7645-5956-7
- eBay For Dummies
0-7645-5654-1
- Fighting Spam For Dummies
0-7645-5965-6
- Genealogy Online For Dummies
0-7645-5964-8
- Google For Dummies
0-7645-4420-9

- Home Recording For Musicians For Dummies
0-7645-1634-5
- The Internet For Dummies
0-7645-4173-0
- iPod & iTunes For Dummies
0-7645-7772-7
- Preventing Identity Theft For Dummies
0-7645-7336-5
- Pro Tools All-in-One Desk Reference For Dummies
0-7645-5714-9
- Roxio Easy Media Creator For Dummies
0-7645-7131-1

SPORTS, FITNESS, PARENTING, RELIGION & SPIRITUALITY

0-7645-5146-9

0-7645-5418-2

Also available:
- Adoption For Dummies
  0-7645-5488-3
- Basketball For Dummies
  0-7645-5248-1
- The Bible For Dummies
  0-7645-5296-1
- Buddhism For Dummies
  0-7645-5359-3
- Catholicism For Dummies
  0-7645-5391-7
- Hockey For Dummies
  0-7645-5228-7

- Judaism For Dummies
  0-7645-5299-6
- Martial Arts For Dummies
  0-7645-5358-5
- Pilates For Dummies
  0-7645-5397-6
- Religion For Dummies
  0-7645-5264-3
- Teaching Kids to Read For Dummies
  0-7645-4043-2
- Weight Training For Dummies
  0-7645-5168-X
- Yoga For Dummies
  0-7645-5117-5

TRAVEL

0-7645-5438-7

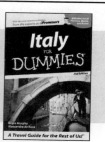

0-7645-5453-0

Also available:
- Alaska For Dummies
  0-7645-1761-9
- Arizona For Dummies
  0-7645-6938-4
- Cancún and the Yucatán For Dummies
  0-7645-2437-2
- Cruise Vacations For Dummies
  0-7645-6941-4
- Europe For Dummies
  0-7645-5456-5
- Ireland For Dummies
  0-7645-5455-7

- Las Vegas For Dummies
  0-7645-5448-4
- London For Dummies
  0-7645-4277-X
- New York City For Dummies
  0-7645-6945-7
- Paris For Dummies
  0-7645-5494-8
- RV Vacations For Dummies
  0-7645-5443-3
- Walt Disney World & Orlando For Dummies
  0-7645-6943-0

GRAPHICS, DESIGN & WEB DEVELOPMENT

0-7645-4345-8

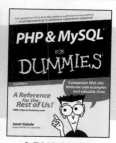

0-7645-5589-8

Also available:
- Adobe Acrobat 6 PDF For Dummies
  0-7645-3760-1
- Building a Web Site For Dummies
  0-7645-7144-3
- Dreamweaver MX 2004 For Dummies
  0-7645-4342-3
- FrontPage 2003 For Dummies
  0-7645-3882-9
- HTML 4 For Dummies
  0-7645-1995-6
- Illustrator CS For Dummies
  0-7645-4084-X

- Macromedia Flash MX 2004 For Dummies
  0-7645-4358-X
- Photoshop 7 All-in-One Desk
  Reference For Dummies
  0-7645-1667-1
- Photoshop CS Timesaving Techniques
  For Dummies
  0-7645-6782-9
- PHP 5 For Dummies
  0-7645-4166-8
- PowerPoint 2003 For Dummies
  0-7645-3908-6
- QuarkXPress 6 For Dummies
  0-7645-2593-X

NETWORKING, SECURITY, PROGRAMMING & DATABASES

0-7645-6852-3

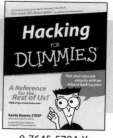

0-7645-5784-X

Also available:
- A+ Certification For Dummies
  0-7645-4187-0
- Access 2003 All-in-One Desk
  Reference For Dummies
  0-7645-3988-4
- Beginning Programming For Dummies
  0-7645-4997-9
- C For Dummies
  0-7645-7068-4
- Firewalls For Dummies
  0-7645-4048-3
- Home Networking For Dummies
  0-7645-42796

- Network Security For Dummies
  0-7645-1679-5
- Networking For Dummies
  0-7645-1677-9
- TCP/IP For Dummies
  0-7645-1760-0
- VBA For Dummies
  0-7645-3989-2
- Wireless All In-One Desk Reference
  For Dummies
  0-7645-7496-5
- Wireless Home Networking For Dummies
  0-7645-3910-8